THE DEVIL IS A PART-TIMER! HIGH SCHOOL!

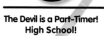

3

The Devil is a Part-Timer!
High School!

ART
**KURONE
MISHIMA**

ORIGINAL STORY
SATOSHI WAGAHARA

CHARACTER DESIGN
029 (ONIKU)

The Devil is a Part-Timer! High School! 3

CONTENTS

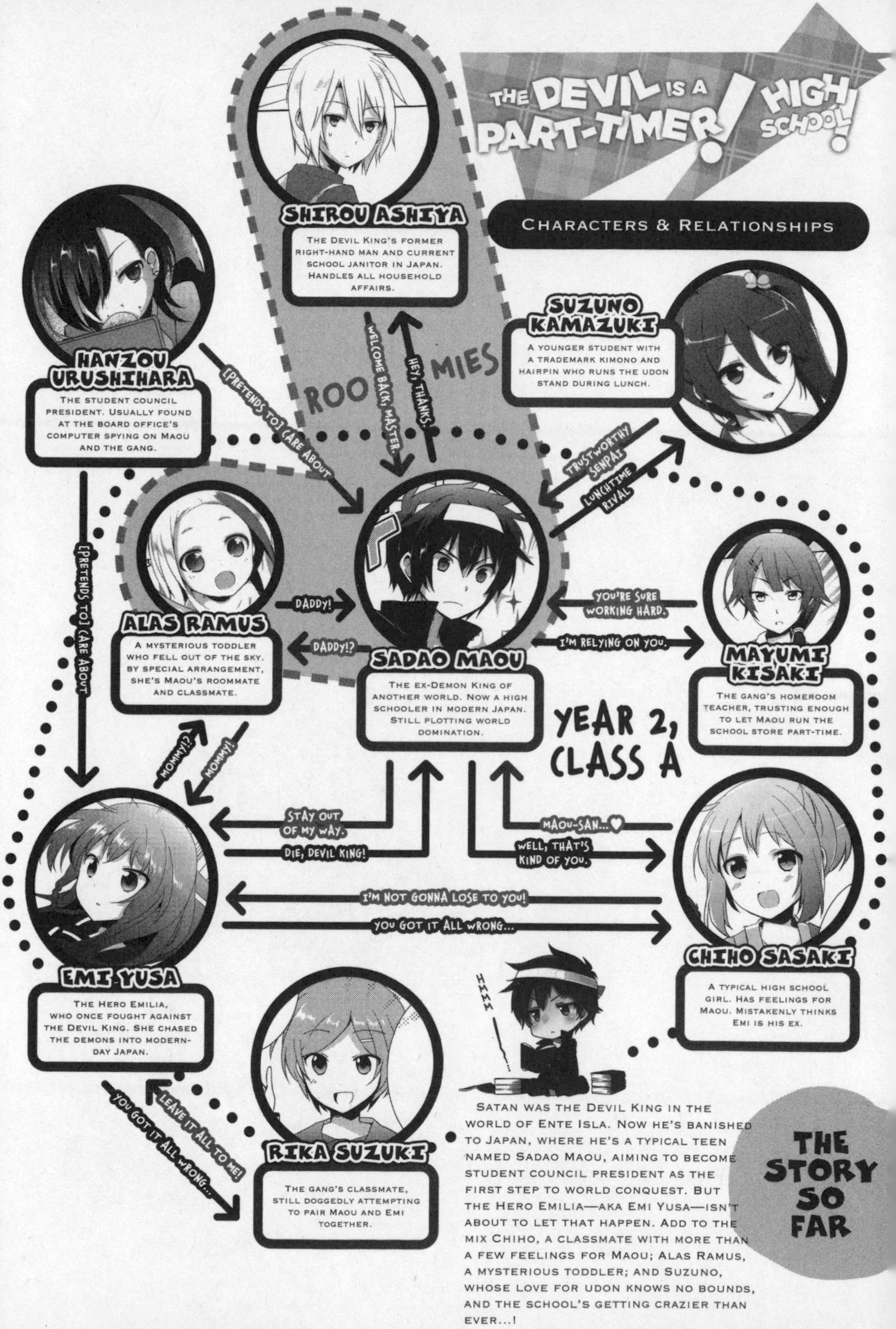

THE DEVIL IS A PART-TIMER! HIGH SCHOOL!
CHARACTERS & RELATIONSHIPS
SHIROU ASHIYA
THE DEVIL KING'S FORMER RIGHT-HAND MAN AND CURRENT SCHOOL JANITOR IN JAPAN. HANDLES ALL HOUSEHOLD AFFAIRS.
WELCOME BACK, MASTER.
HEY, THANKS.
ROO MIES
HANZOU URUSHIHARA
THE STUDENT COUNCIL PRESIDENT. USUALLY FOUND AT THE BOARD OFFICE'S COMPUTER SPYING ON MAOU AND THE GANG.
[PRETENDS TO] CARE ABOUT
SUZUNO KAMAZUKI
A YOUNGER STUDENT WITH A TRADEMARK KIMONO AND HAIRPIN WHO RUNS THE UDON STAND DURING LUNCH.
TRUSTWORTHY SENPAI
LUNCHTIME RIVAL
ALAS RAMUS
A MYSTERIOUS TODDLER WHO FELL OUT OF THE SKY. BY SPECIAL ARRANGEMENT, SHE'S MAOU'S ROOMMATE AND CLASSMATE.
DADDY!
DADDY!?
SADAO MAOU
THE EX-DEMON KING OF ANOTHER WORLD. NOW A HIGH SCHOOLER IN MODERN JAPAN. STILL PLOTTING WORLD DOMINATION.
YOU'RE SURE WORKING HARD.
I'M RELYING ON YOU.
MAYUMI KISAKI
THE GANG'S HOMEROOM TEACHER, TRUSTING ENOUGH TO LET MAOU RUN THE SCHOOL STORE PART-TIME.
YEAR 2, CLASS A
[PRETENDS TO] CARE ABOUT
MOMMY!?
MOMMY!
STAY OUT OF MY WAY.
DIE, DEVIL KING!
MAOU-SAN...♥
WELL, THAT'S KIND OF YOU.
I'M NOT GONNA LOSE TO YOU!
YOU GOT IT ALL WRONG...
EMI YUSA
THE HERO EMILIA, WHO ONCE FOUGHT AGAINST THE DEVIL KING. SHE CHASED THE DEMONS INTO MODERN-DAY JAPAN.
CHIHO SASAKI
A TYPICAL HIGH SCHOOL GIRL. HAS FEELINGS FOR MAOU. MISTAKENLY THINKS EMI IS HIS EX.
HMMM
LEAVE IT ALL TO ME!
YOU GOT IT ALL WRONG...
RIKA SUZUKI
THE GANG'S CLASSMATE, STILL DOGGEDLY ATTEMPTING TO PAIR MAOU AND EMI TOGETHER.

THE STORY SO FAR

SATAN WAS THE DEVIL KING IN THE WORLD OF ENTE ISLA. NOW HE'S BANISHED TO JAPAN, WHERE HE'S A TYPICAL TEEN NAMED SADAO MAOU, AIMING TO BECOME STUDENT COUNCIL PRESIDENT AS THE FIRST STEP TO WORLD CONQUEST. BUT THE HERO EMILIA—AKA EMI YUSA—ISN'T ABOUT TO LET THAT HAPPEN. ADD TO THE MIX CHIHO, A CLASSMATE WITH MORE THAN A FEW FEELINGS FOR MAOU; ALAS RAMUS, A MYSTERIOUS TODDLER; AND SUZUNO, WHOSE LOVE FOR UDON KNOWS NO BOUNDS, AND THE SCHOOL'S GETTING CRAZIER THAN EVER...!

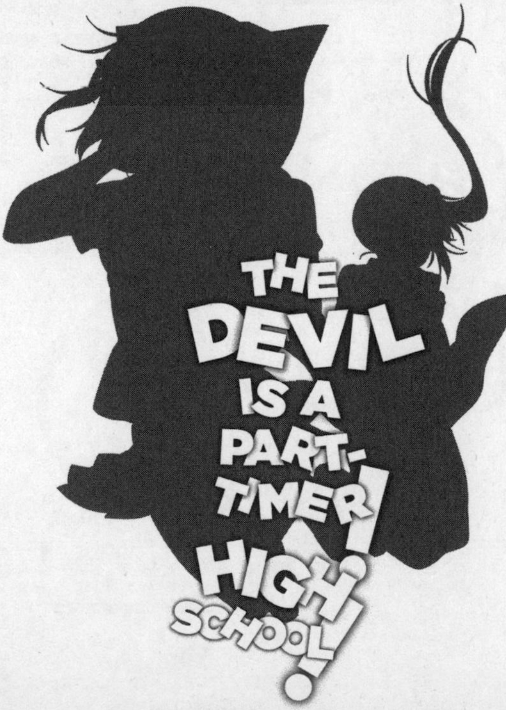
THE DEVIL IS A PART-TIMER! HIGH SCHOOL!

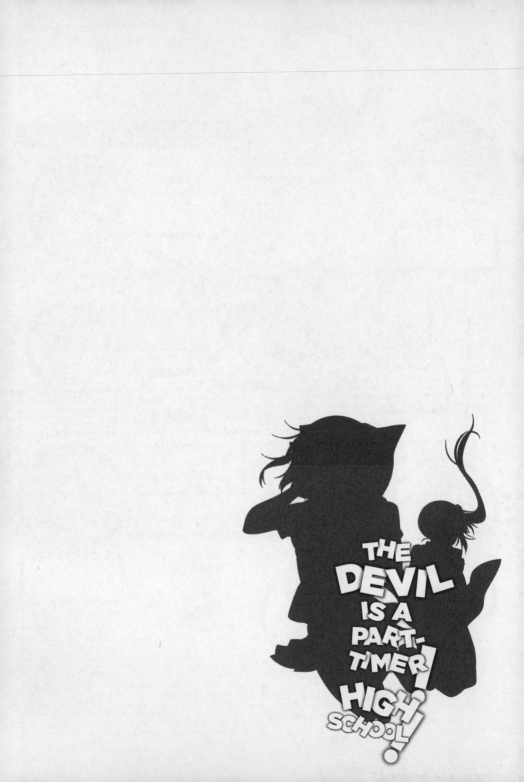

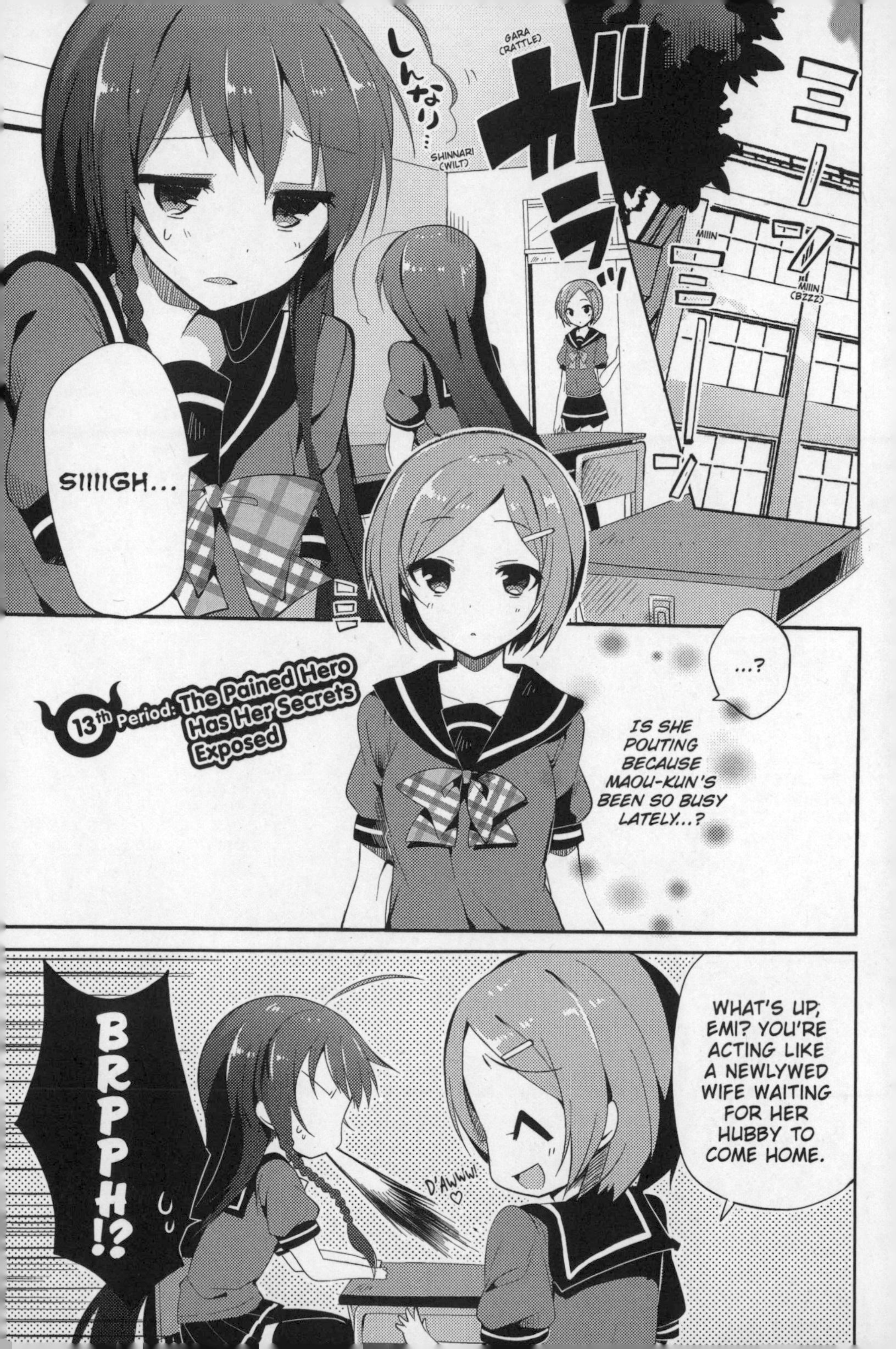
MIIIN
MIIIN (BZZZ)
GARA (RATTLE)
しんなり…
SHINNARI (WILT)
SIIIIGH...
...?
IS SHE POUTING BECAUSE MAOU-KUN'S BEEN SO BUSY LATELY...?
13th Period: The Pained Hero Has Her Secrets Exposed
WHAT'S UP, EMI? YOU'RE ACTING LIKE A NEWLYWED WIFE WAITING FOR HER HUBBY TO COME HOME.
D'AWWW! ♡
BRPPH!?

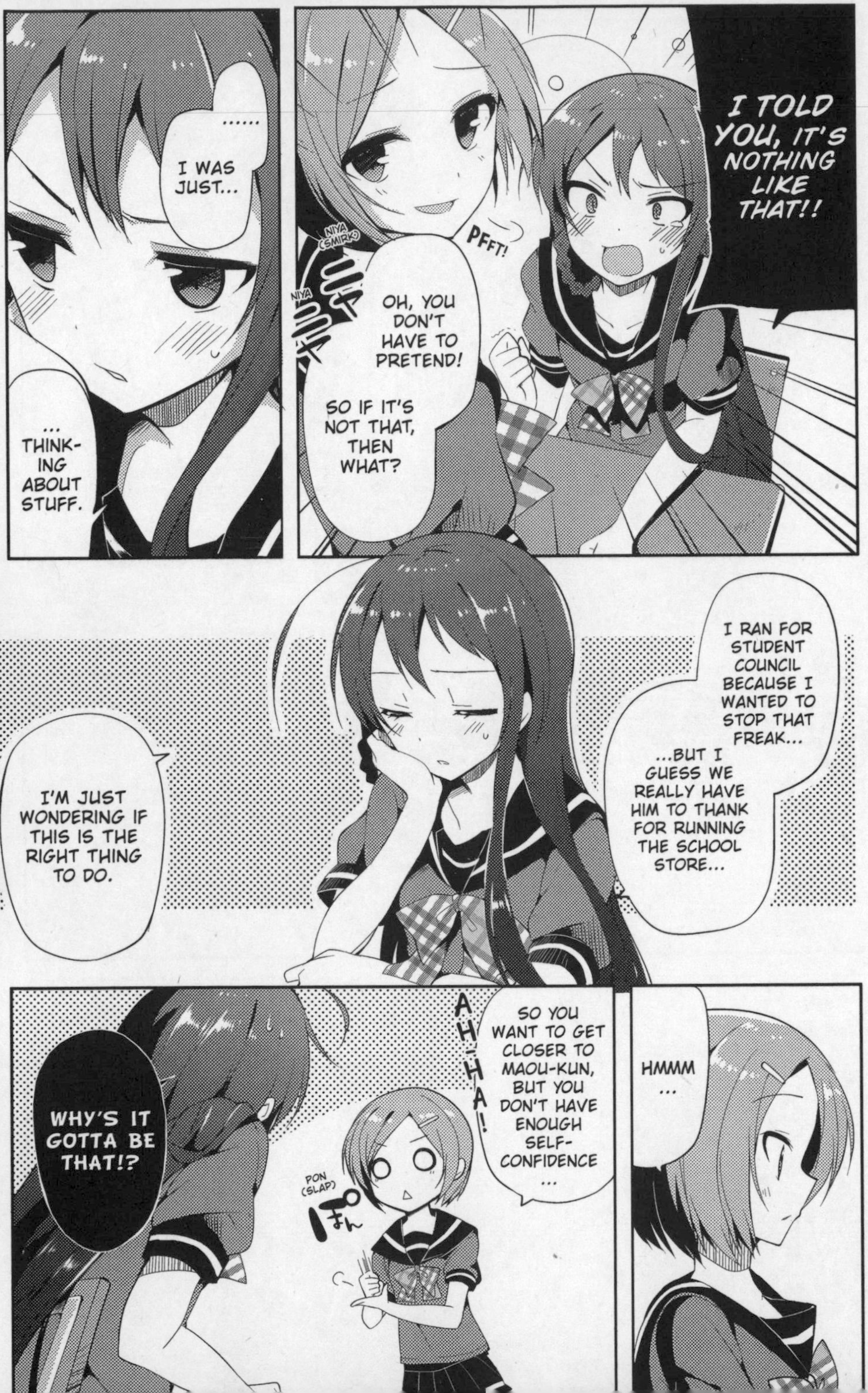
I TOLD YOU, IT'S NOTHING LIKE THAT!!
PFFT!
OH, YOU DON'T HAVE TO PRETEND!
NIYA (SMIRK)
NIYA
SO IF IT'S NOT THAT, THEN WHAT?
......
I WAS JUST...
...THINKING ABOUT STUFF.
I RAN FOR STUDENT COUNCIL BECAUSE I WANTED TO STOP THAT FREAK...
...BUT I GUESS WE REALLY HAVE HIM TO THANK FOR RUNNING THE SCHOOL STORE...
I'M JUST WONDERING IF THIS IS THE RIGHT THING TO DO.
HMMM...
AH-HA!
SO YOU WANT TO GET CLOSER TO MAOU-KUN, BUT YOU DON'T HAVE ENOUGH SELF-CONFIDENCE...
PON (SLAP)
WHY'S IT GOTTA BE THAT!?

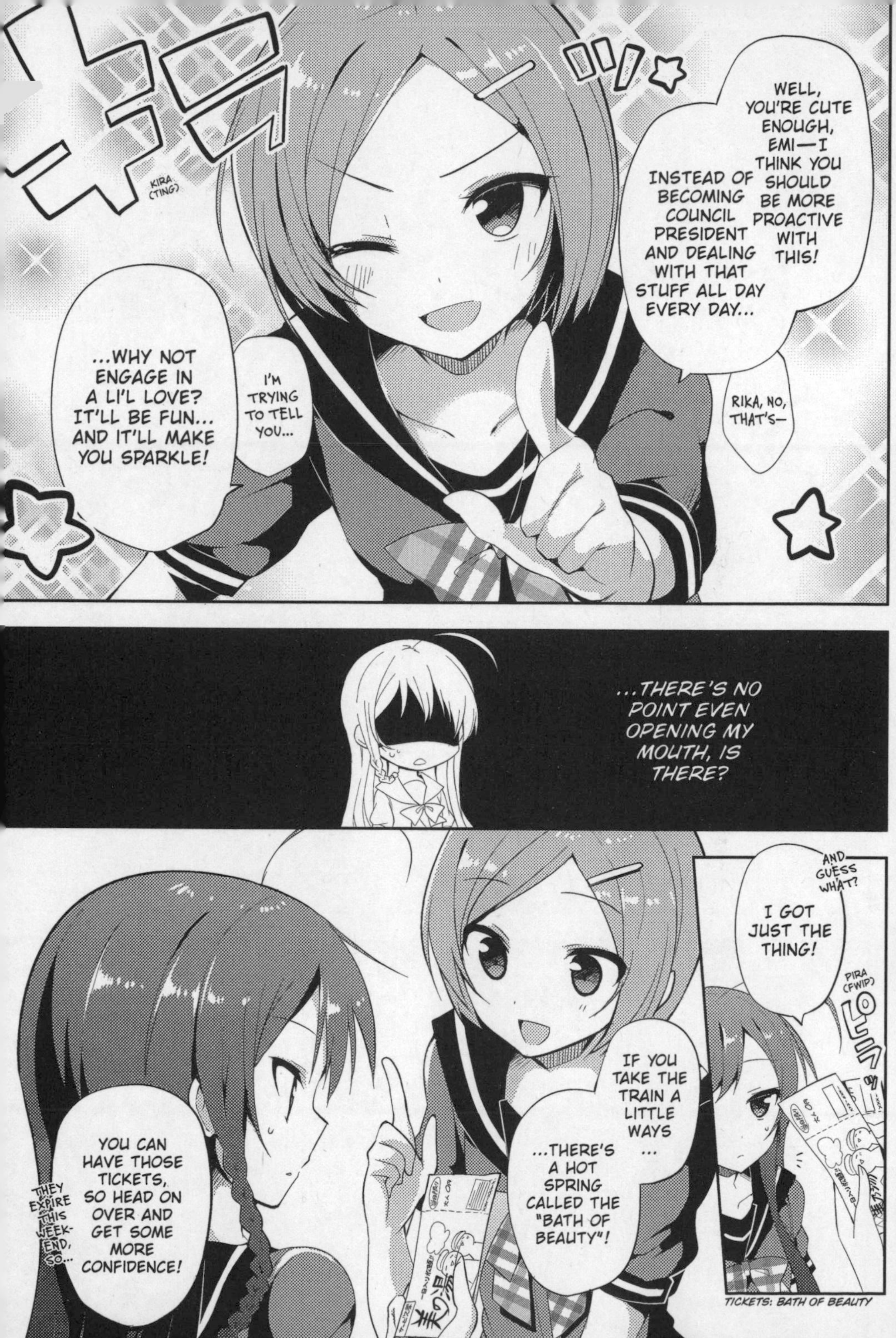
WELL, YOU'RE CUTE ENOUGH, EMI—I THINK YOU SHOULD BE MORE PROACTIVE WITH THIS!
INSTEAD OF BECOMING COUNCIL PRESIDENT AND DEALING WITH THAT STUFF ALL DAY EVERY DAY...
RIKA, NO, THAT'S—
KIRA (TING)
I'M TRYING TO TELL YOU...
...WHY NOT ENGAGE IN A LI'L LOVE? IT'LL BE FUN... AND IT'LL MAKE YOU SPARKLE!
...THERE'S NO POINT EVEN OPENING MY MOUTH, IS THERE?
AND GUESS WHAT?
I GOT JUST THE THING!
PIRA (FWIP)
TICKETS: BATH OF BEAUTY
IF YOU TAKE THE TRAIN A LITTLE WAYS ...
...THERE'S A HOT SPRING CALLED THE "BATH OF BEAUTY"!
YOU CAN HAVE THOSE TICKETS, SO HEAD ON OVER AND GET SOME MORE CONFIDENCE!
THEY EXPIRE THIS WEEK-END, SO...

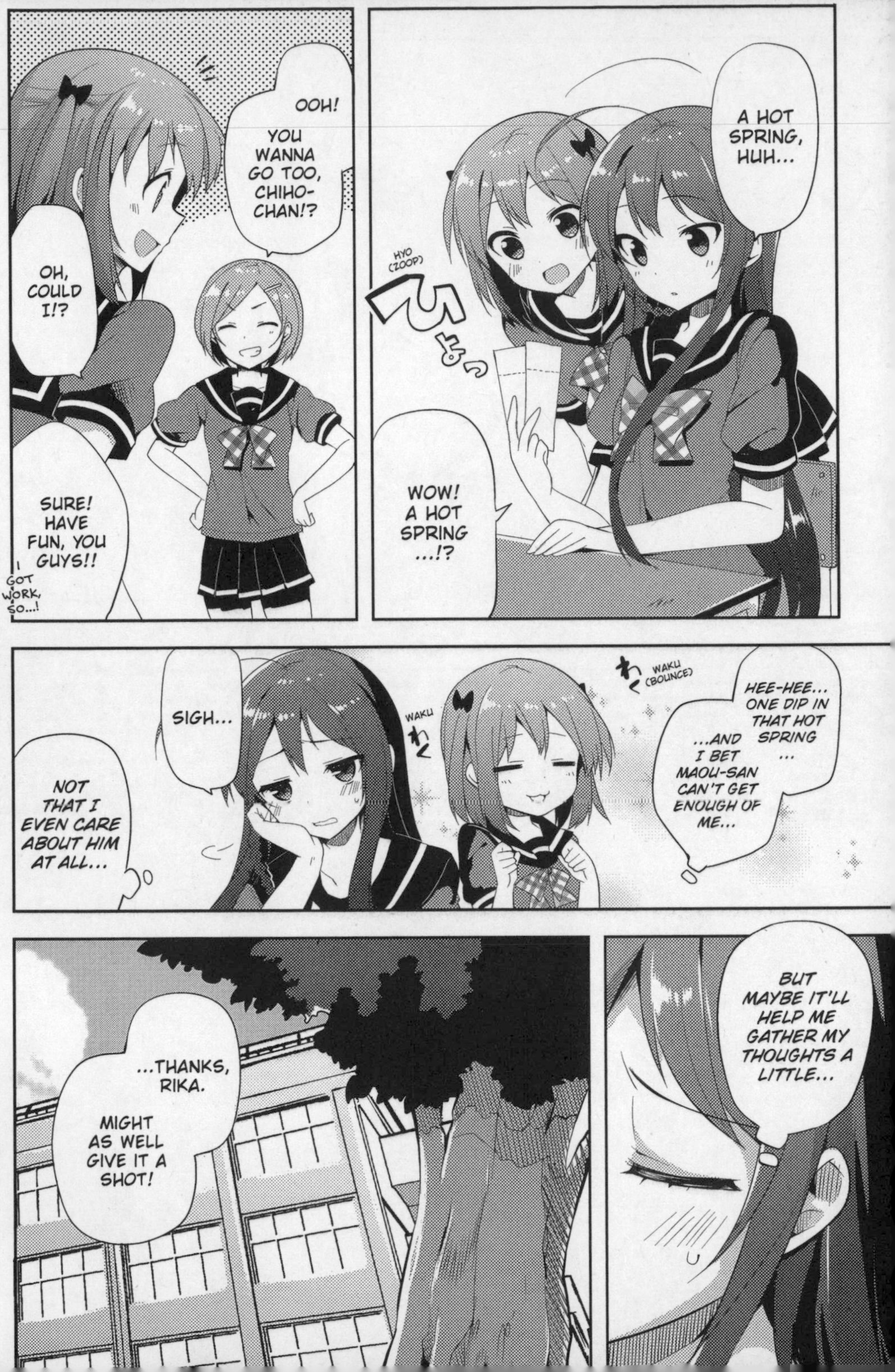
A HOT SPRING, HUH...
HYO (ZOOP)
ひょっ
WOW! A HOT SPRING ...!?
OOH!
YOU WANNA GO TOO, CHIHO-CHAN!?
OH, COULD I!?
SURE! HAVE FUN, YOU GUYS!!
I GOT WORK, SO...!
HEE-HEE... ONE DIP IN THAT HOT SPRING ...
...AND I BET MAOU-SAN CAN'T GET ENOUGH OF ME...
わく WAKU (BOUNCE)
WAKU わく
SIGH...
NOT THAT I EVEN CARE ABOUT HIM AT ALL...
BUT MAYBE IT'LL HELP ME GATHER MY THOUGHTS A LITTLE...
...THANKS, RIKA.
MIGHT AS WELL GIVE IT A SHOT!

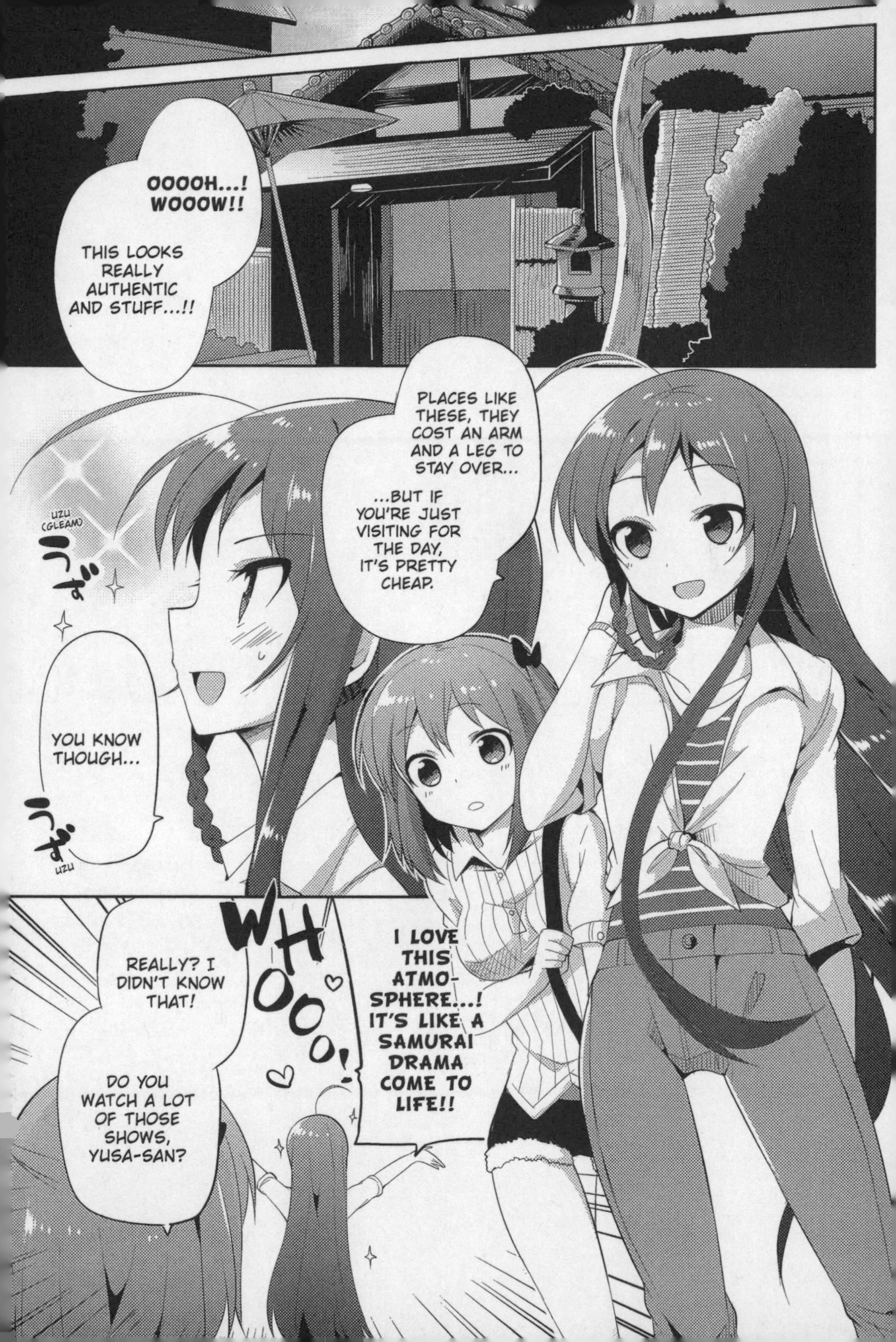
OOOOH...! WOOOW!!
THIS LOOKS REALLY AUTHENTIC AND STUFF...!!
PLACES LIKE THESE, THEY COST AN ARM AND A LEG TO STAY OVER...
...BUT IF YOU'RE JUST VISITING FOR THE DAY, IT'S PRETTY CHEAP.
UZU (GLEAM)
うず
YOU KNOW THOUGH...
うず
UZU
I LOVE THIS ATMO-SPHERE...! IT'S LIKE A SAMURAI DRAMA COME TO LIFE!!
WHOOO!
REALLY? I DIDN'T KNOW THAT!
DO YOU WATCH A LOT OF THOSE SHOWS, YUSA-SAN?

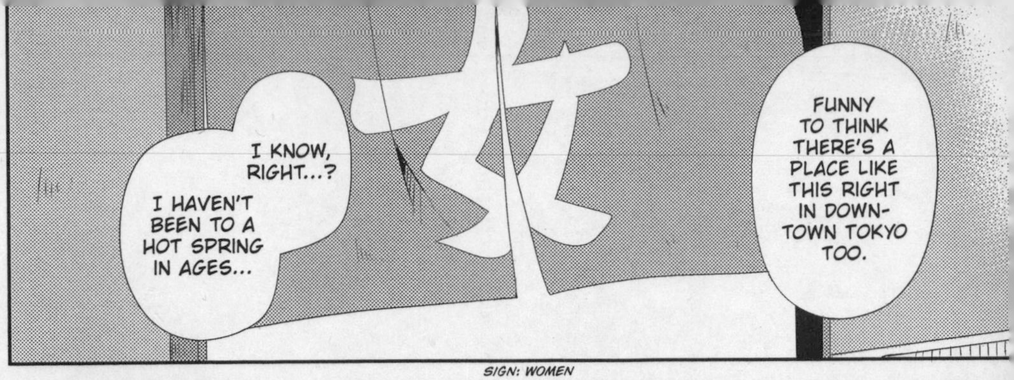
FUNNY TO THINK THERE'S A PLACE LIKE THIS RIGHT IN DOWN-TOWN TOKYO TOO.
I KNOW, RIGHT...?
I HAVEN'T BEEN TO A HOT SPRING IN AGES...

SIGN: WOMEN

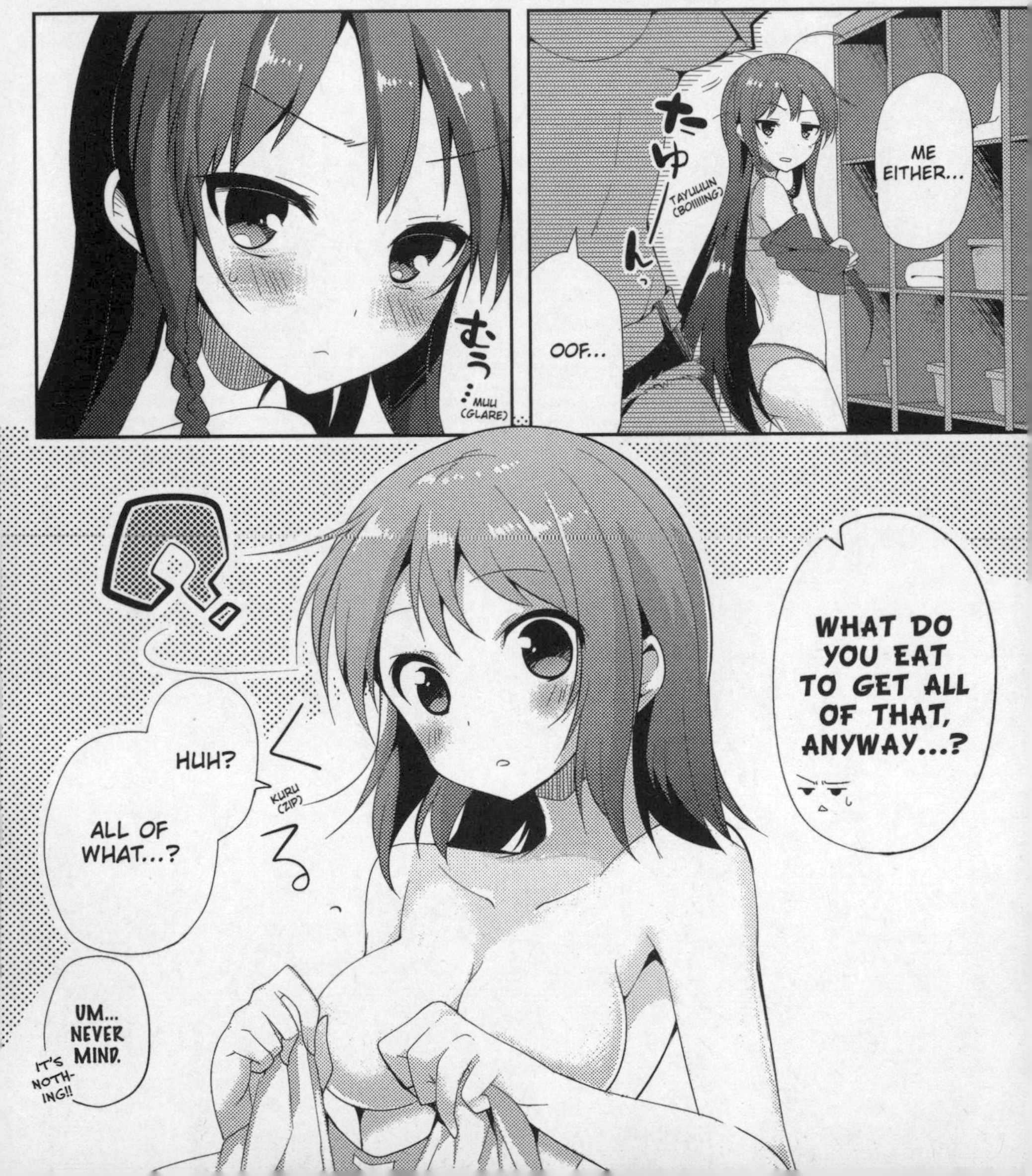
ME EITHER...
たゆ～ん
TAYUUUN (BOIIIING)
OOF...
むぅ…
MUU (GLARE)
WHAT DO YOU EAT TO GET ALL OF THAT, ANYWAY...?
HUH?
ALL OF WHAT...?
KURU (ZIP)
UM... NEVER MIND.
IT'S NOTH-ING!!

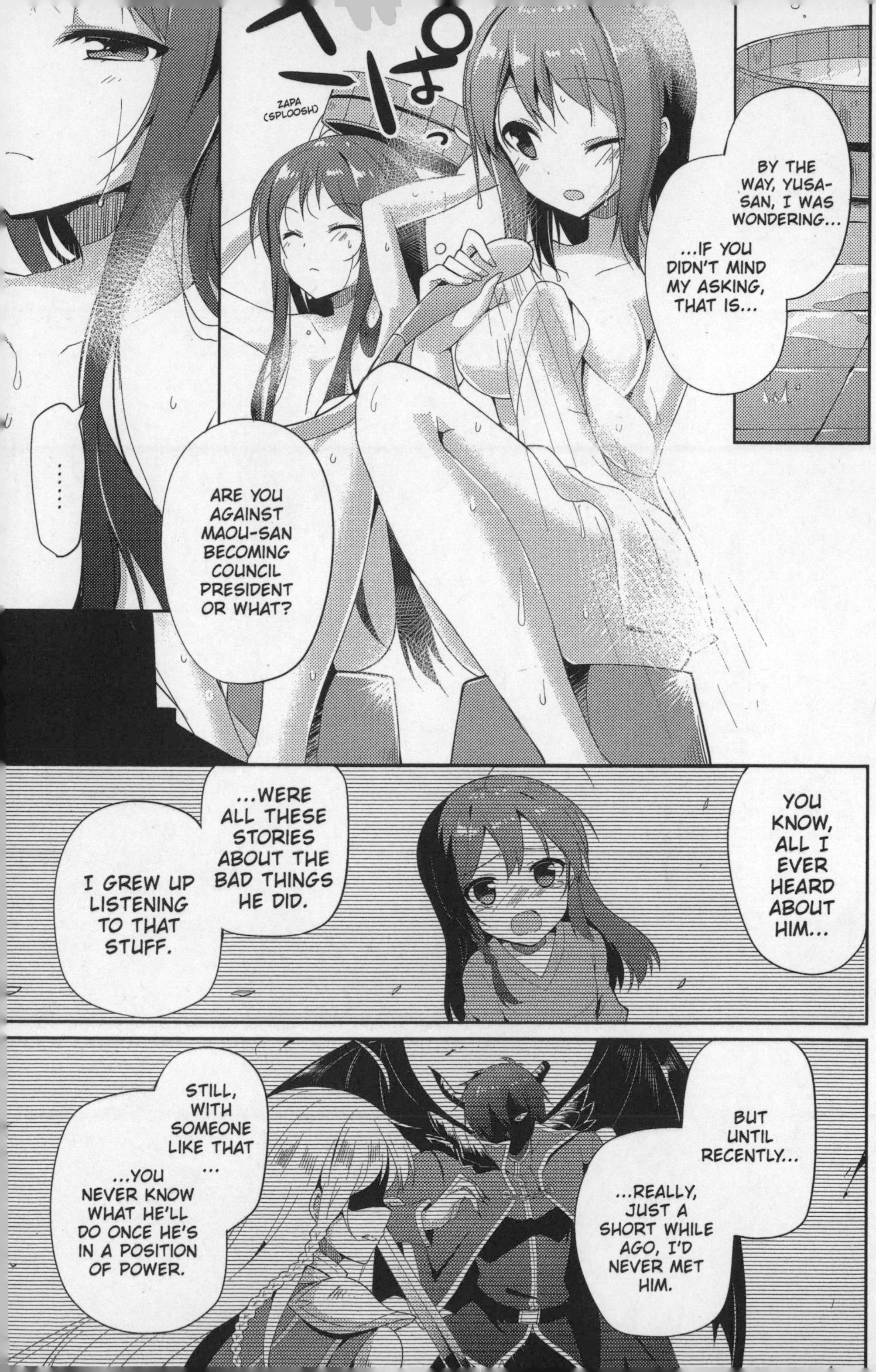
ZAPA (SPLOOSH)
BY THE WAY, YUSA-SAN, I WAS WONDERING...
...IF YOU DIDN'T MIND MY ASKING, THAT IS...
ARE YOU AGAINST MAOU-SAN BECOMING COUNCIL PRESIDENT OR WHAT?
......
YOU KNOW, ALL I EVER HEARD ABOUT HIM...
...WERE ALL THESE STORIES ABOUT THE BAD THINGS HE DID.
I GREW UP LISTENING TO THAT STUFF.
BUT UNTIL RECENTLY...
...REALLY, JUST A SHORT WHILE AGO, I'D NEVER MET HIM.
STILL, WITH SOMEONE LIKE THAT...
...YOU NEVER KNOW WHAT HE'LL DO ONCE HE'S IN A POSITION OF POWER.

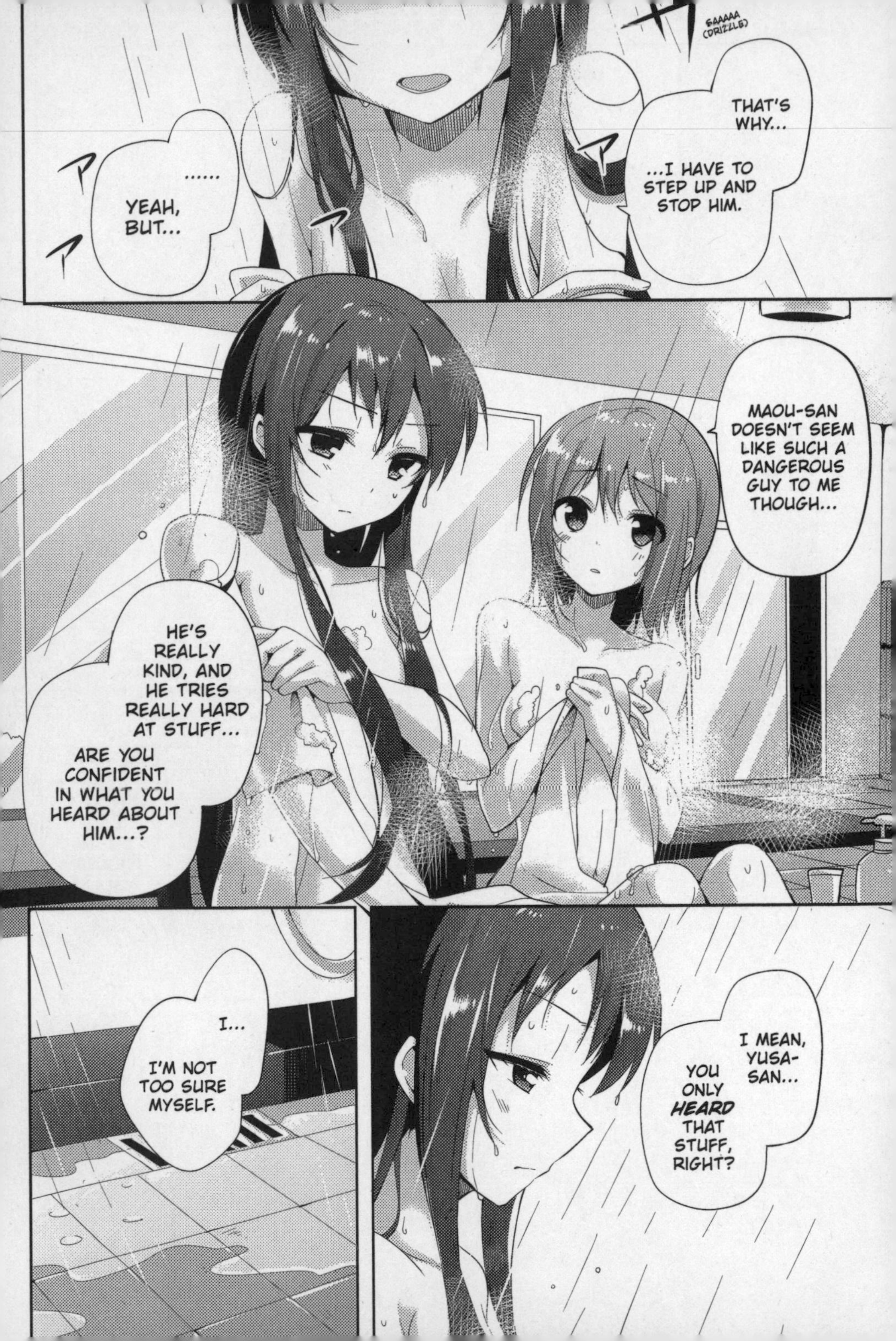
SAAAAA (DRIZZLE)
THAT'S WHY...
...I HAVE TO STEP UP AND STOP HIM.
......
YEAH, BUT...
MAOU-SAN DOESN'T SEEM LIKE SUCH A DANGEROUS GUY TO ME THOUGH...
HE'S REALLY KIND, AND HE TRIES REALLY HARD AT STUFF...
ARE YOU CONFIDENT IN WHAT YOU HEARD ABOUT HIM...?
I MEAN, YUSA-SAN...
YOU ONLY *HEARD* THAT STUFF, RIGHT?
I...
I'M NOT TOO SURE MYSELF.

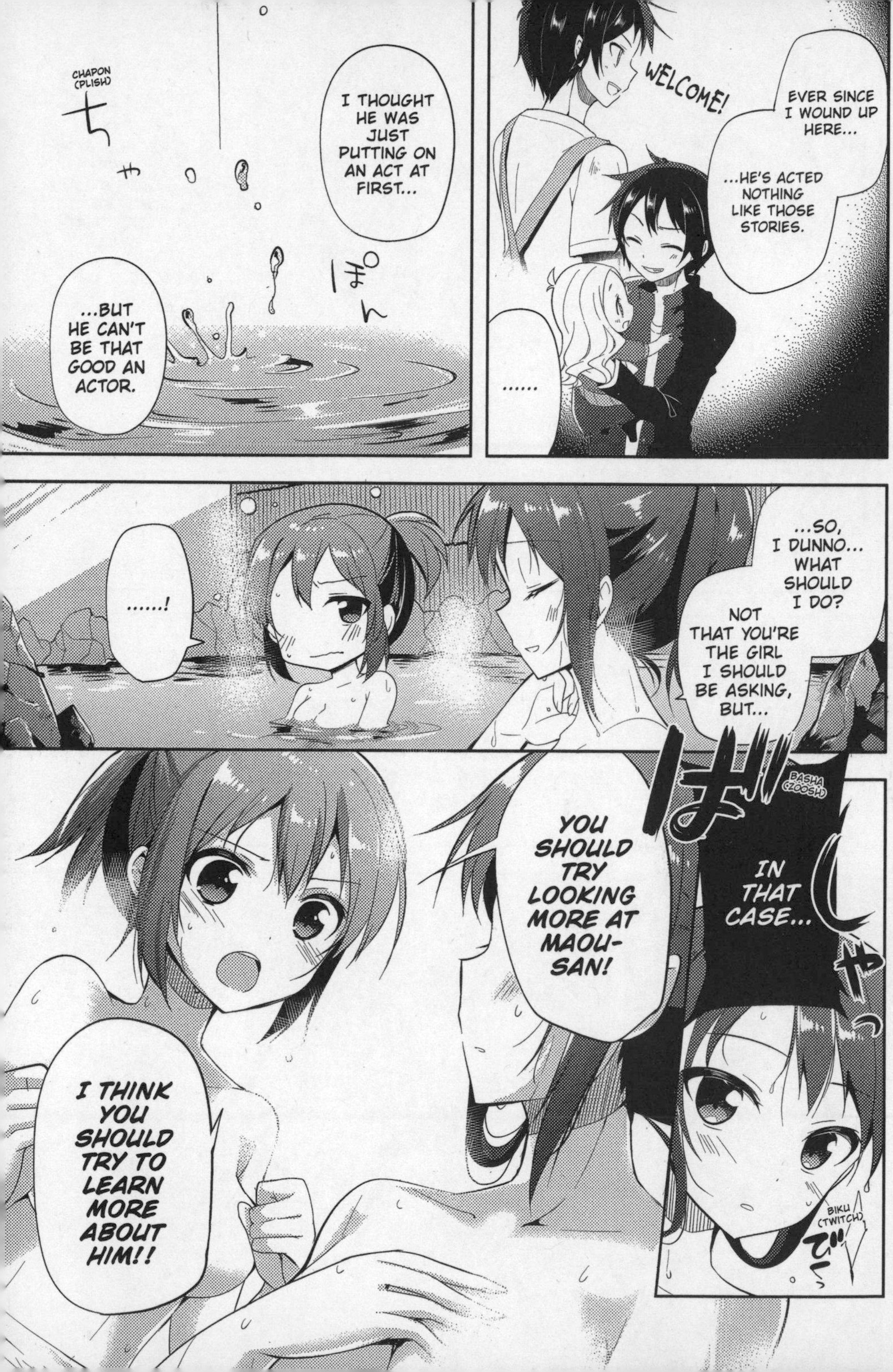
WELCOME!
EVER SINCE I WOUND UP HERE...
...HE'S ACTED NOTHING LIKE THOSE STORIES.
......
I THOUGHT HE WAS JUST PUTTING ON AN ACT AT FIRST...
CHAPON (PLISH)
...BUT HE CAN'T BE THAT GOOD AN ACTOR.
...SO, I DUNNO... WHAT SHOULD I DO?
NOT THAT YOU'RE THE GIRL I SHOULD BE ASKING, BUT...
......!
BASHA (ZOOSH)
IN THAT CASE...
BIKU (TWITCH)
YOU SHOULD TRY LOOKING MORE AT MAOU-SAN!
I THINK YOU SHOULD TRY TO LEARN MORE ABOUT HIM!!

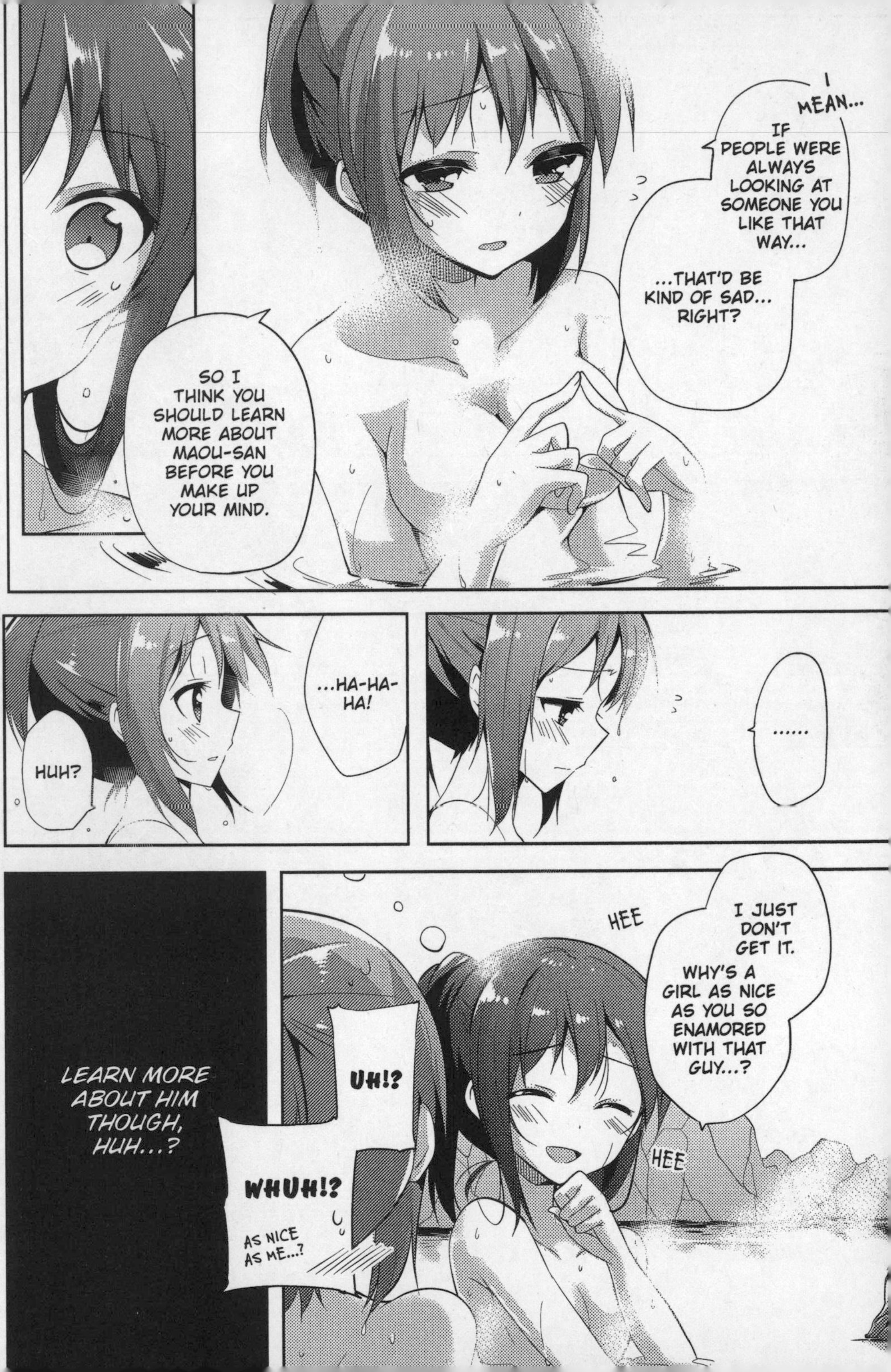
I MEAN...
IF PEOPLE WERE ALWAYS LOOKING AT SOMEONE YOU LIKE THAT WAY...
...THAT'D BE KIND OF SAD... RIGHT?
SO I THINK YOU SHOULD LEARN MORE ABOUT MAOU-SAN BEFORE YOU MAKE UP YOUR MIND.
......
...HA-HA-HA!
HUH?
I JUST DON'T GET IT.
WHY'S A GIRL AS NICE AS YOU SO ENAMORED WITH THAT GUY...?
HEE
HEE
UH!?
WHUH!?
AS NICE AS ME...?
LEARN MORE ABOUT HIM THOUGH, HUH...?

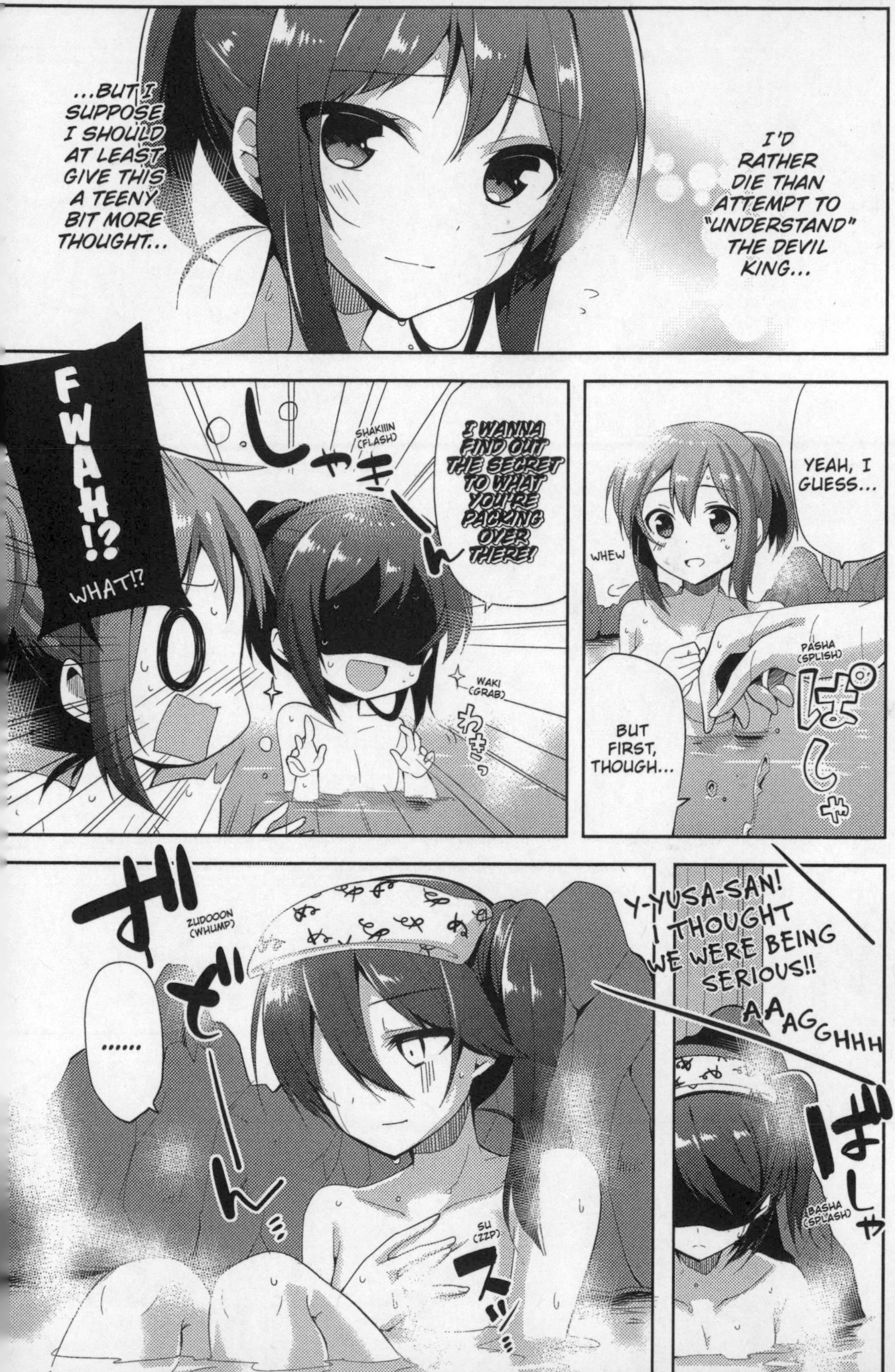
I'D RATHER DIE THAN ATTEMPT TO "UNDERSTAND" THE DEVIL KING...
...BUT I SUPPOSE I SHOULD AT LEAST GIVE THIS A TEENY BIT MORE THOUGHT...
YEAH, I GUESS...
WHEW
ぱしゃ
PASHA (SPLISH)
BUT FIRST, THOUGH...
I WANNA FIND OUT THE SECRET TO WHAT YOU'RE PACKING OVER THERE!
しゃきーん
SHAKIIIN (FLASH)
わきっ
WAKI (GRAB)
FWAH!?
WHAT!?
Y-YUSA-SAN! I THOUGHT WE WERE BEING SERIOUS!!
AAAGGHHH
ばしゃ
BASHA (SPLASH)
ずどーん
ZUDOOON (WHUMP)
......
ス
SU (ZZP)

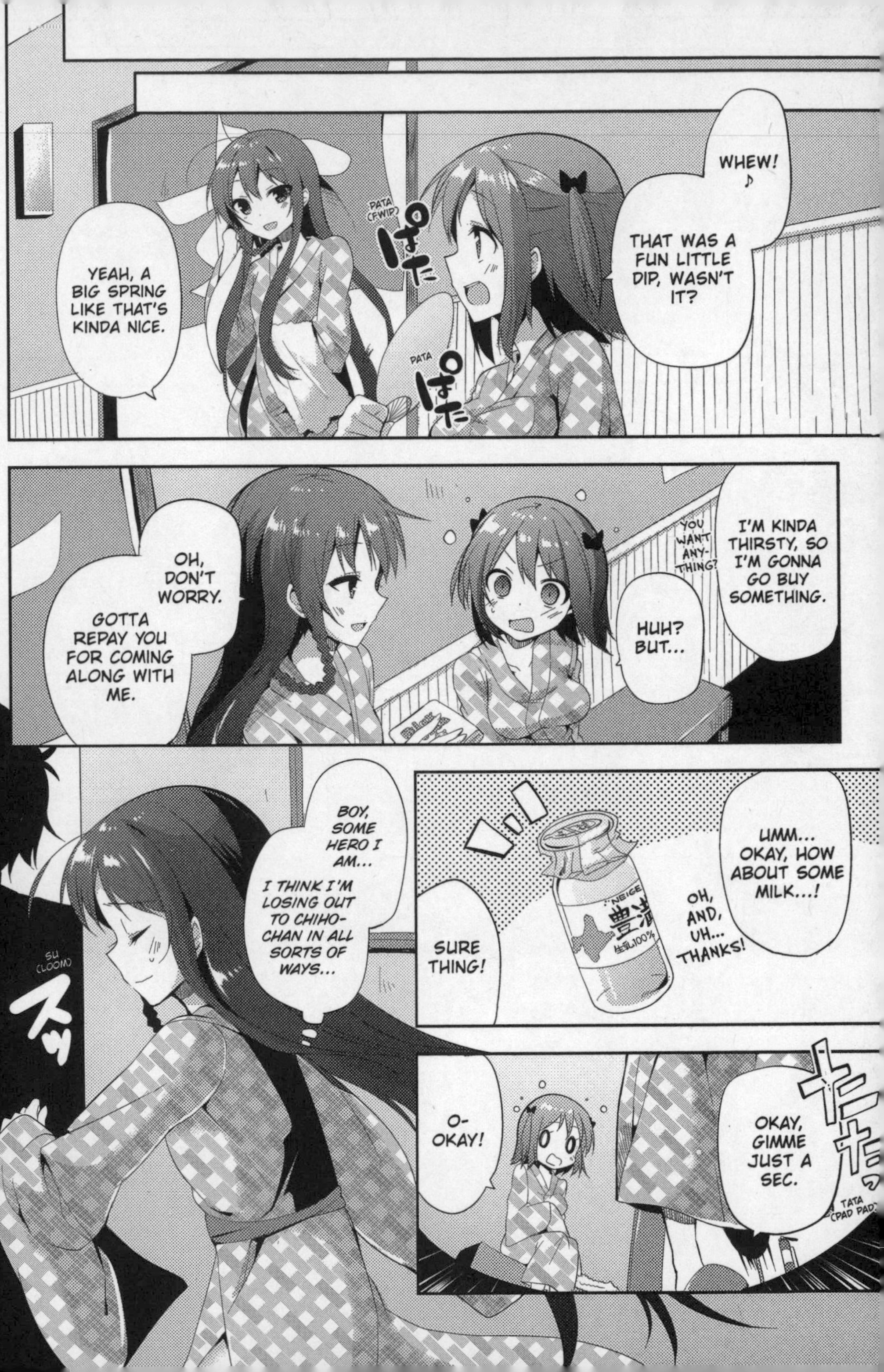
WHEW! ♪
THAT WAS A FUN LITTLE DIP, WASN'T IT?
PATA (FWIP)
ぱた
PATA
ぱた
YEAH, A BIG SPRING LIKE THAT'S KINDA NICE.
I'M KINDA THIRSTY, SO I'M GONNA GO BUY SOMETHING.
YOU WANT ANYTHING?
HUH? BUT...
OH, DON'T WORRY.
GOTTA REPAY YOU FOR COMING ALONG WITH ME.
UMM... OKAY, HOW ABOUT SOME MILK...!
OH, AND, UH... THANKS!
SURE THING!
OKAY, GIMME JUST A SEC.
たたっ
TATA (PAD PAD)
O-OKAY!
BOY, SOME HERO I AM...
I THINK I'M LOSING OUT TO CHIHO-CHAN IN ALL SORTS OF WAYS...
SU (LOOM)
スッ

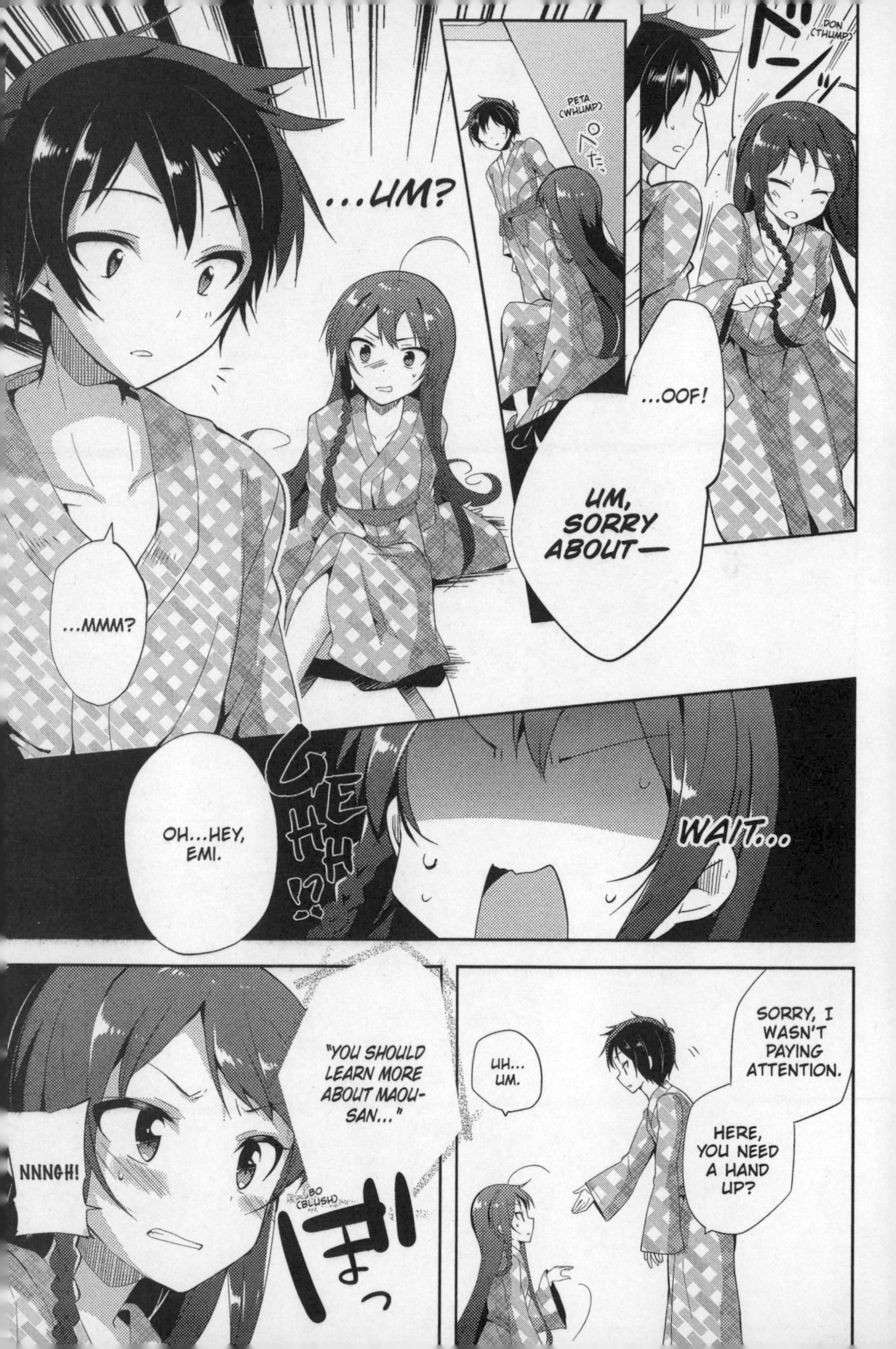

DON (THUMP)
...OOF!
UM, SORRY ABOUT—
PETA (WHUMP)
ぺた、
...UM?
...MMM?
WAIT...
GEHH!?
OH...HEY, EMI.
SORRY, I WASN'T PAYING ATTENTION.
HERE, YOU NEED A HAND UP?
UH... UM.
"YOU SHOULD LEARN MORE ABOUT MAOU-SAN..."
BO (BLUSH)
ぼっ
NNNGH!

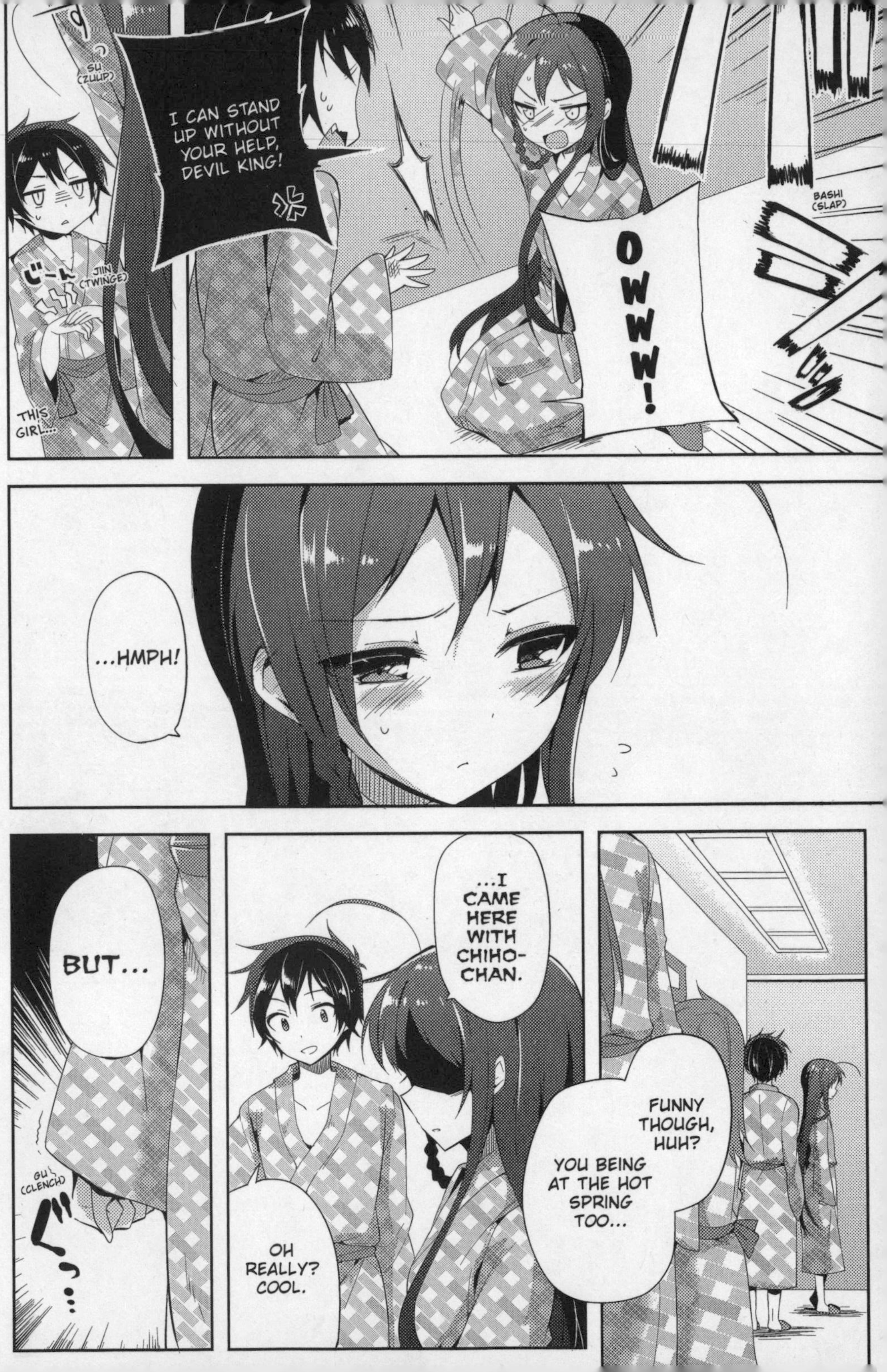
BASHI (SLAP)
OWWW!
I CAN STAND UP WITHOUT YOUR HELP, DEVIL KING!
SU (ZUUP)
JIIN (TWINGE)
THIS GIRL...
...HMPH!
FUNNY THOUGH, HUH?
YOU BEING AT THE HOT SPRING TOO...
...I CAME HERE WITH CHIHO-CHAN.
OH REALLY? COOL.
BUT...
GU (CLENCH)

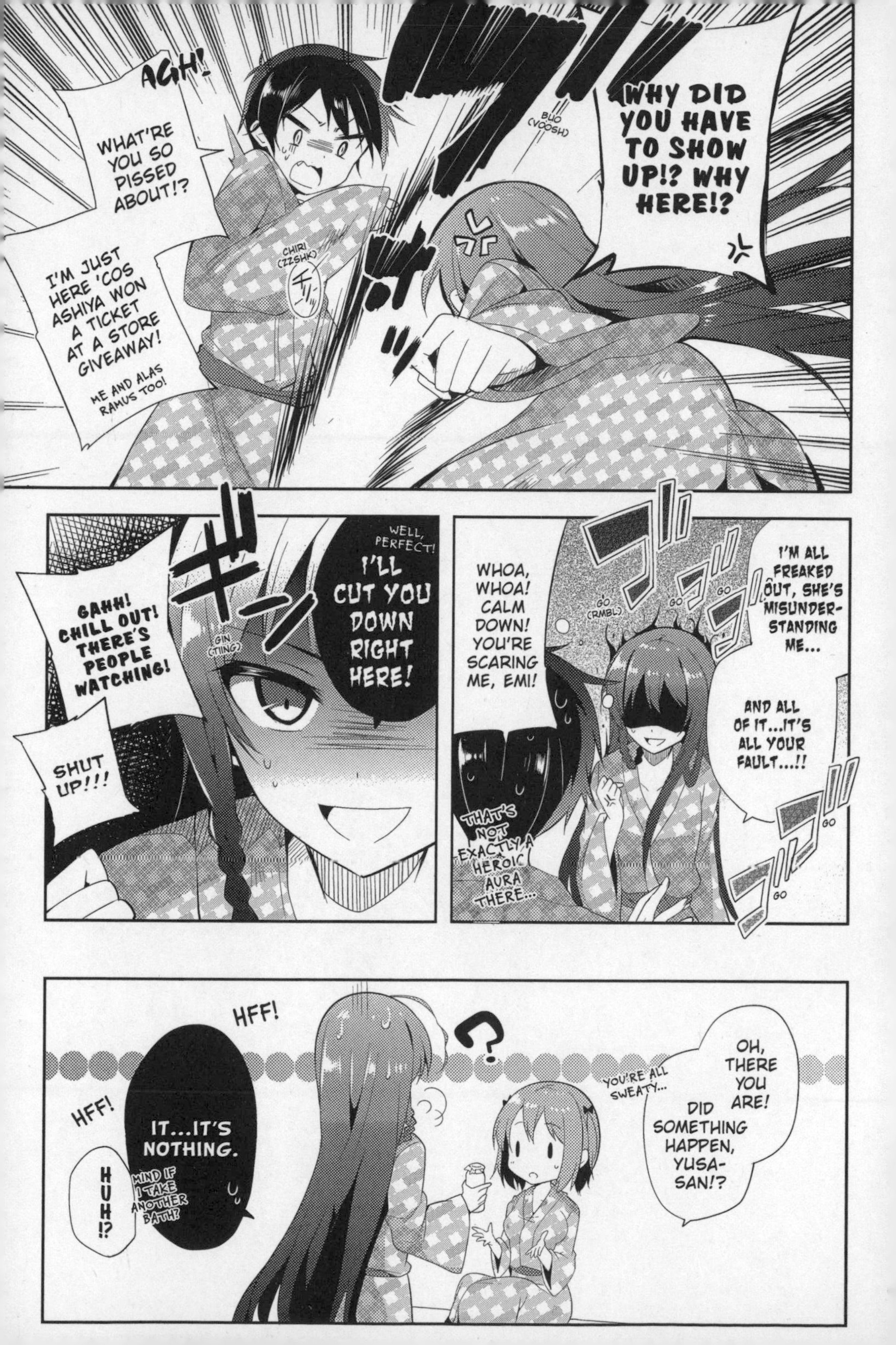

WHY DID YOU HAVE TO SHOW UP!? WHY HERE!?
BUO (VOOSH)
AGH!
WHAT'RE YOU SO PISSED ABOUT!?
CHIRI (ZZSHK)
I'M JUST HERE 'COS ASHIYA WON A TICKET AT A STORE GIVEAWAY!
ME AND ALAS RAMUS TOO!
I'M ALL FREAKED OUT, SHE'S MISUNDER-STANDING ME...
AND ALL OF IT...IT'S ALL YOUR FAULT...!!
GO
GO
GO
GO
GO (RMBL)
WHOA, WHOA! CALM DOWN! YOU'RE SCARING ME, EMI!
THAT'S NOT EXACTLY A HEROIC AURA THERE...
WELL, PERFECT!
I'LL CUT YOU DOWN RIGHT HERE!
GIN (TIING)
GAHH! CHILL OUT! THERE'S PEOPLE WATCHING!
SHUT UP!!!
OH, THERE YOU ARE!
DID SOMETHING HAPPEN, YUSA-SAN!?
YOU'RE ALL SWEATY...
HFF!
IT...IT'S NOTHING.
HFF!
MIND IF I TAKE ANOTHER BATH?
HUH!?

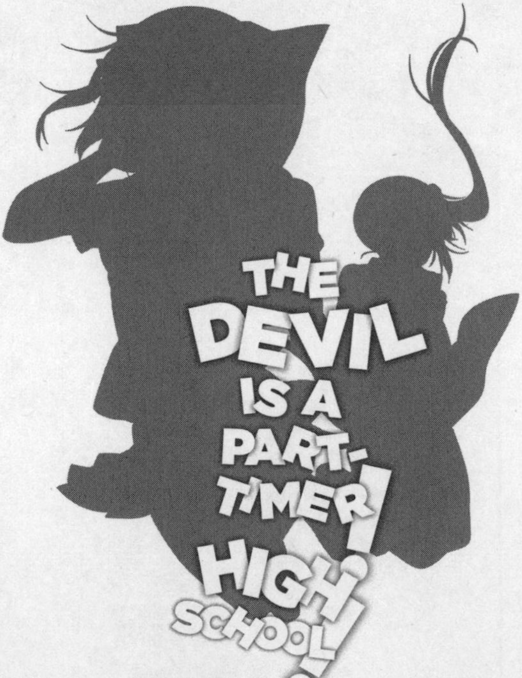
THE DEVIL IS A PART-TIMER! HIGH SCHOOL!

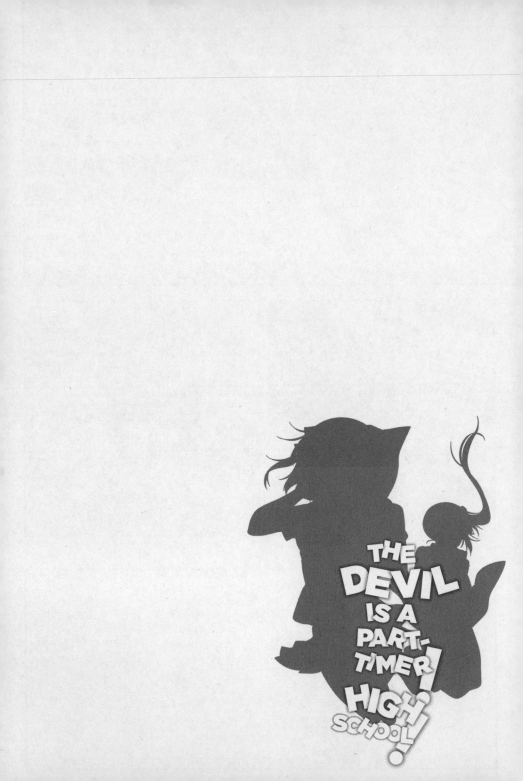

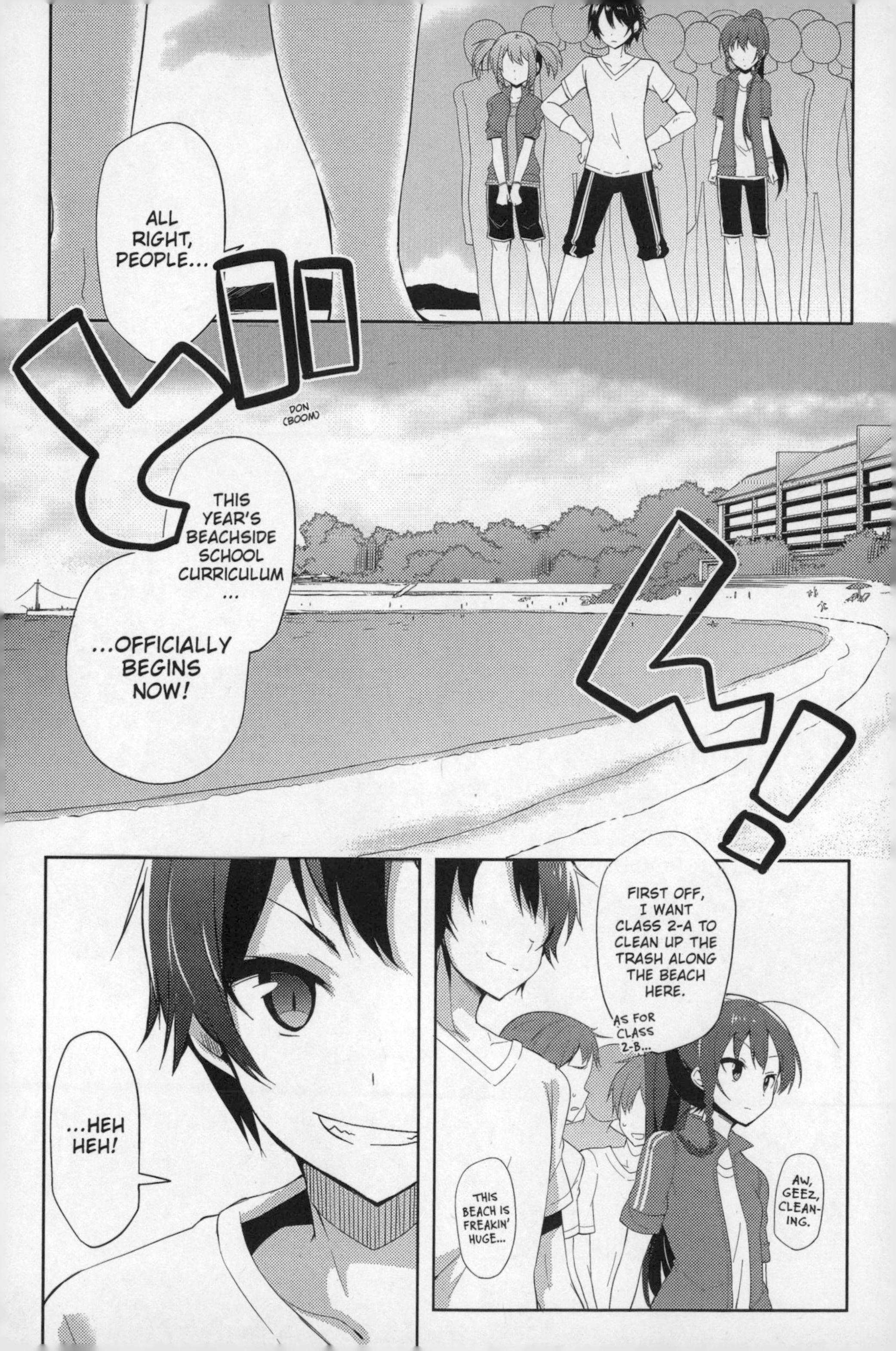
ALL RIGHT, PEOPLE...
DON (BOOM)
THIS YEAR'S BEACHSIDE SCHOOL CURRICULUM ...
...OFFICIALLY BEGINS NOW!
FIRST OFF, I WANT CLASS 2-A TO CLEAN UP THE TRASH ALONG THE BEACH HERE.
AS FOR CLASS 2-B...
AW, GEEZ, CLEAN-ING.
THIS BEACH IS FREAKIN' HUGE...
...HEH HEH!

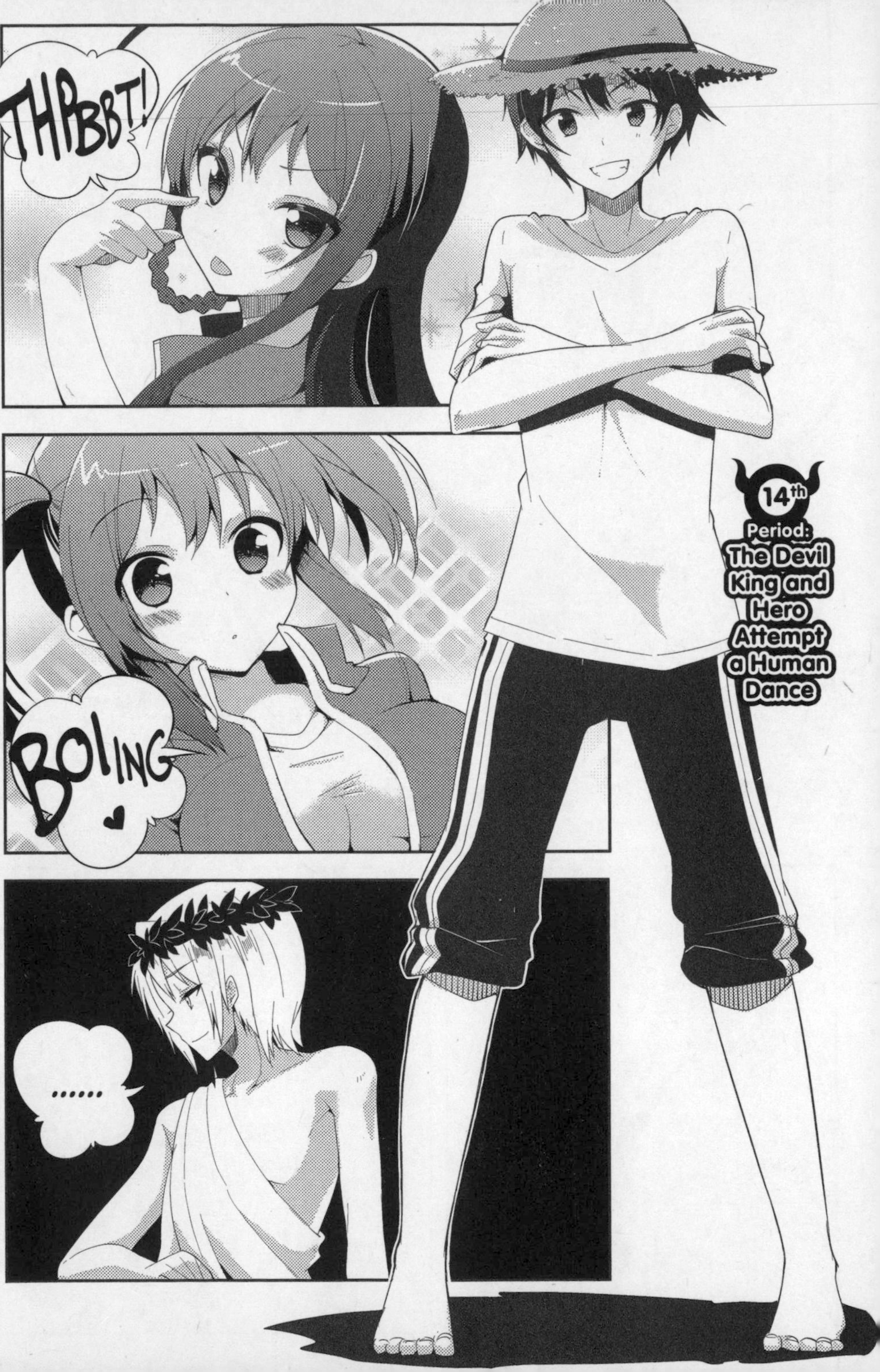
14th Period: The Devil King and Hero Attempt a Human Dance
THPBBT!
BOI!NG ♥
......

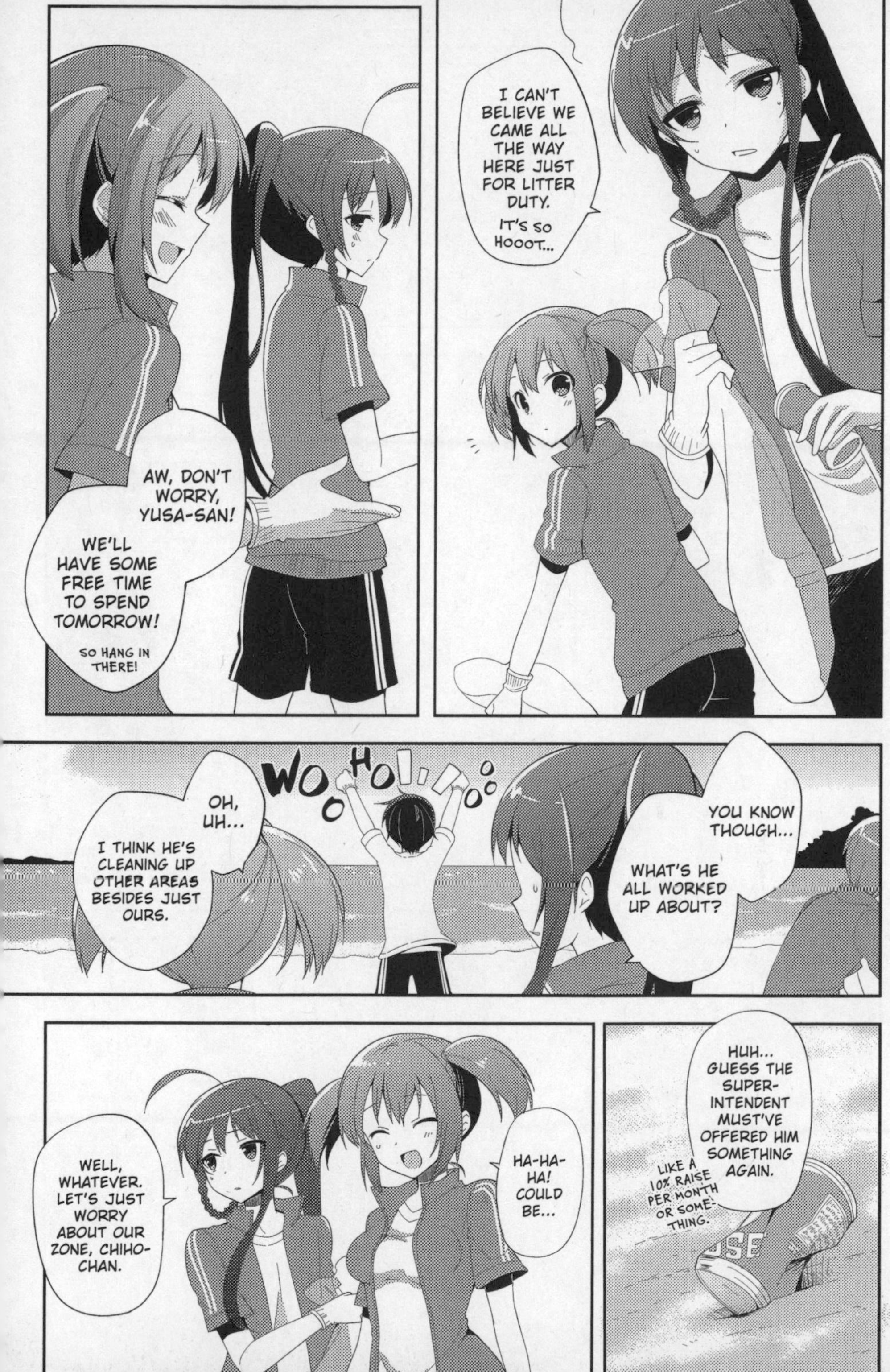
I CAN'T BELIEVE WE CAME ALL THE WAY HERE JUST FOR LITTER DUTY.
IT'S SO HOOOT...
AW, DON'T WORRY, YUSA-SAN!
WE'LL HAVE SOME FREE TIME TO SPEND TOMORROW!
SO HANG IN THERE!
YOU KNOW THOUGH...
WHAT'S HE ALL WORKED UP ABOUT?
WOOHO!!OOO
OH, UH...
I THINK HE'S CLEANING UP OTHER AREAS BESIDES JUST OURS.
HUH... GUESS THE SUPER-INTENDENT MUST'VE OFFERED HIM SOMETHING AGAIN.
LIKE A 10% RAISE PER MONTH OR SOME-THING.
HA-HA-HA! COULD BE...
WELL, WHATEVER. LET'S JUST WORRY ABOUT OUR ZONE, CHIHO-CHAN.

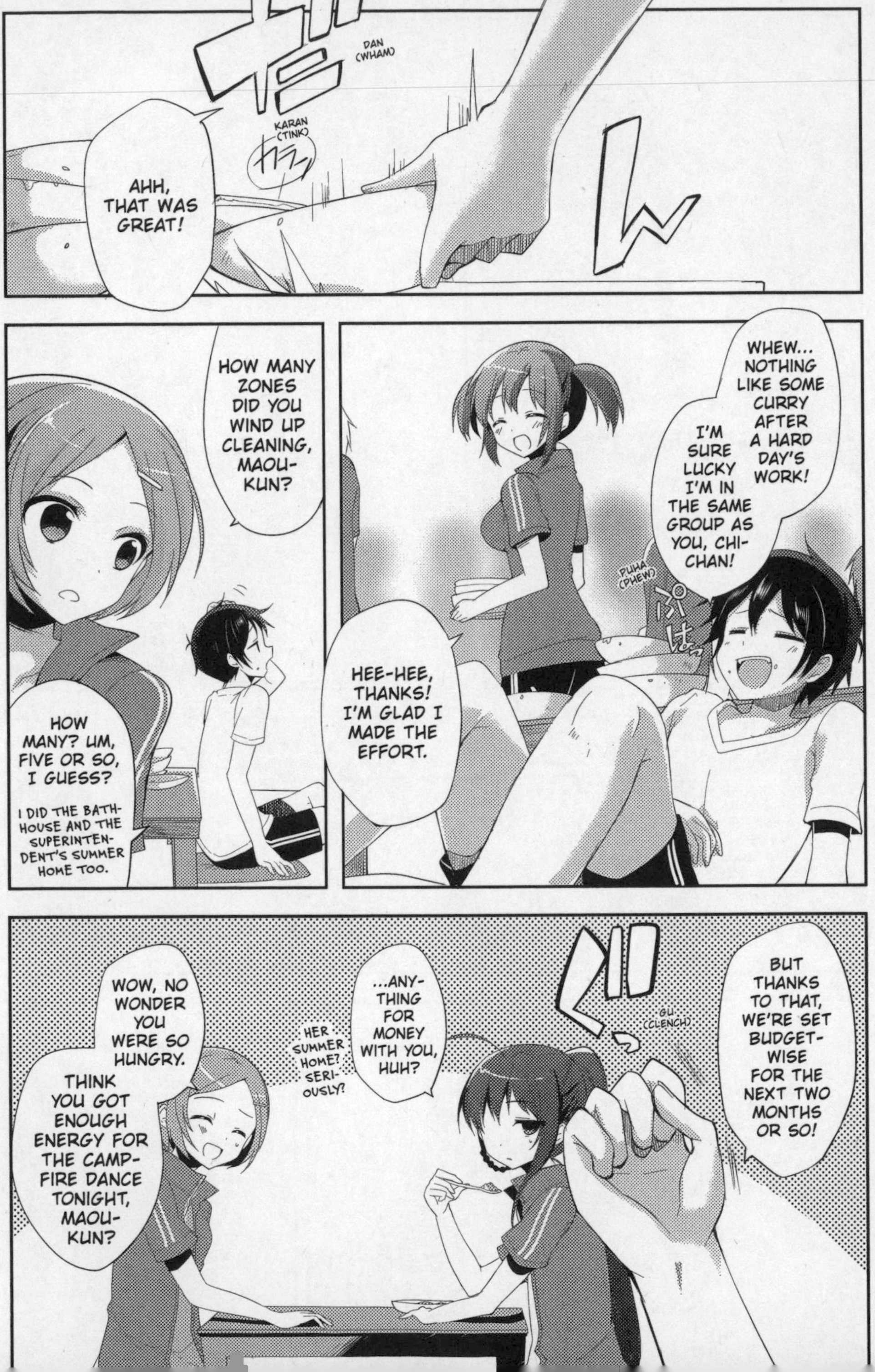
DAN (WHAM)
KARAN (TINK)
AHH, THAT WAS GREAT!
WHEW... NOTHING LIKE SOME CURRY AFTER A HARD DAY'S WORK!
I'M SURE LUCKY I'M IN THE SAME GROUP AS YOU, CHI-CHAN!
PUHA (PHEW)
HEE-HEE, THANKS! I'M GLAD I MADE THE EFFORT.
HOW MANY ZONES DID YOU WIND UP CLEANING, MAOU-KUN?
HOW MANY? UM, FIVE OR SO, I GUESS?
I DID THE BATHHOUSE AND THE SUPERINTENDENT'S SUMMER HOME TOO.
BUT THANKS TO THAT, WE'RE SET BUDGET-WISE FOR THE NEXT TWO MONTHS OR SO!
GU (CLENCH)
...ANYTHING FOR MONEY WITH YOU, HUH?
HER SUMMER HOME? SERIOUSLY?
WOW, NO WONDER YOU WERE SO HUNGRY.
THINK YOU GOT ENOUGH ENERGY FOR THE CAMPFIRE DANCE TONIGHT, MAOU-KUN?

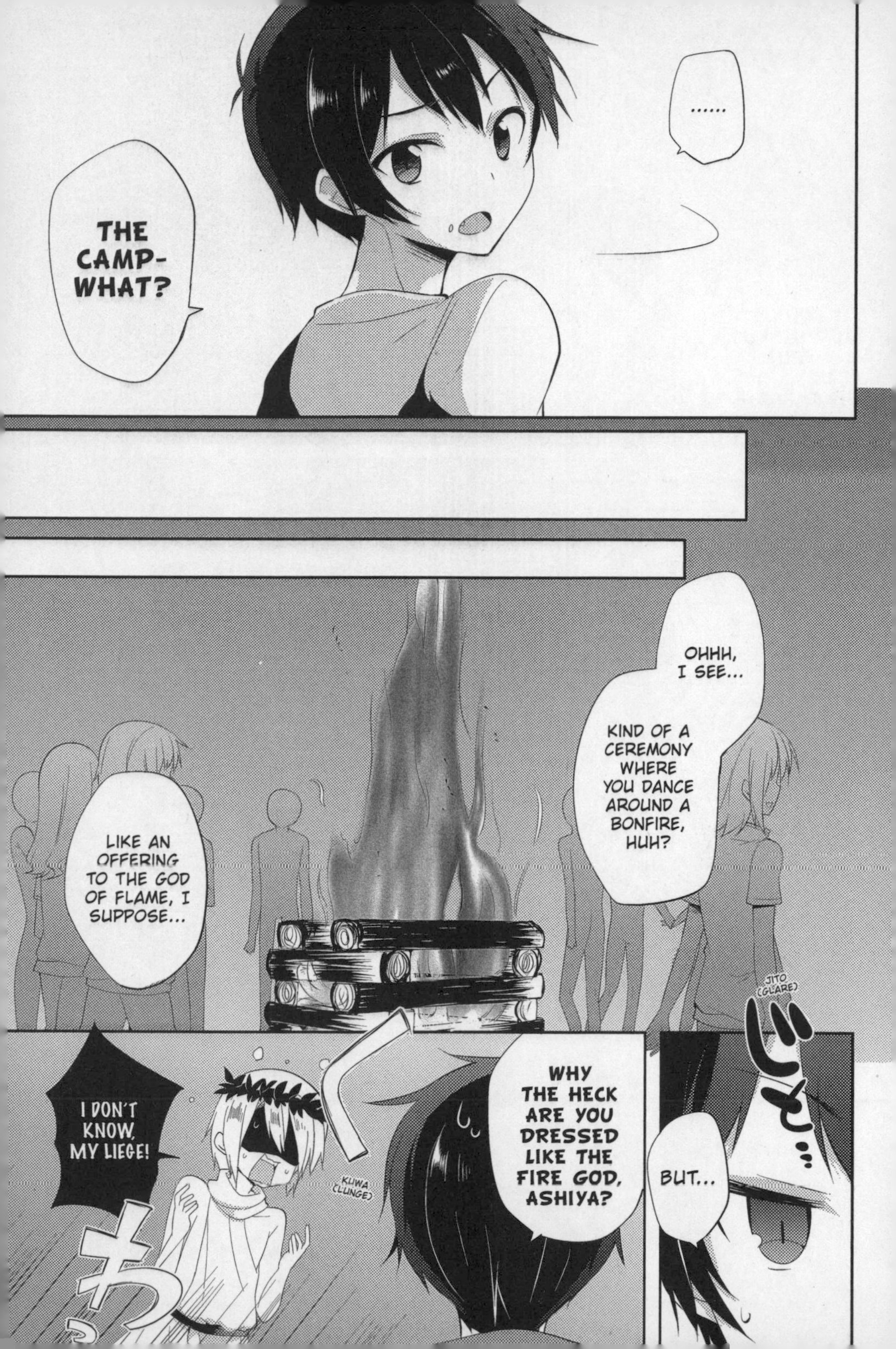
……
THE CAMP-WHAT?
OHHH, I SEE...
KIND OF A CEREMONY WHERE YOU DANCE AROUND A BONFIRE, HUH?
LIKE AN OFFERING TO THE GOD OF FLAME, I SUPPOSE...
JITO (GLARE)
BUT...
WHY THE HECK ARE YOU DRESSED LIKE THE FIRE GOD, ASHIYA?
KUWA (LUNGE)
I DON'T KNOW, MY LIEGE!

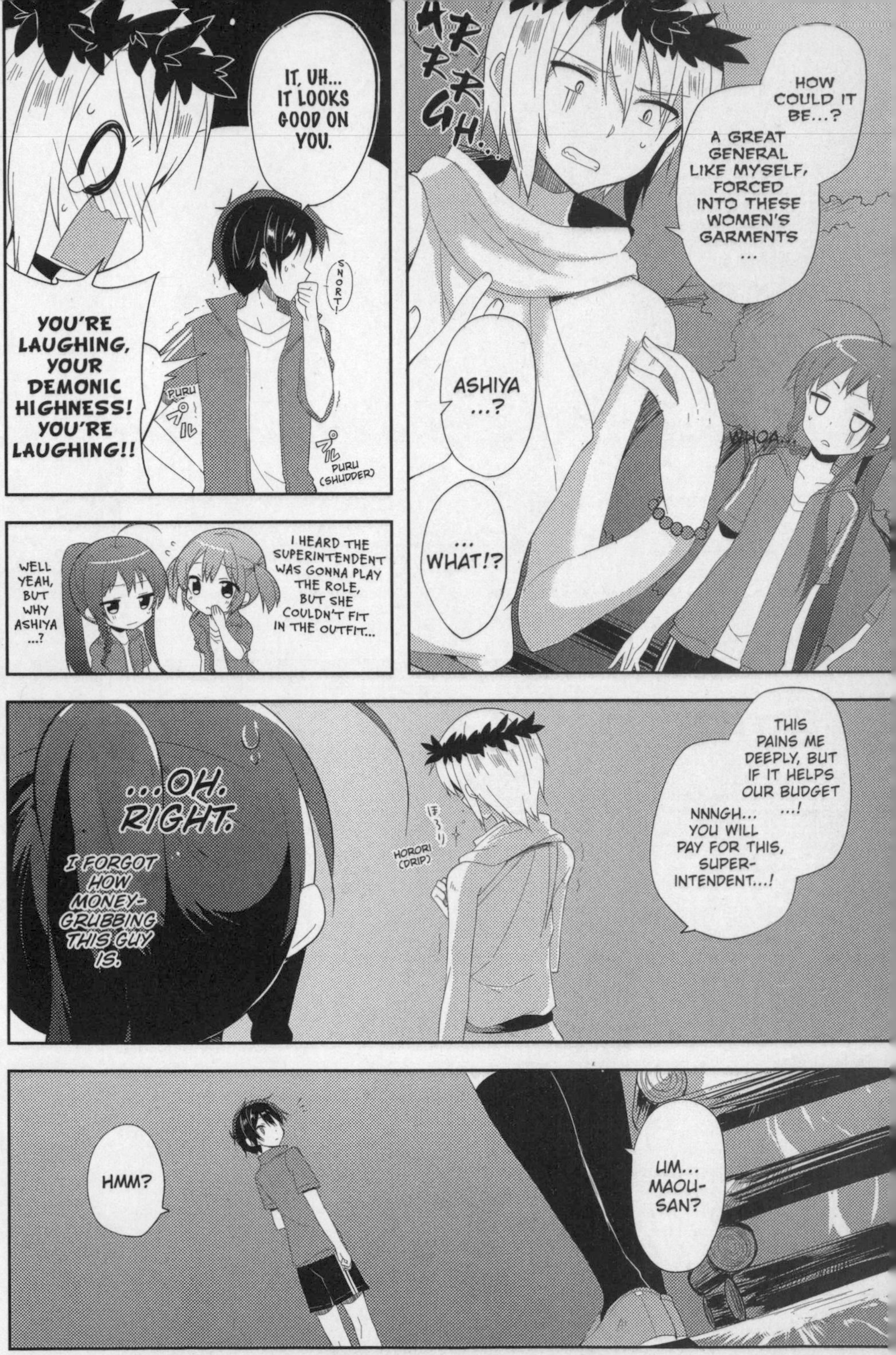
HOW COULD IT BE...? A GREAT GENERAL LIKE MYSELF, FORCED INTO THESE WOMEN'S GARMENTS...
ARRRGH...
WHOA...
ASHIYA...?
...WHAT!?
IT, UH... IT LOOKS GOOD ON YOU.
SNORT!
YOU'RE LAUGHING, YOUR DEMONIC HIGHNESS! YOU'RE LAUGHING!!
PURU
PURU (SHUDDER)
I HEARD THE SUPERINTENDENT WAS GONNA PLAY THE ROLE, BUT SHE COULDN'T FIT IN THE OUTFIT...
WELL YEAH, BUT WHY ASHIYA...?
THIS PAINS ME DEEPLY, BUT IF IT HELPS OUR BUDGET...!
NNNGH... YOU WILL PAY FOR THIS, SUPER-INTENDENT...!
ほろり
HORORI (DRIP)
...OH. RIGHT.
I FORGOT HOW MONEY-GRUBBING THIS GUY IS.
UM... MAOU-SAN?
HMM?

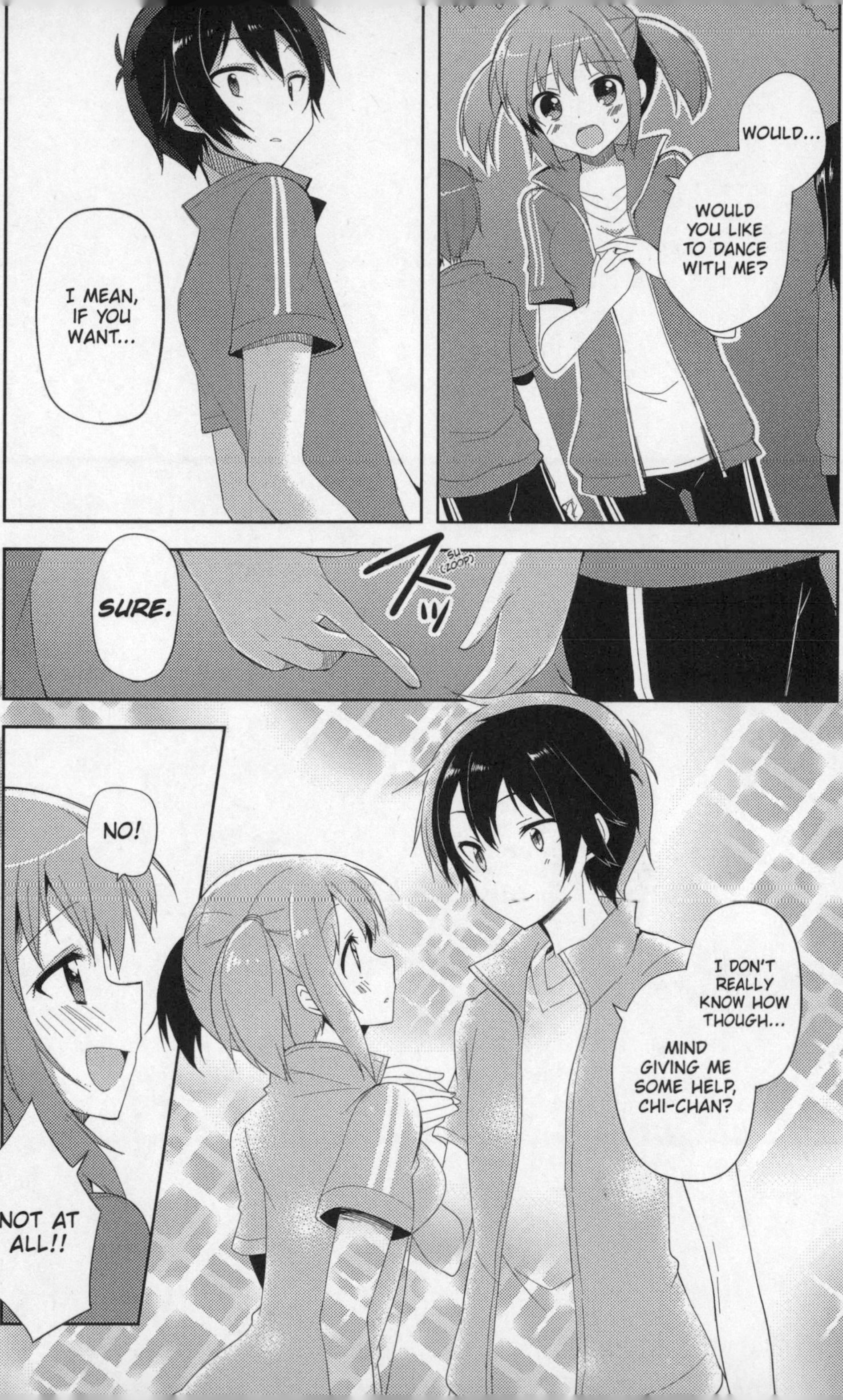
WOULD...
WOULD YOU LIKE TO DANCE WITH ME?
I MEAN, IF YOU WANT...
スッ
SU (ZOOP)
SURE.
I DON'T REALLY KNOW HOW THOUGH...
MIND GIVING ME SOME HELP, CHI-CHAN?
NO!
NOT AT ALL!!

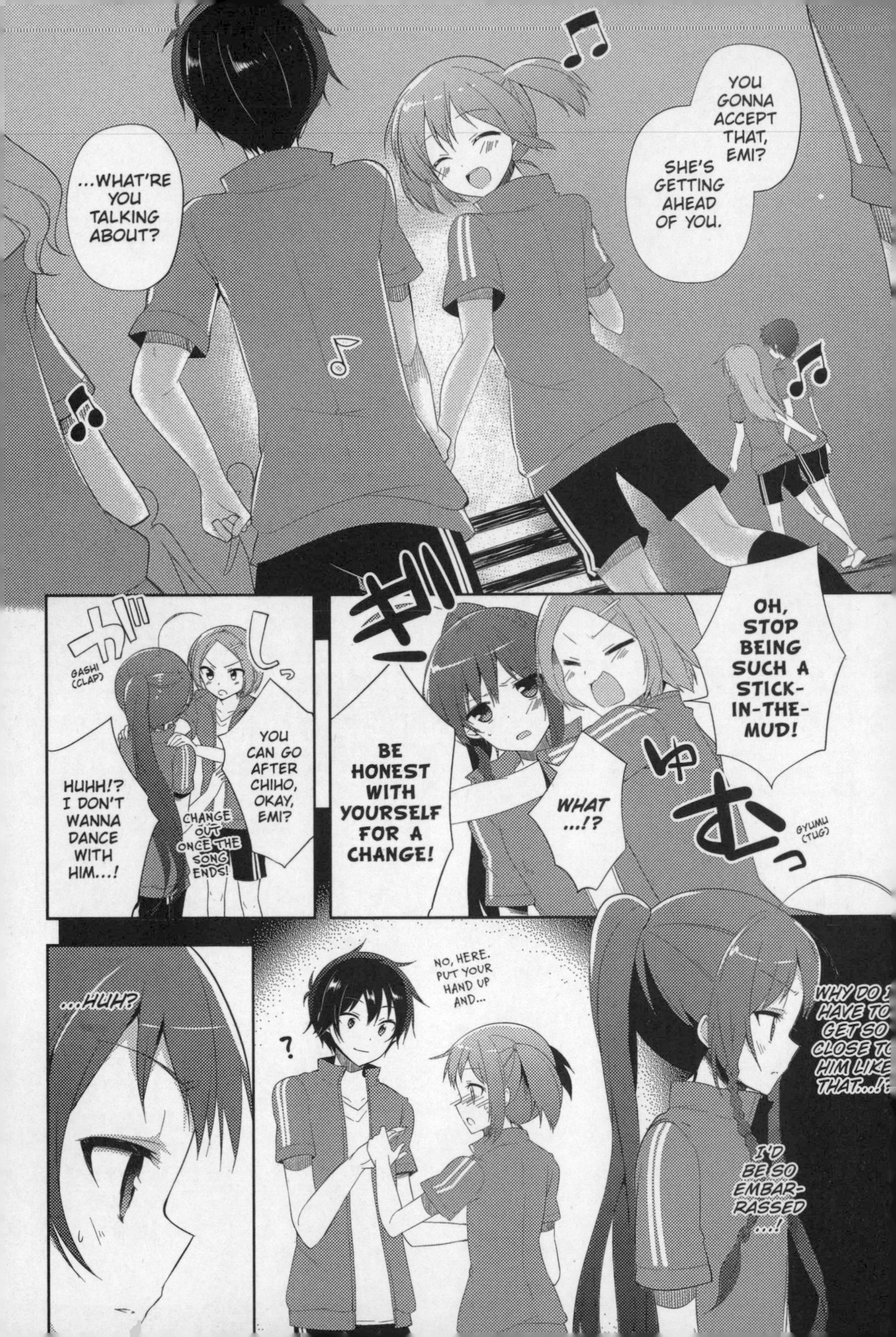

YOU GONNA ACCEPT THAT, EMI?
SHE'S GETTING AHEAD OF YOU.
...WHAT'RE YOU TALKING ABOUT?
OH, STOP BEING SUCH A STICK-IN-THE-MUD!
GYUMU (TUG)
WHAT ...!?
BE HONEST WITH YOURSELF FOR A CHANGE!
GASHI (CLAP)
YOU CAN GO AFTER CHIHO, OKAY, EMI?
CHANGE OUT ONCE THE SONG ENDS!
HUHH!? I DON'T WANNA DANCE WITH HIM...!
WHY DO I HAVE TO GET SO CLOSE TO HIM LIKE THAT...!?
I'D BE SO EMBARRASSED...!
NO, HERE. PUT YOUR HAND UP AND...
?
...HUH?

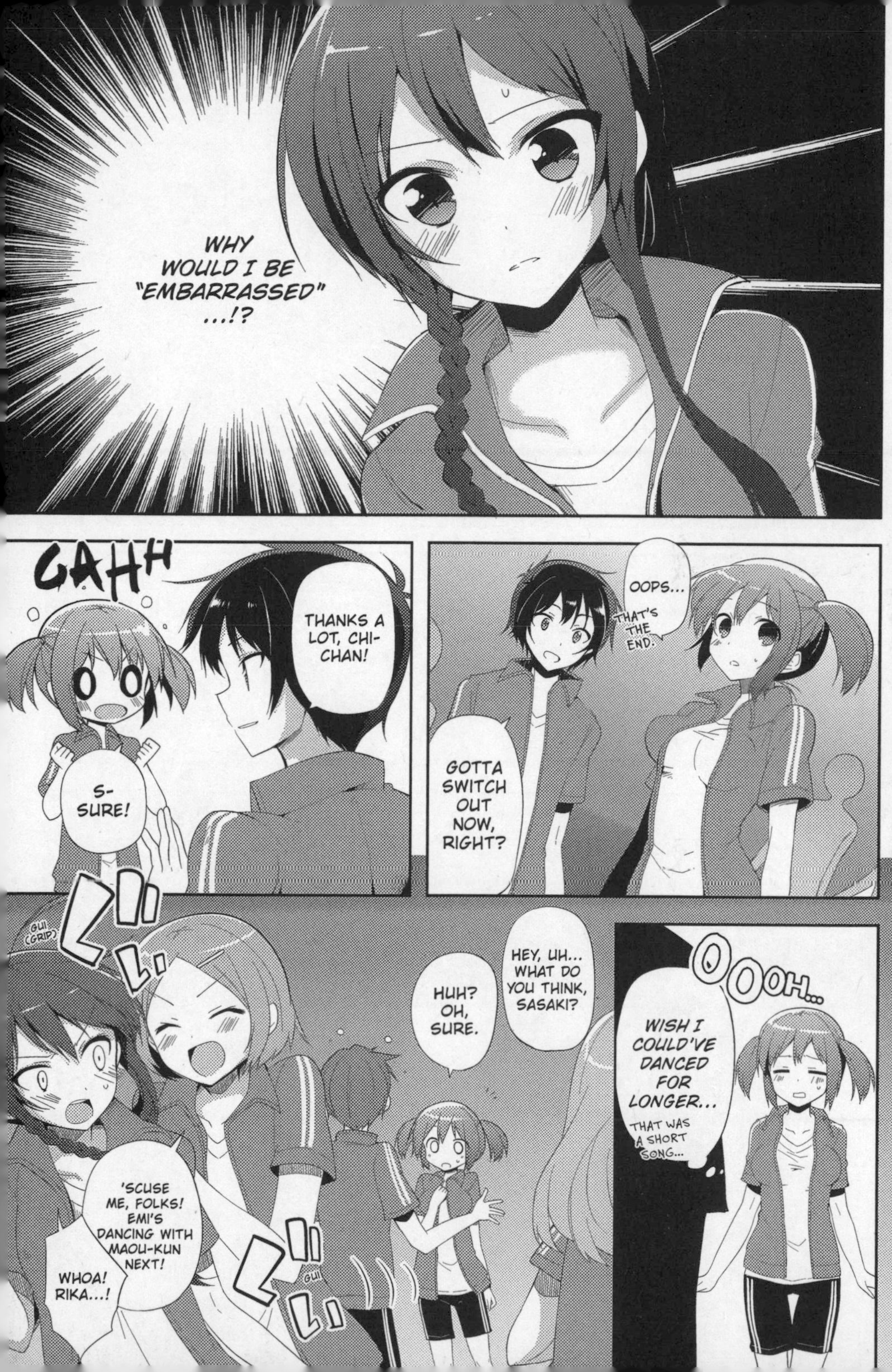
WHY WOULD I BE "EMBARRASSED" ...!?
OOPS...
THAT'S THE END.
GOTTA SWITCH OUT NOW, RIGHT?
GAHH
THANKS A LOT, CHI-CHAN!
S-SURE!
OOOH...
WISH I COULD'VE DANCED FOR LONGER...
THAT WAS A SHORT SONG...
HEY, UH... WHAT DO YOU THINK, SASAKI?
HUH? OH, SURE.
GUI (GRIP)
'SCUSE ME, FOLKS! EMI'S DANCING WITH MAOU-KUN NEXT!
WHOA! RIKA...!
GUI

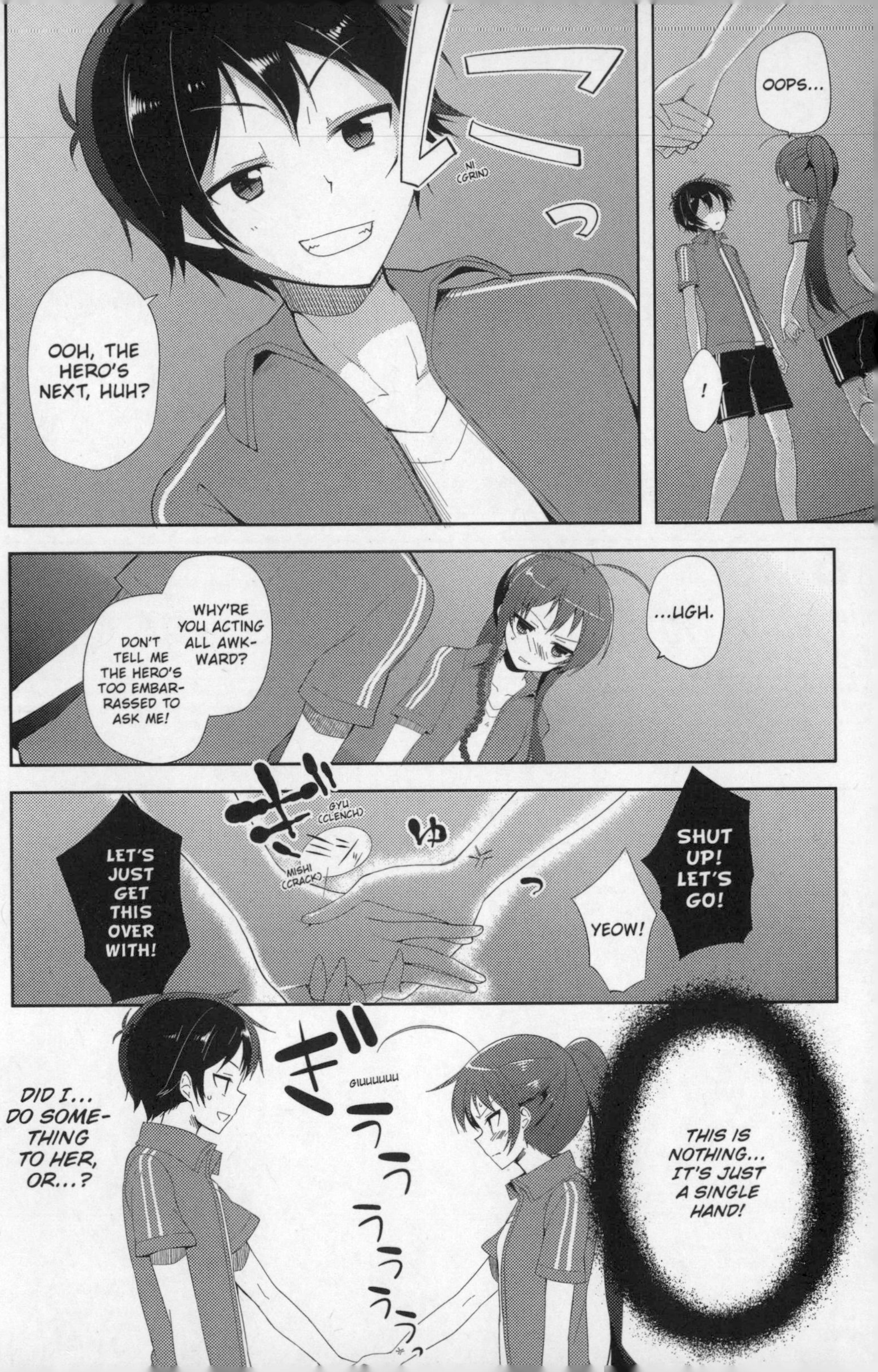
OOPS...
!
NI (GRIN)
OOH, THE HERO'S NEXT, HUH?
...UGH.
WHY'RE YOU ACTING ALL AWK-WARD?
DON'T TELL ME THE HERO'S TOO EMBAR-RASSED TO ASK ME!
SHUT UP! LET'S GO!
YEOW!
GYU (CLENCH)
MISHI (CRACK)
LET'S JUST GET THIS OVER WITH!
THIS IS NOTHING... IT'S JUST A SINGLE HAND!
GIUUUUUUU
DID I... DO SOME-THING TO HER, OR...?

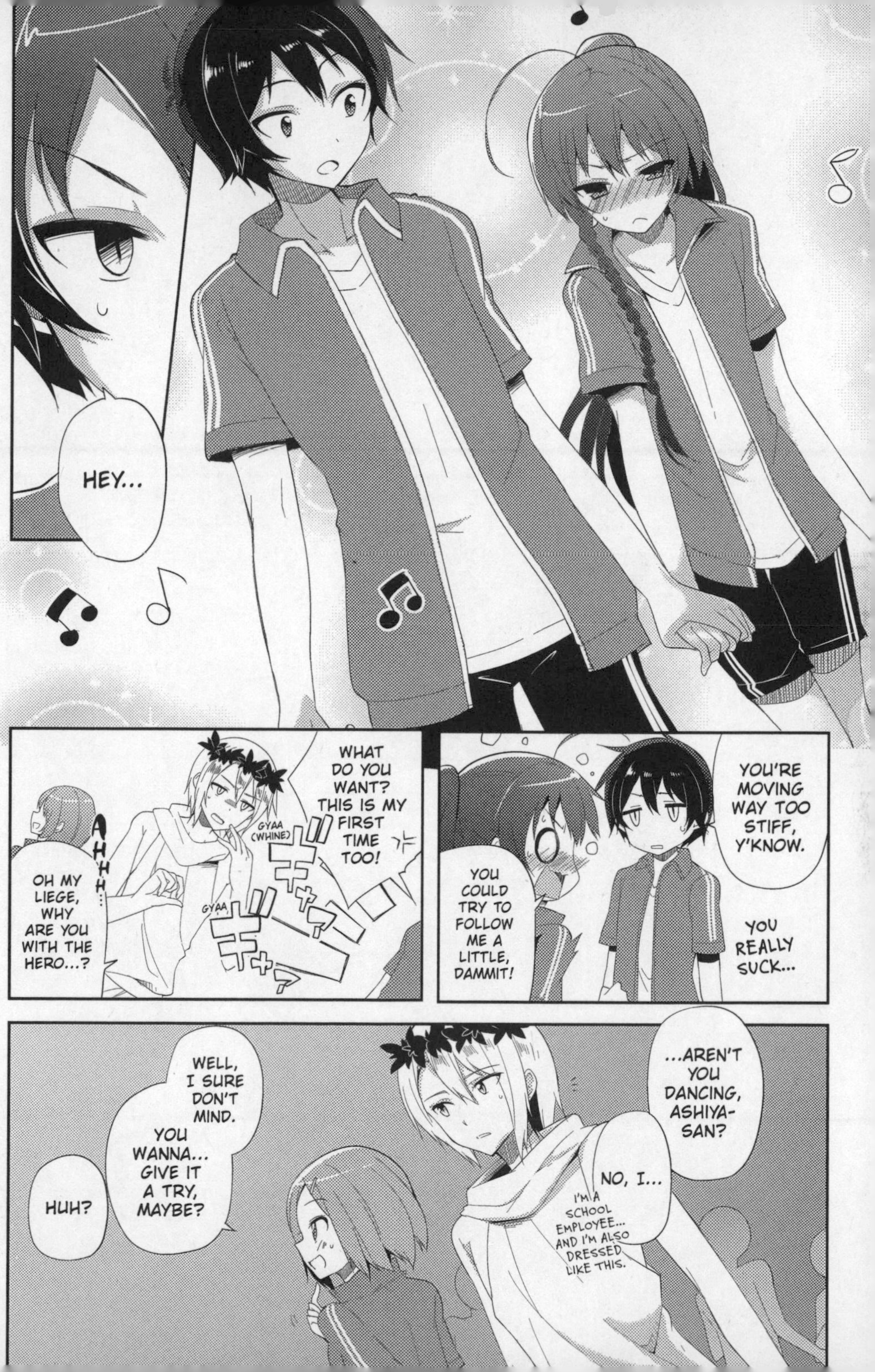
HEY...
YOU'RE MOVING WAY TOO STIFF, Y'KNOW.
YOU REALLY SUCK...
YOU COULD TRY TO FOLLOW ME A LITTLE, DAMMIT!
WHAT DO YOU WANT? THIS IS MY FIRST TIME TOO!
GYAA (WHINE)
GYAA
AHHH...
OH MY LIEGE, WHY ARE YOU WITH THE HERO...?
...AREN'T YOU DANCING, ASHIYA-SAN?
NO, I...
I'M A SCHOOL EMPLOYEE... AND I'M ALSO DRESSED LIKE THIS.
WELL, I SURE DON'T MIND.
YOU WANNA... GIVE IT A TRY, MAYBE?
HUH?

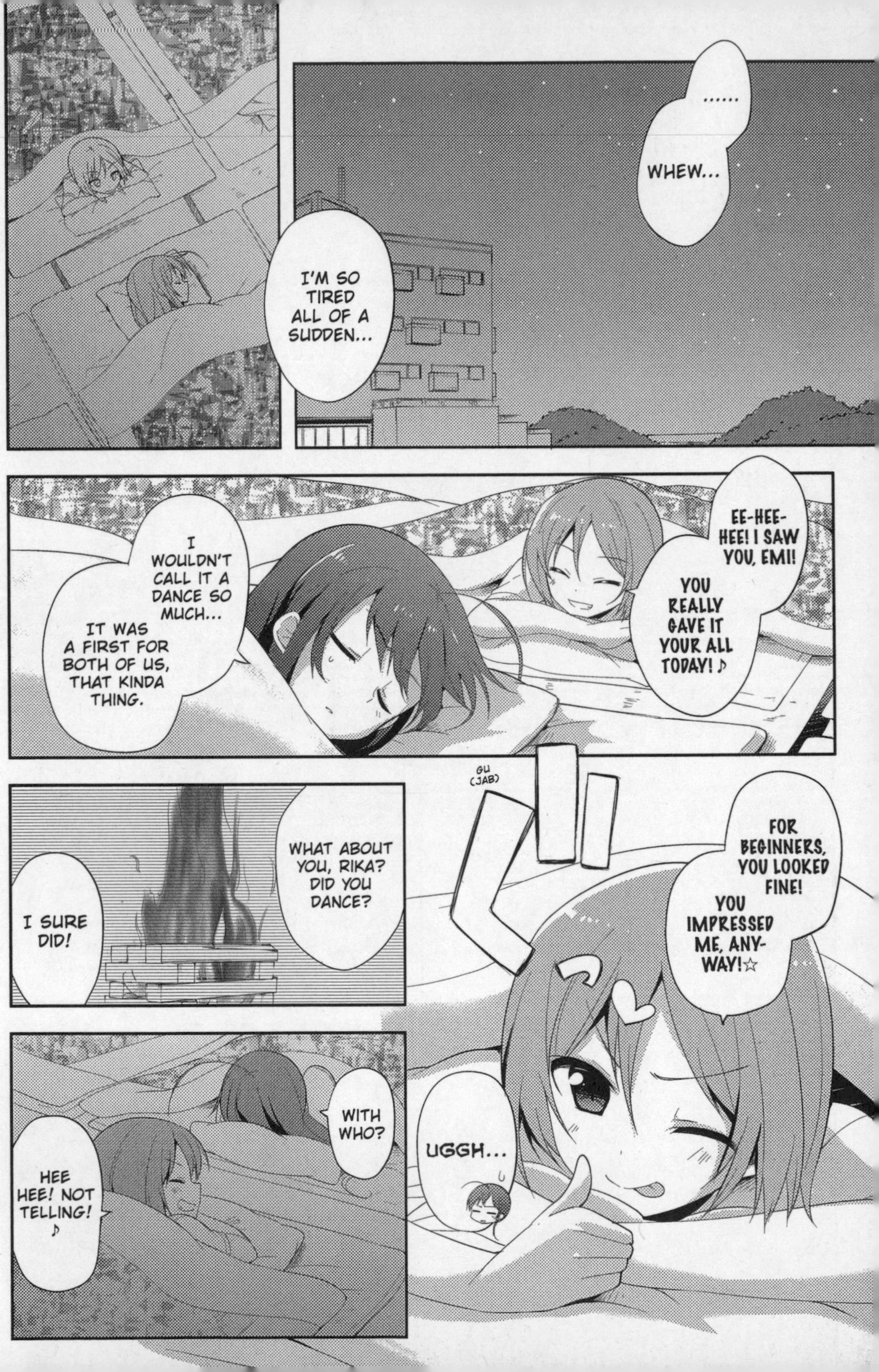
......
WHEW...
I'M SO TIRED ALL OF A SUDDEN...
EE-HEE-HEE! I SAW YOU, EMI!
YOU REALLY GAVE IT YOUR ALL TODAY! ♪
I WOULDN'T CALL IT A DANCE SO MUCH...
IT WAS A FIRST FOR BOTH OF US, THAT KINDA THING.
GU (JAB)
FOR BEGINNERS, YOU LOOKED FINE!
YOU IMPRESSED ME, ANY-WAY!☆
UGGH...
WHAT ABOUT YOU, RIKA? DID YOU DANCE?
I SURE DID!
WITH WHO?
HEE HEE! NOT TELLING! ♪

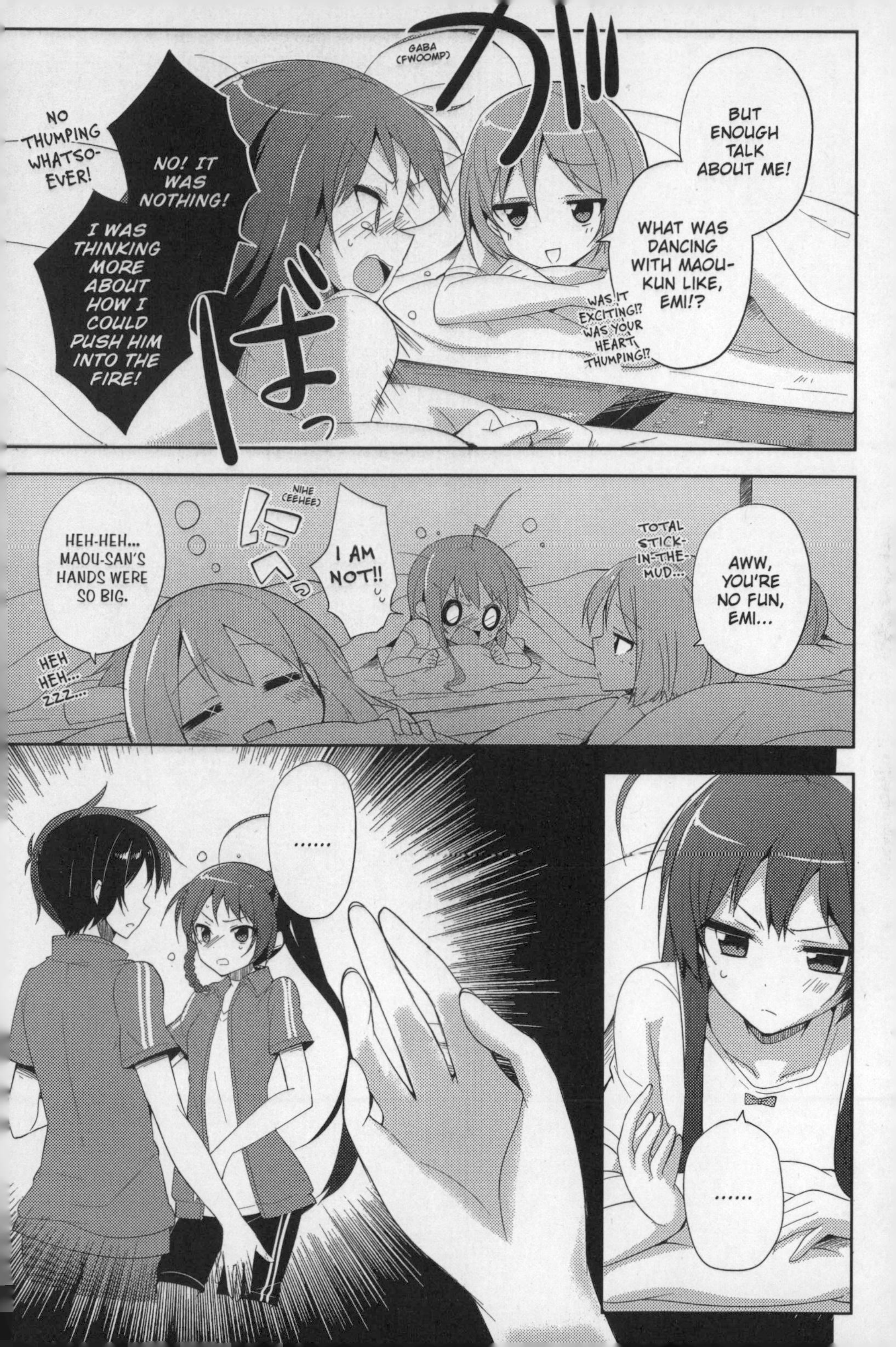
BUT ENOUGH TALK ABOUT ME!
WHAT WAS DANCING WITH MAOU-KUN LIKE, EMI!?
WAS IT EXCITING!? WAS YOUR HEART THUMPING!?
GABA (FWOOMP)
NO! IT WAS NOTHING!
I WAS THINKING MORE ABOUT HOW I COULD PUSH HIM INTO THE FIRE!
NO THUMPING WHATSO-EVER!
AWW, YOU'RE NO FUN, EMI...
TOTAL STICK-IN-THE-MUD...
I AM NOT!!
NIHE (EEHEE)
HEH-HEH... MAOU-SAN'S HANDS WERE SO BIG.
HEH HEH... ZZZ...
......
......

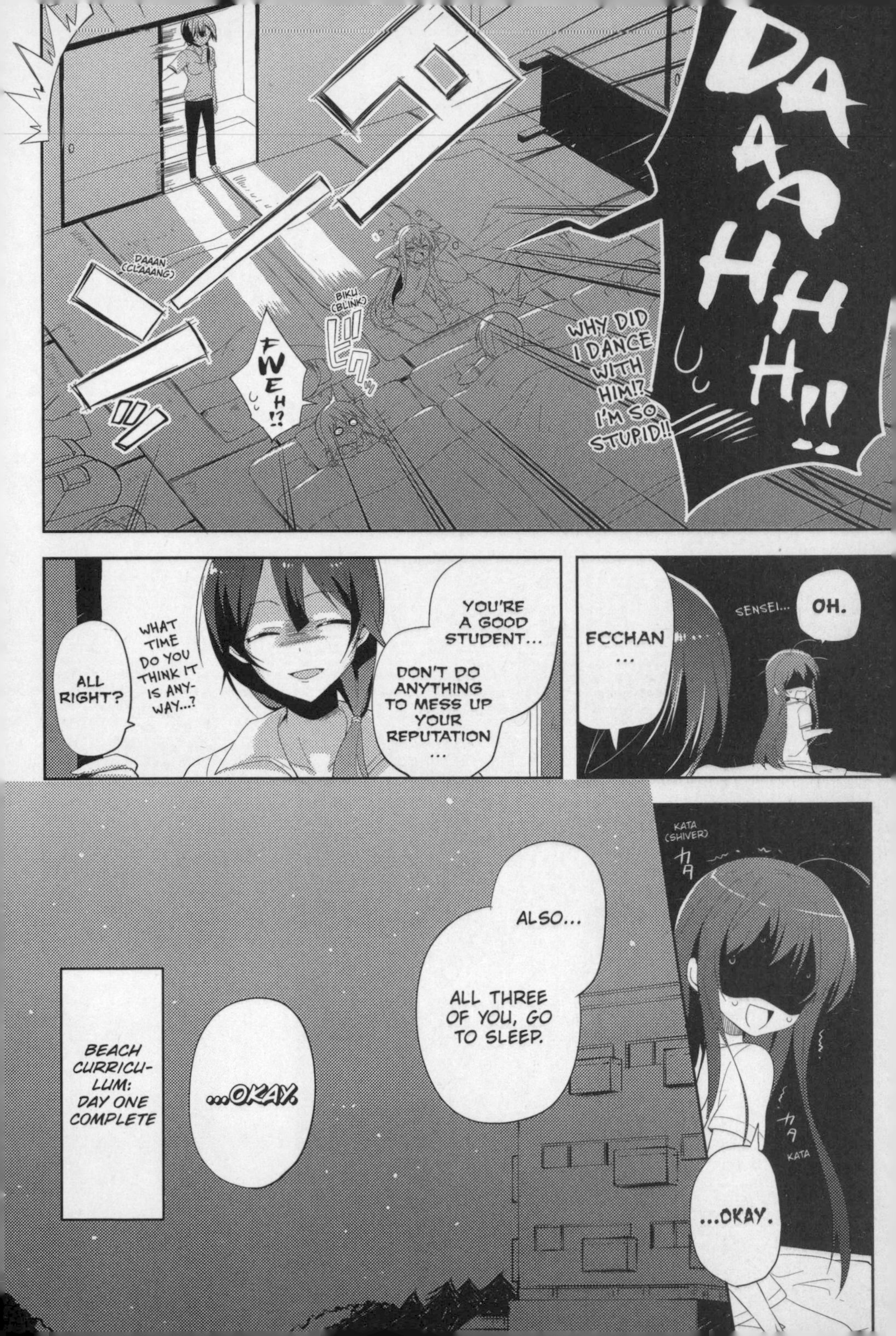
DAAHHHH!!
WHY DID I DANCE WITH HIM!? I'M SO STUPID!!
BIKU (BLINK)
FWEH!?
DAAAN (CLAAANG)
SENSEI...
OH.
ECCHAN ...
YOU'RE A GOOD STUDENT...
DON'T DO ANYTHING TO MESS UP YOUR REPUTATION ...
WHAT TIME DO YOU THINK IT IS ANY-WAY...?
ALL RIGHT?
KATA (SHIVER)
ALSO...
ALL THREE OF YOU, GO TO SLEEP.
KATA
...OKAY.
...OKAY.
BEACH CURRICU-LUM: DAY ONE COMPLETE

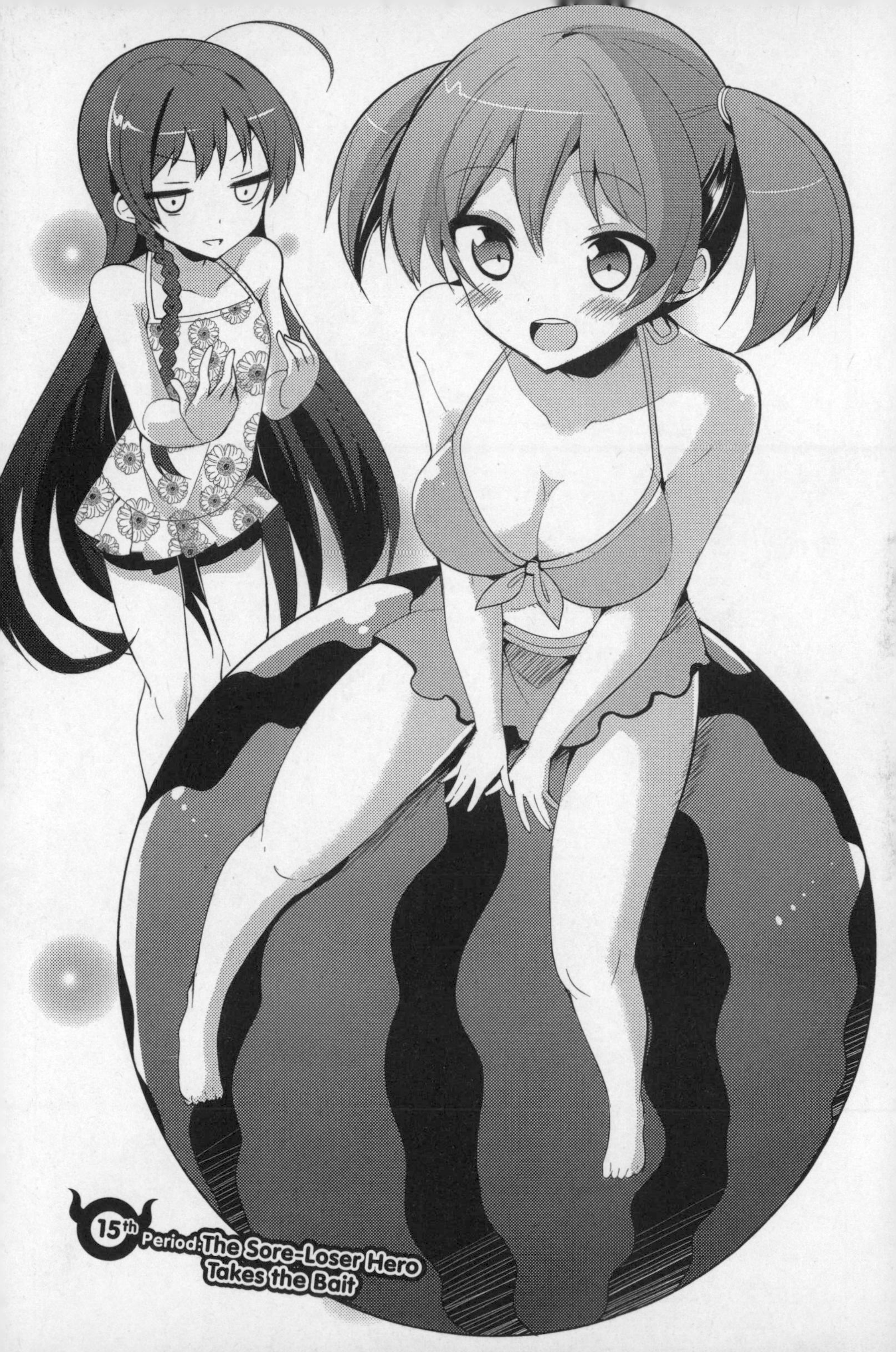

15th Period: The Sore-Loser Hero Takes the Bait

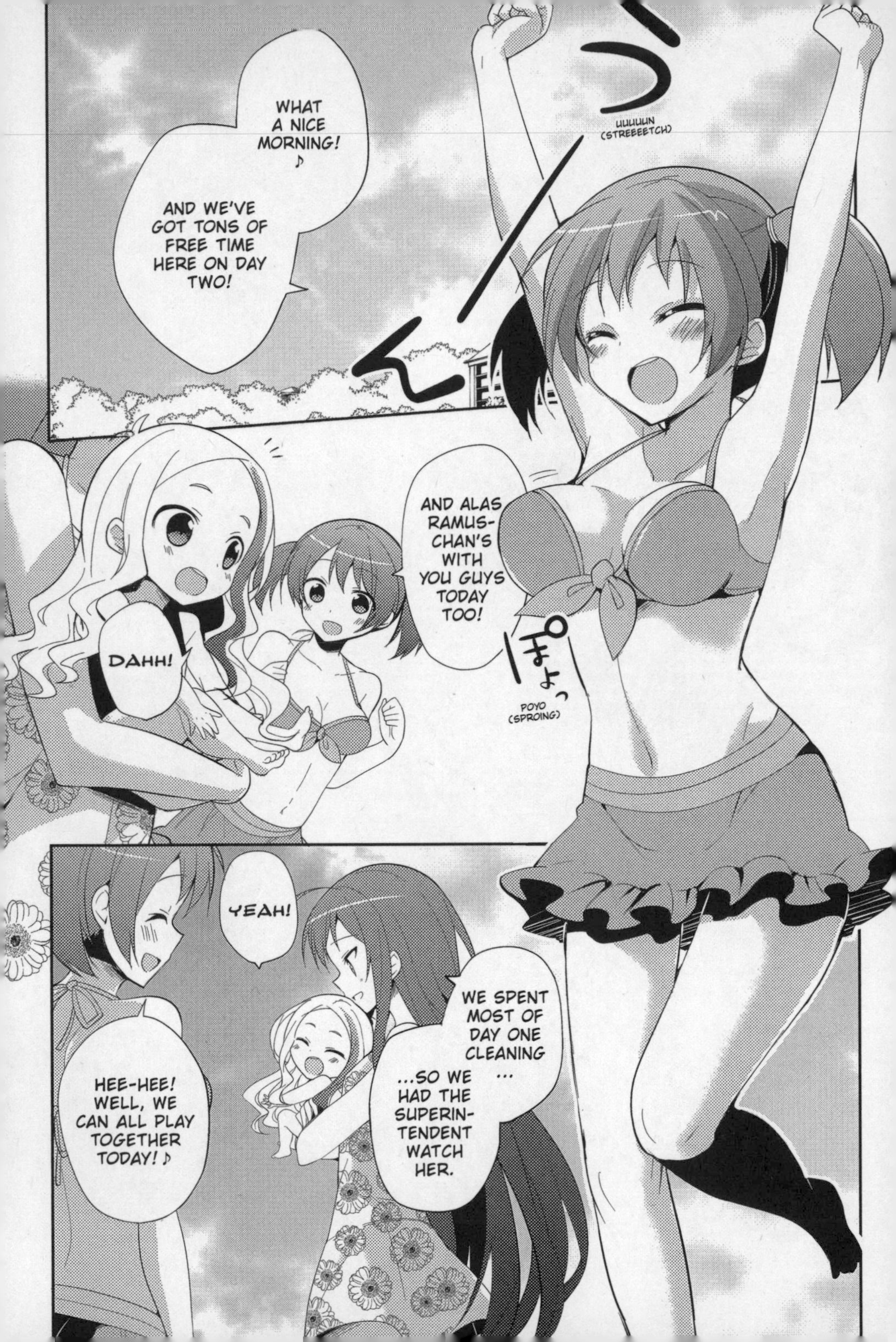
UUUUUN (STREEEETCH)
WHAT A NICE MORNING! ♪
AND WE'VE GOT TONS OF FREE TIME HERE ON DAY TWO!
AND ALAS RAMUS-CHAN'S WITH YOU GUYS TODAY TOO!
POYO (SPROING)
DAHH!
WE SPENT MOST OF DAY ONE CLEANING ...
...SO WE HAD THE SUPERINTENDENT WATCH HER.
YEAH!
HEE-HEE! WELL, WE CAN ALL PLAY TOGETHER TODAY! ♪

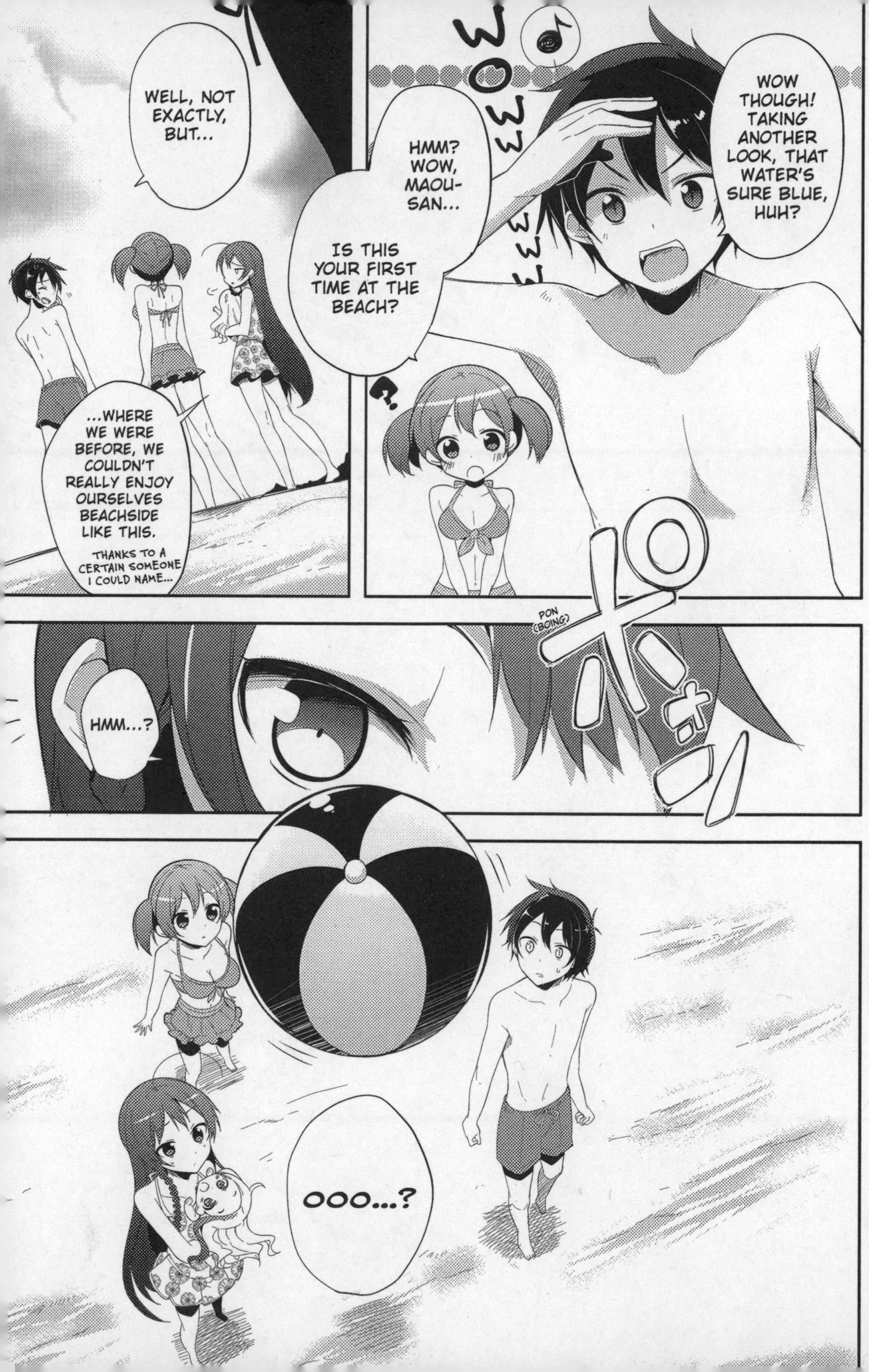
WOW THOUGH! TAKING ANOTHER LOOK, THAT WATER'S SURE BLUE, HUH?
WOWWWWWW
HMM? WOW, MAOU-SAN...
IS THIS YOUR FIRST TIME AT THE BEACH?
WELL, NOT EXACTLY, BUT...
...WHERE WE WERE BEFORE, WE COULDN'T REALLY ENJOY OURSELVES BEACHSIDE LIKE THIS.
THANKS TO A CERTAIN SOMEONE I COULD NAME...
PON (BOING)
HMM...?
OOO...?

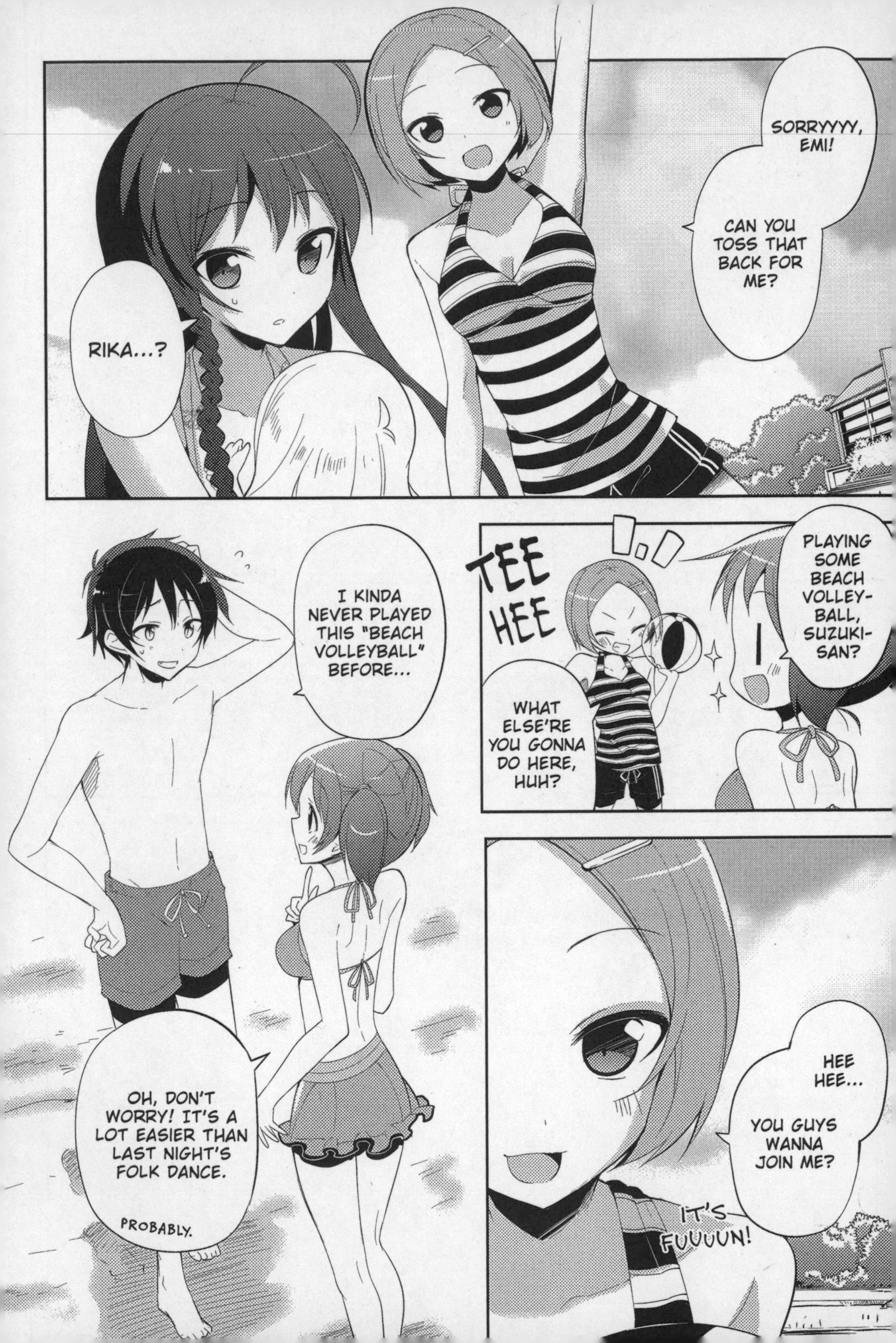
SORRYYYY, EMI!
CAN YOU TOSS THAT BACK FOR ME?
RIKA...?
PLAYING SOME BEACH VOLLEY-BALL, SUZUKI-SAN?
!!
TEE HEE
WHAT ELSE'RE YOU GONNA DO HERE, HUH?
HEE HEE...
YOU GUYS WANNA JOIN ME?
IT'S FUUUUN!
I KINDA NEVER PLAYED THIS "BEACH VOLLEYBALL" BEFORE...
OH, DON'T WORRY! IT'S A LOT EASIER THAN LAST NIGHT'S FOLK DANCE.
PROBABLY.

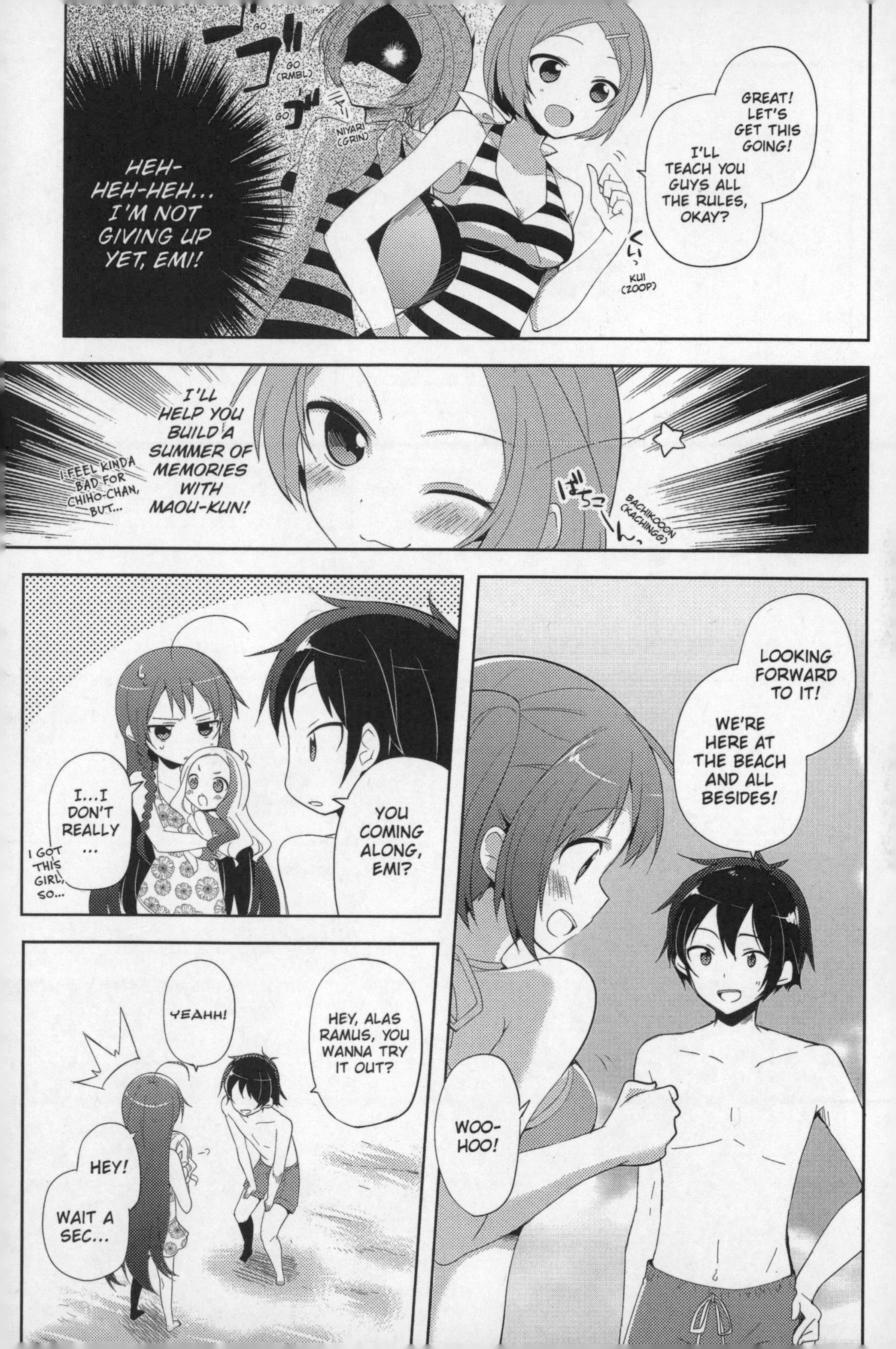
GREAT! LET'S GET THIS GOING!
I'LL TEACH YOU GUYS ALL THE RULES, OKAY?
くいっ
KUI (ZOOP)
GO
GO (RMBL)
GO
NIYARI (GRIN)
HEH-HEH-HEH... I'M NOT GIVING UP YET, EMI!
ばちこーん
BACHIKOOON (KACHINGG)
I'LL HELP YOU BUILD A SUMMER OF MEMORIES WITH MAOU-KUN!
I FEEL KINDA BAD FOR CHIHO-CHAN, BUT...
LOOKING FORWARD TO IT!
WE'RE HERE AT THE BEACH AND ALL BESIDES!
WOO-HOO!
YOU COMING ALONG, EMI?
I...I DON'T REALLY ...
I GOT THIS GIRL, SO...
HEY, ALAS RAMUS, YOU WANNA TRY IT OUT?
YEAHH!
HEY!
WAIT A SEC...

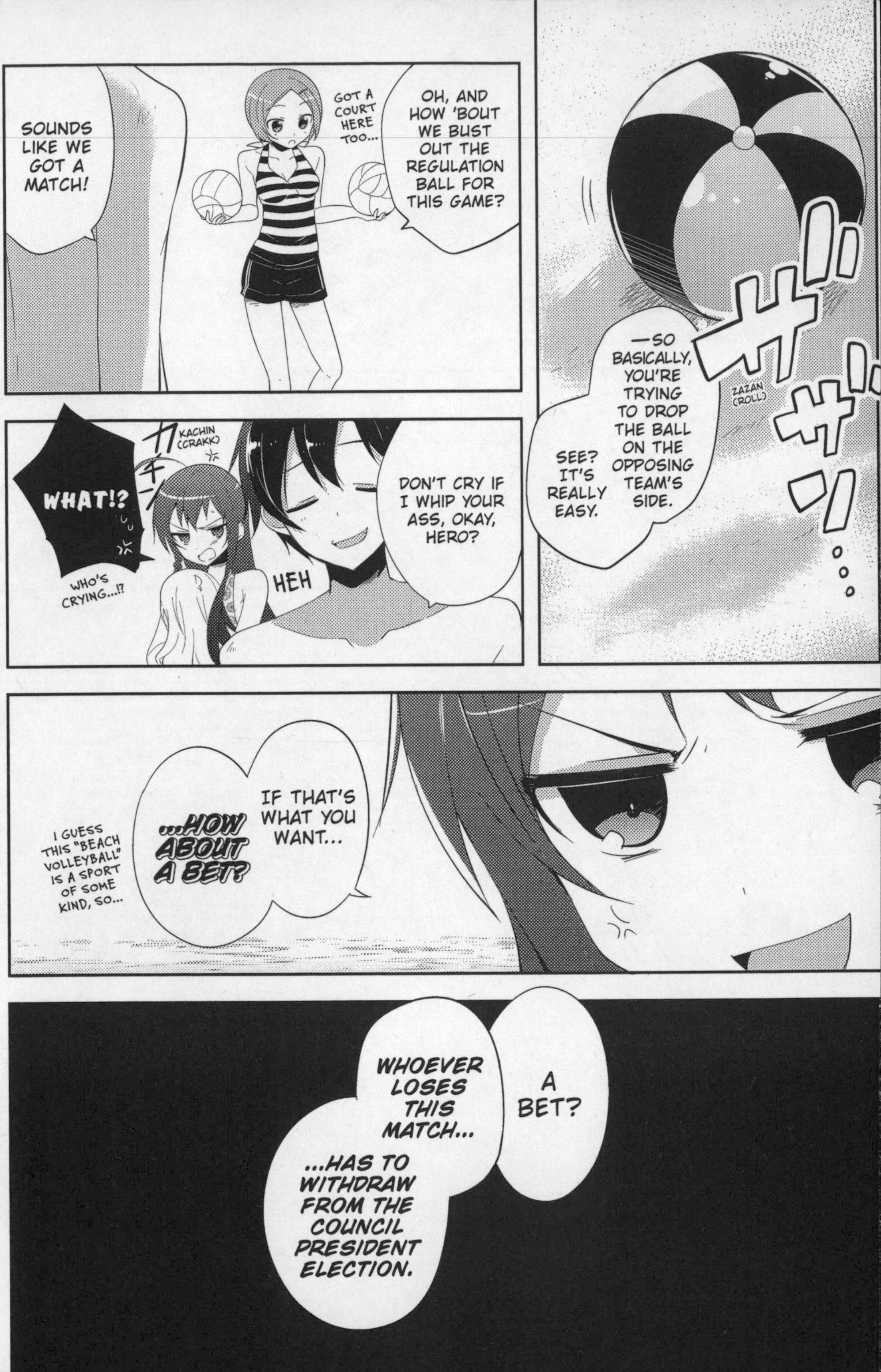

ZAZAN (ROLL)
—SO BASICALLY, YOU'RE TRYING TO DROP THE BALL ON THE OPPOSING TEAM'S SIDE.
SEE? IT'S REALLY EASY.
OH, AND HOW 'BOUT WE BUST OUT THE REGULATION BALL FOR THIS GAME?
GOT A COURT HERE TOO...
SOUNDS LIKE WE GOT A MATCH!
DON'T CRY IF I WHIP YOUR ASS, OKAY, HERO?
HEH
KACHIN (CRAKK)
WHAT!?
WHO'S CRYING...!?
IF THAT'S WHAT YOU WANT...
...HOW ABOUT A BET?
I GUESS THIS "BEACH VOLLEYBALL" IS A SPORT OF SOME KIND, SO...
A BET?
WHOEVER LOSES THIS MATCH...
...HAS TO WITHDRAW FROM THE COUNCIL PRESIDENT ELECTION.

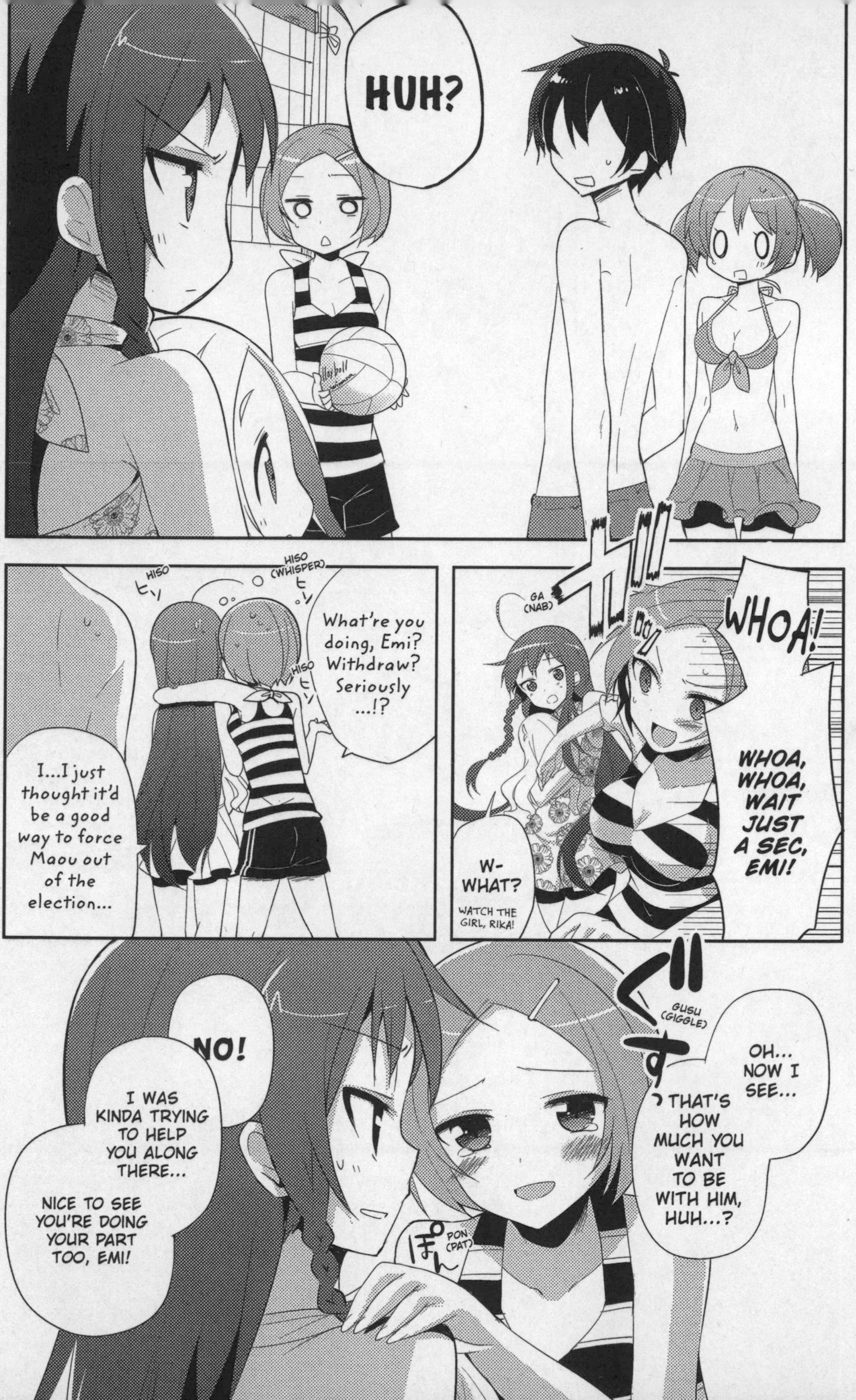
HUH?
GA (NAB)
WHOA!
WHOA, WHOA, WAIT JUST A SEC, EMI!
W- WHAT?
WATCH THE GIRL, RIKA!
HISO
HISO (WHISPER)
HISO
What're you doing, Emi? Withdraw? Seriously ...!?
I...I just thought it'd be a good way to force Maou out of the election...
GUSU (GIGGLE)
OH... NOW I SEE...
THAT'S HOW MUCH YOU WANT TO BE WITH HIM, HUH...?
NO!
I WAS KINDA TRYING TO HELP YOU ALONG THERE...
NICE TO SEE YOU'RE DOING YOUR PART TOO, EMI!
PON (PAT)

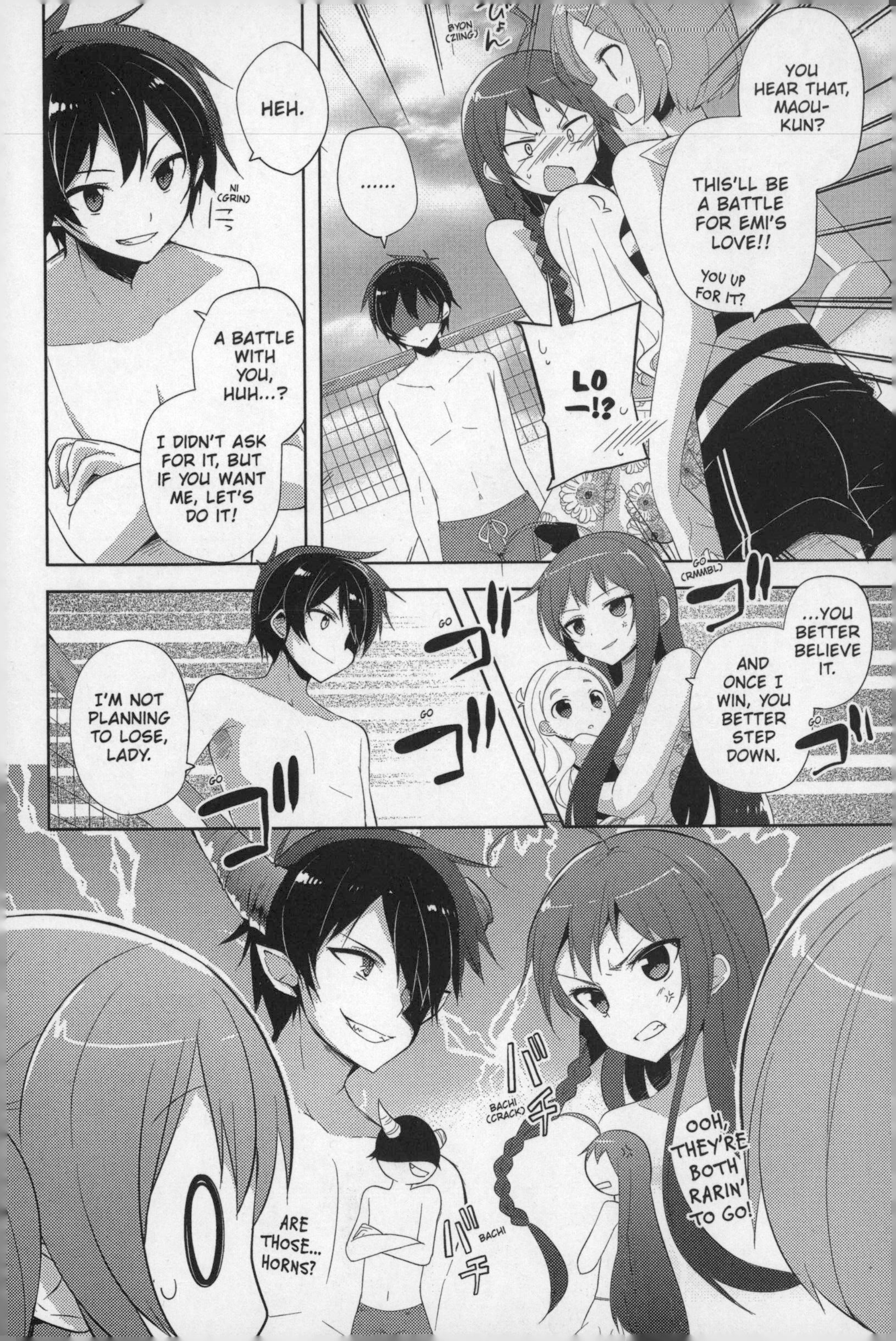
BYON (ZIING)
YOU HEAR THAT, MAOU-KUN?
......
THIS'LL BE A BATTLE FOR EMI'S LOVE!!
YOU UP FOR IT?
LO—!?
HEH.
NI (GRIN)
A BATTLE WITH YOU, HUH...?
I DIDN'T ASK FOR IT, BUT IF YOU WANT ME, LET'S DO IT!
GO (RMMBL)
...YOU BETTER BELIEVE IT.
AND ONCE I WIN, YOU BETTER STEP DOWN.
GO
GO
GO
I'M NOT PLANNING TO LOSE, LADY.
GO
BACHI (CRACK)
OOH, THEY'RE BOTH RARIN' TO GO!
BACHI
ARE THOSE... HORNS?

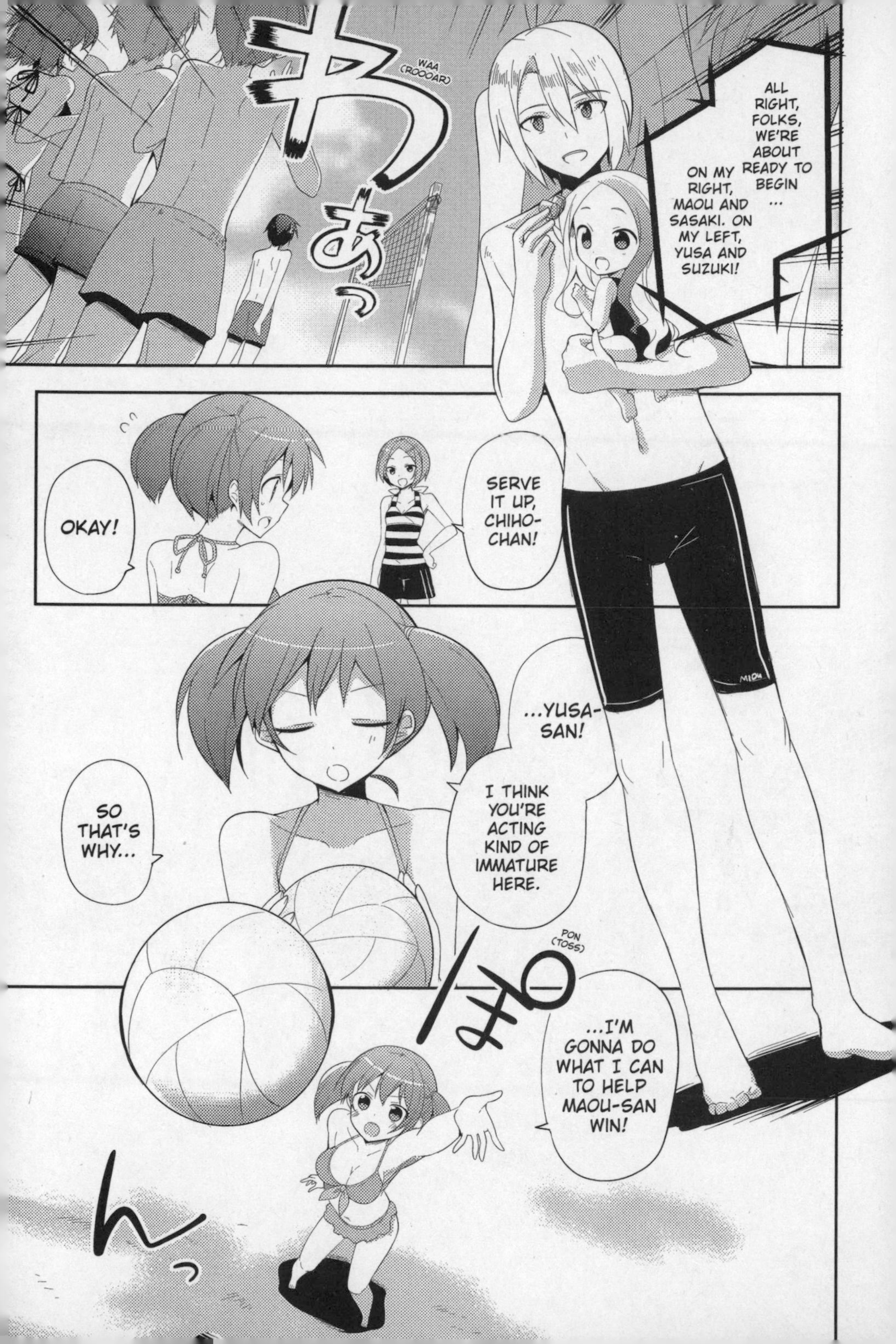
WAA (ROOOAR)
ALL RIGHT, FOLKS, WE'RE ABOUT READY TO BEGIN ...
ON MY RIGHT, MAOU AND SASAKI. ON MY LEFT, YUSA AND SUZUKI!
SERVE IT UP, CHIHO-CHAN!
OKAY!
...YUSA-SAN!
I THINK YOU'RE ACTING KIND OF IMMATURE HERE.
SO THAT'S WHY...
PON (TOSS)
...I'M GONNA DO WHAT I CAN TO HELP MAOU-SAN WIN!

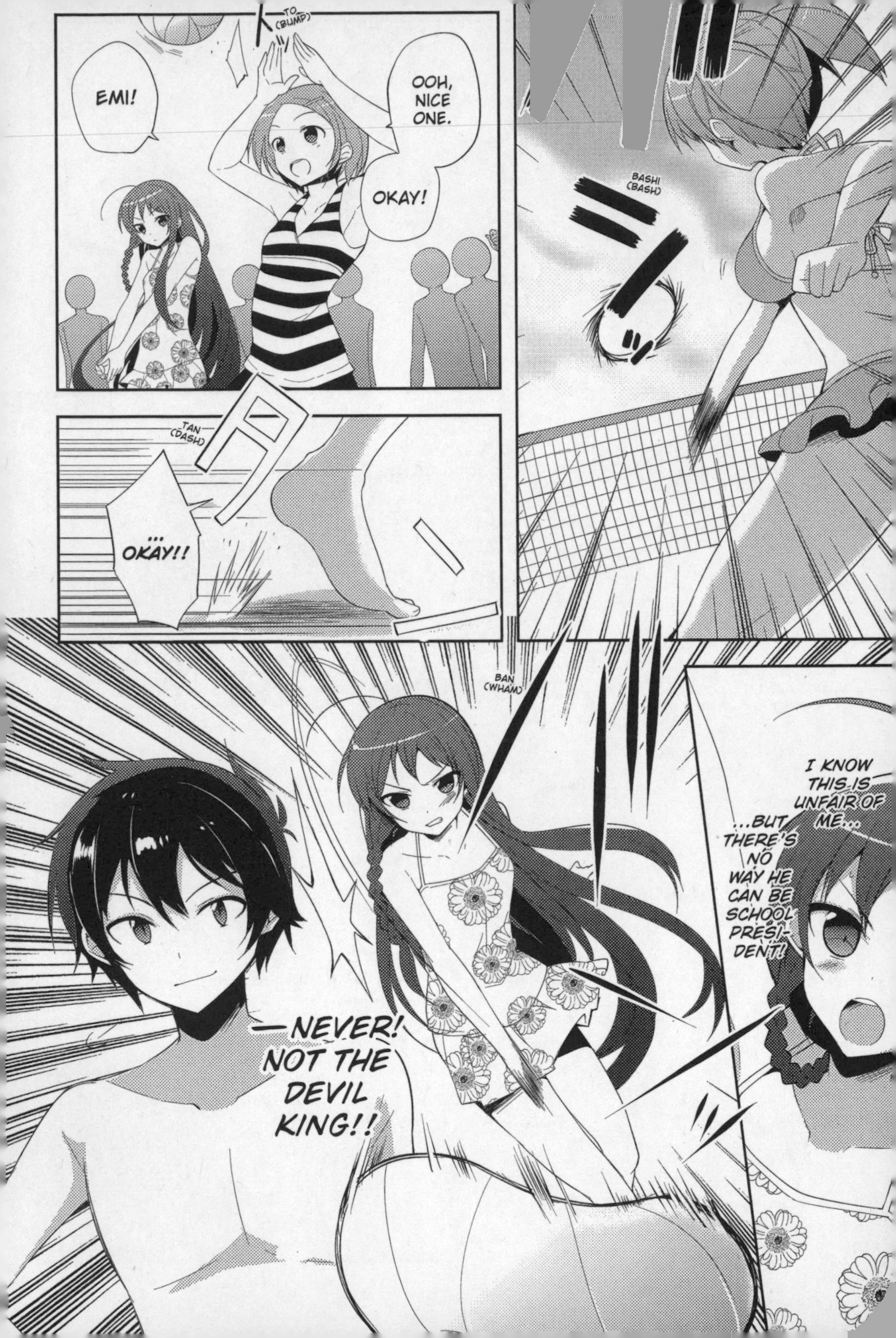
BASHI (BASH)
TO (BUMP)
OOH, NICE ONE.
EMI!
OKAY!
TAN (DASH)
...OKAY!!
I KNOW THIS IS UNFAIR OF ME...
...BUT THERE'S NO WAY HE CAN BE SCHOOL PRESI-DENT!
BAN (WHAM)
—NEVER! NOT THE DEVIL KING!!

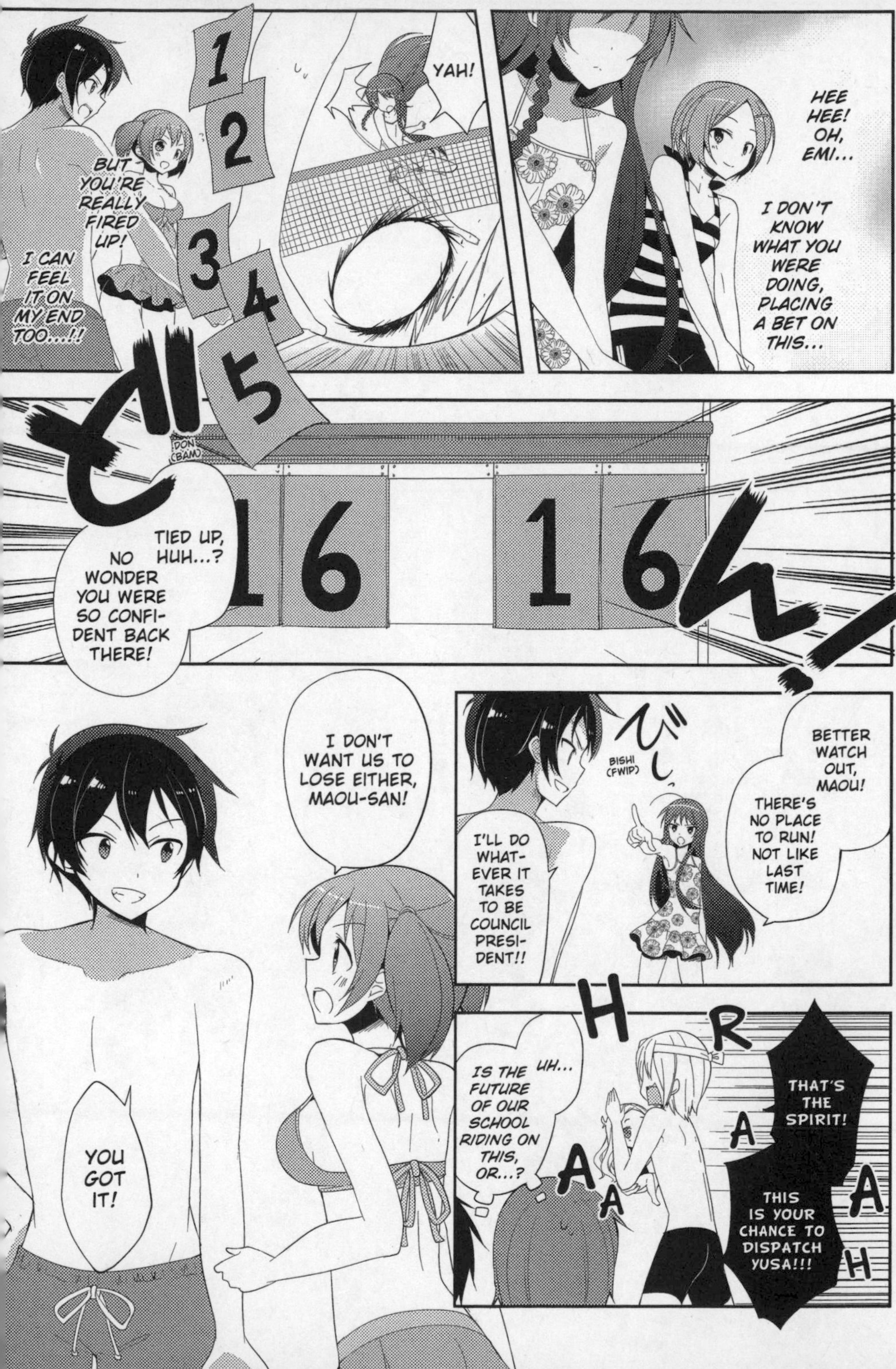

HEE HEE! OH, EMI...
I DON'T KNOW WHAT YOU WERE DOING, PLACING A BET ON THIS...
YAH!
1
2
BUT YOU'RE REALLY FIRED UP!
I CAN FEEL IT ON MY END TOO...!!
3
4
5
DON (BAM)
16 16
TIED UP, HUH...?
NO WONDER YOU WERE SO CONFIDENT BACK THERE!
BISHI (FWIP)
BETTER WATCH OUT, MAOU!
THERE'S NO PLACE TO RUN! NOT LIKE LAST TIME!
I'LL DO WHATEVER IT TAKES TO BE COUNCIL PRESIDENT!!
HRAAAAH
THAT'S THE SPIRIT!
THIS IS YOUR CHANCE TO DISPATCH YUSA!!!
UH...
IS THE FUTURE OF OUR SCHOOL RIDING ON THIS, OR...?
I DON'T WANT US TO LOSE EITHER, MAOU-SAN!
YOU GOT IT!

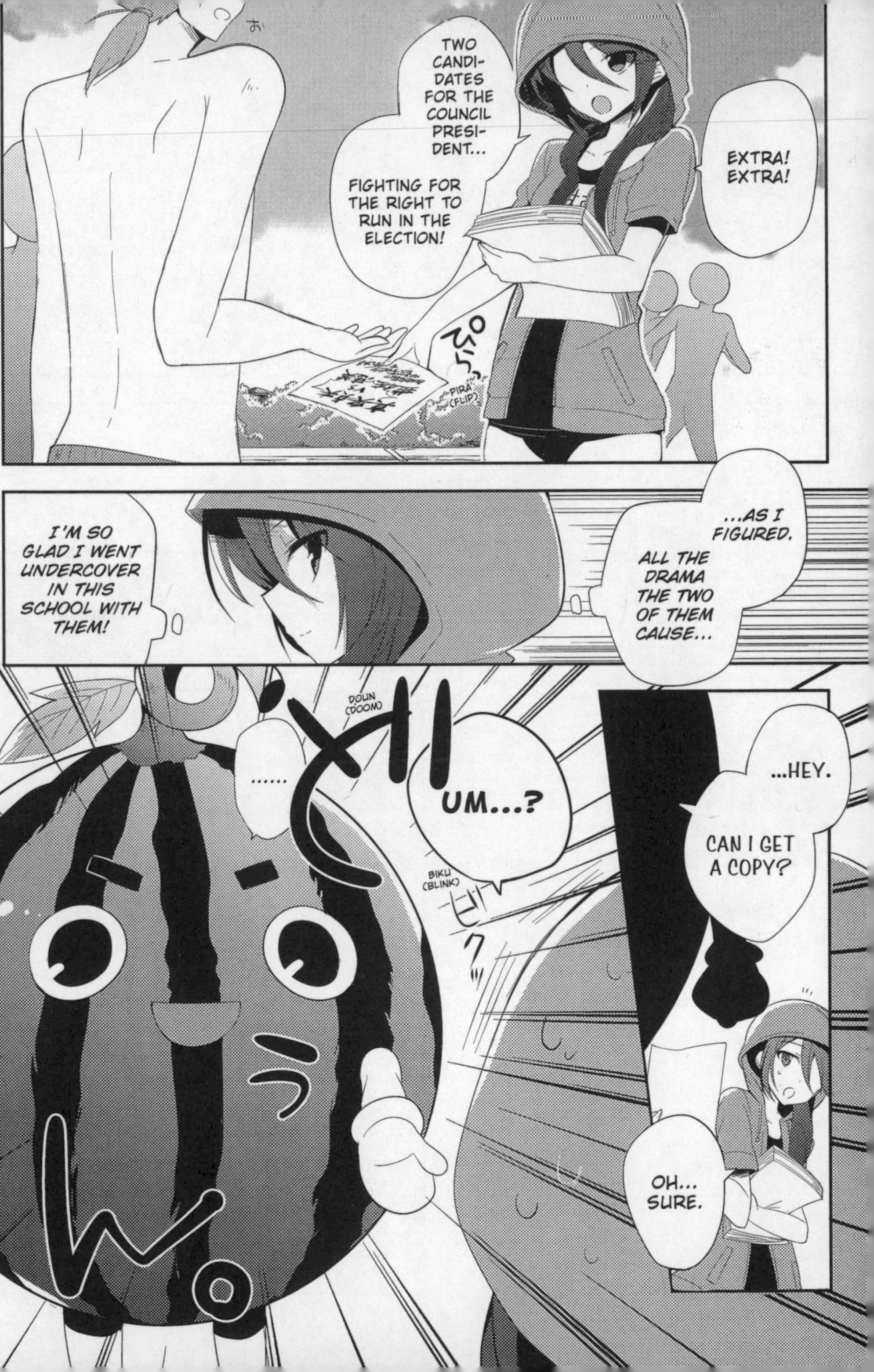
EXTRA! EXTRA!
TWO CANDIDATES FOR THE COUNCIL PRESIDENT...
FIGHTING FOR THE RIGHT TO RUN IN THE ELECTION!
PIRA (FLIP)
...AS I FIGURED.
ALL THE DRAMA THE TWO OF THEM CAUSE...
I'M SO GLAD I WENT UNDERCOVER IN THIS SCHOOL WITH THEM!
...HEY.
CAN I GET A COPY?
OH... SURE.
DOUN (DOOM)
UM...?
......
BIKU (BLINK)

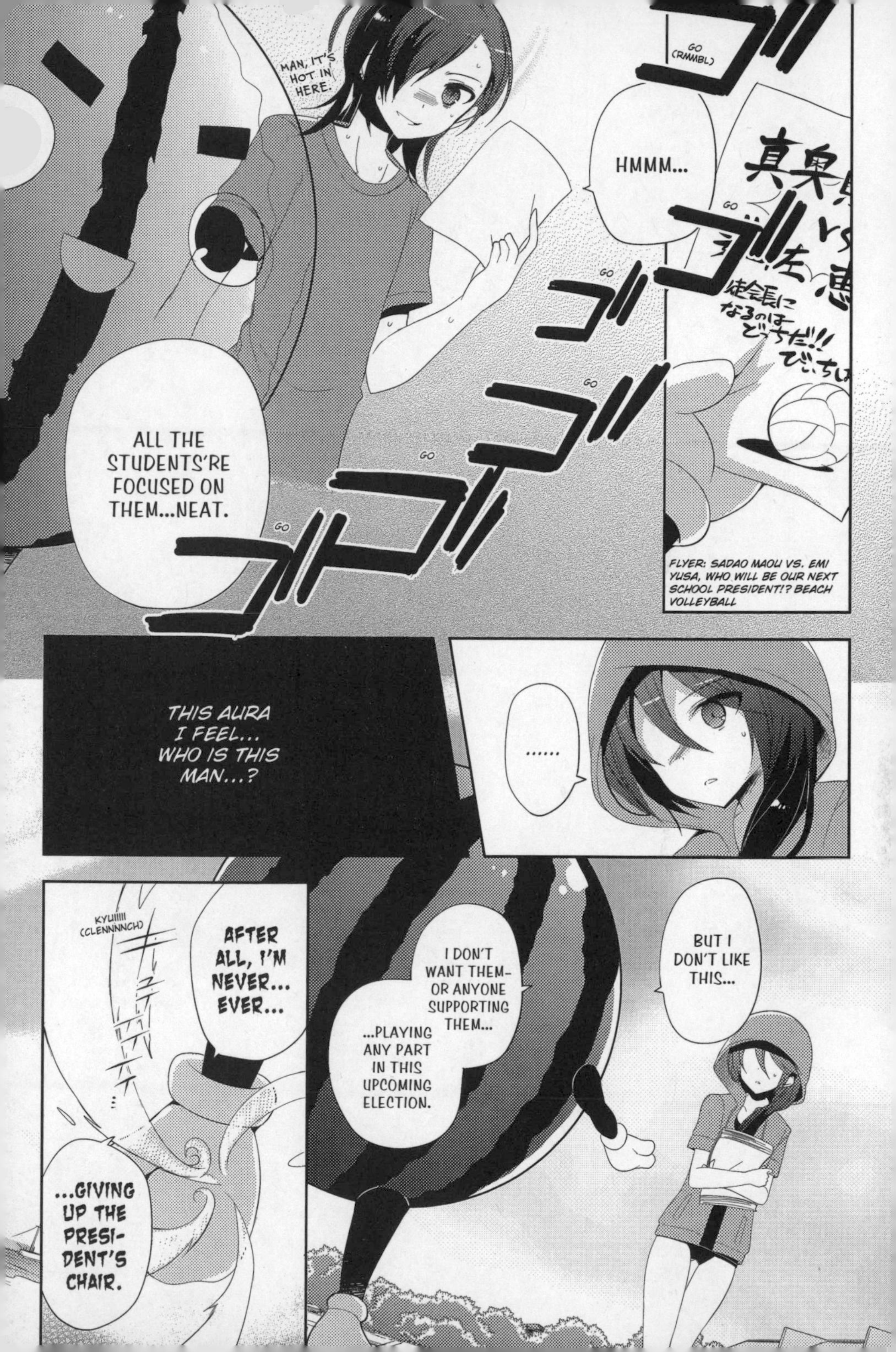
GO (RMMBL)
HMMM...
GO
FLYER: SADAO MAOU VS. EMI YUSA, WHO WILL BE OUR NEXT SCHOOL PRESIDENT!? BEACH VOLLEYBALL
MAN, IT'S HOT IN HERE.
GO
GO
GO
GO
ALL THE STUDENTS'RE FOCUSED ON THEM...NEAT.
......
THIS AURA I FEEL... WHO IS THIS MAN...?
BUT I DON'T LIKE THIS...
I DON'T WANT THEM- OR ANYONE SUPPORTING THEM...
...PLAYING ANY PART IN THIS UPCOMING ELECTION.
AFTER ALL, I'M NEVER... EVER...
KYUIIII (CLENNNNCH)
...GIVING UP THE PRESI-DENT'S CHAIR.

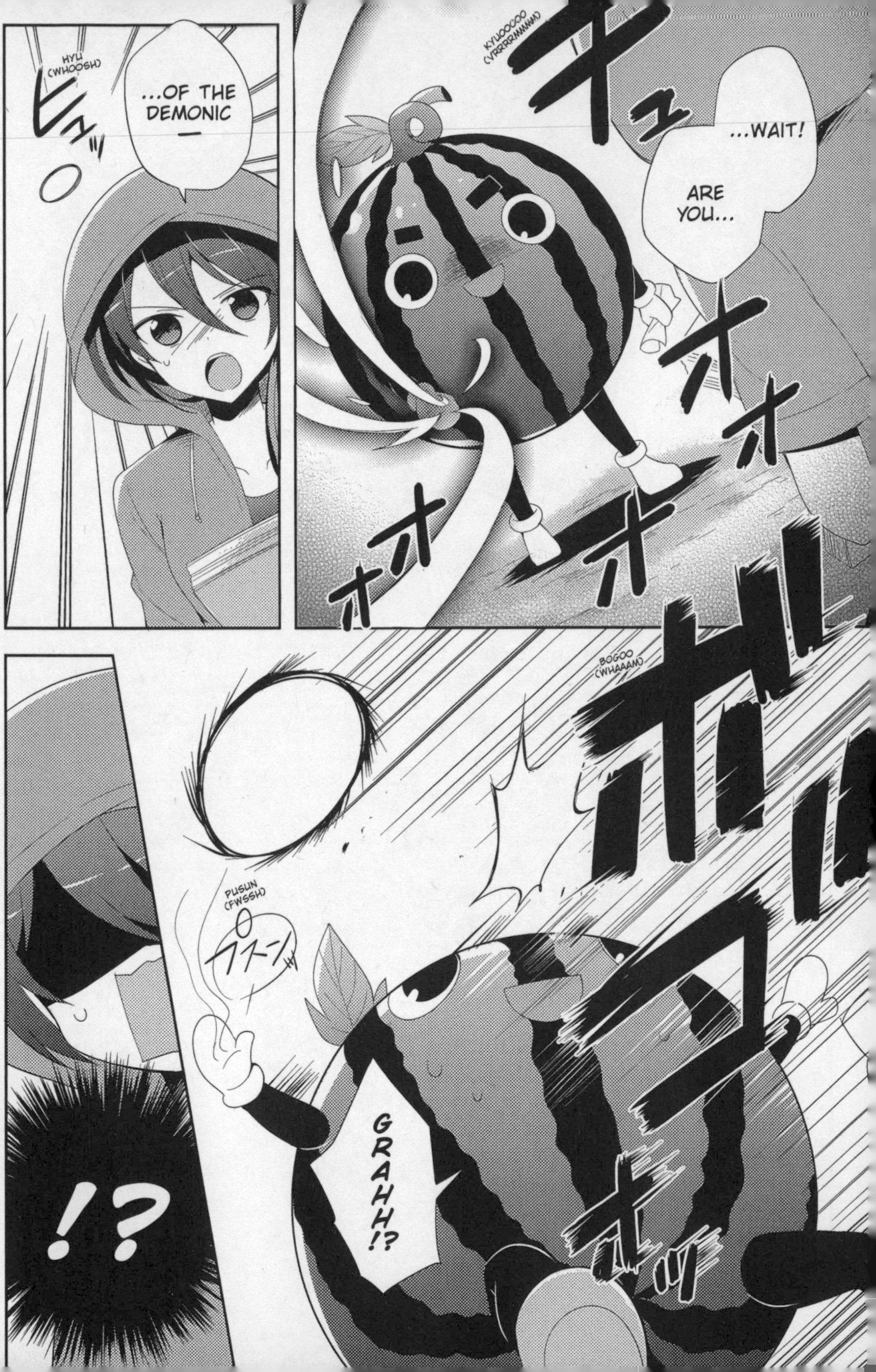
KYUOOOOO (VRRRRMMMM)
...WAIT!
ARE YOU...
HYU (WHOOSH)
...OF THE DEMONIC—
BOGOO (WHAAAM)
PUSUN (FWSSH)
GRAHH!?
!?

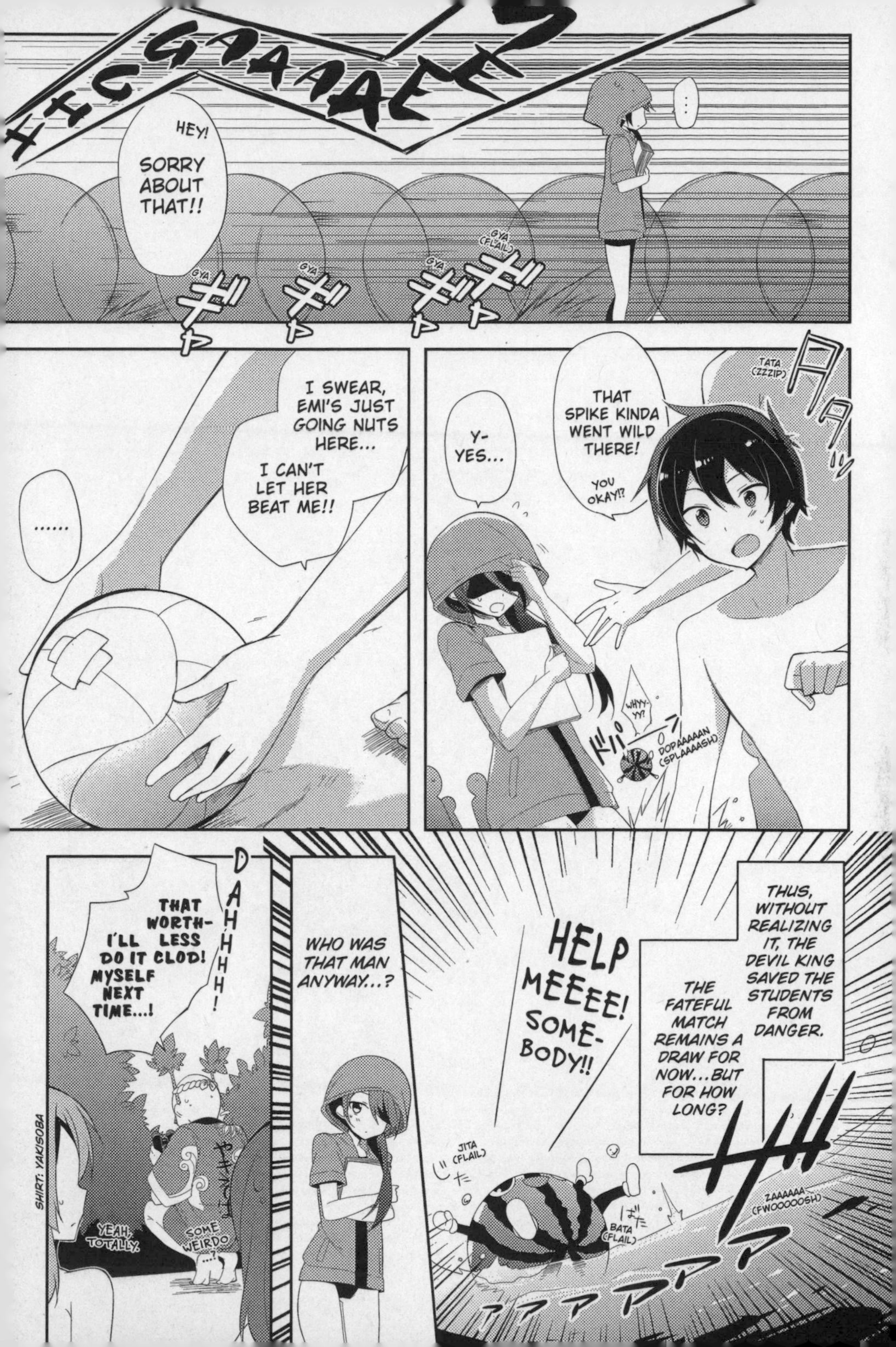
...
HEY! SORRY ABOUT THAT!!
GYA (FLAIL)
GYA
GYA
GYA
TATA (ZZZIP)
THAT SPIKE KINDA WENT WILD THERE!
YOU OKAY!?
Y-YES...
WHYY-YY?
DOPAAAAAN (SPLAAAASH)
I SWEAR, EMI'S JUST GOING NUTS HERE...
I CAN'T LET HER BEAT ME!!
......
THUS, WITHOUT REALIZING IT, THE DEVIL KING SAVED THE STUDENTS FROM DANGER.
THE FATEFUL MATCH REMAINS A DRAW FOR NOW...BUT FOR HOW LONG?
HELP MEEEE! SOMEBODY!!
ZAAAAAA (FWOOOOOSH)
BATA (FLAIL)
JITA (FLAIL)
WHO WAS THAT MAN ANYWAY...?
DAHHHHH!
THAT WORTHLESS CLOD!
I'LL DO IT MYSELF NEXT TIME...!
SOME WEIRDO...?
YEAH, TOTALLY.
SHIRT: YAKISOBA

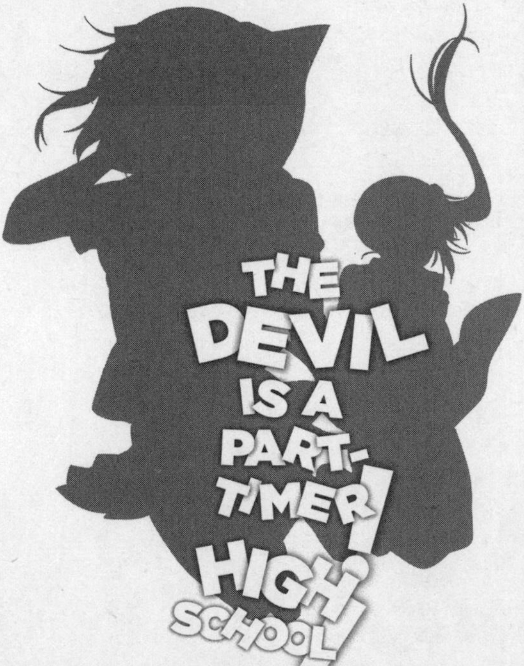
THE DEVIL IS A PART-TIMER!
HIGH SCHOOL!

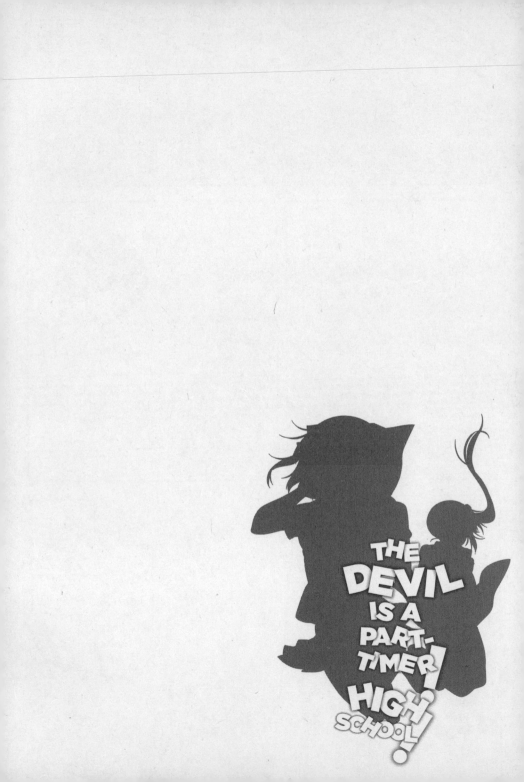

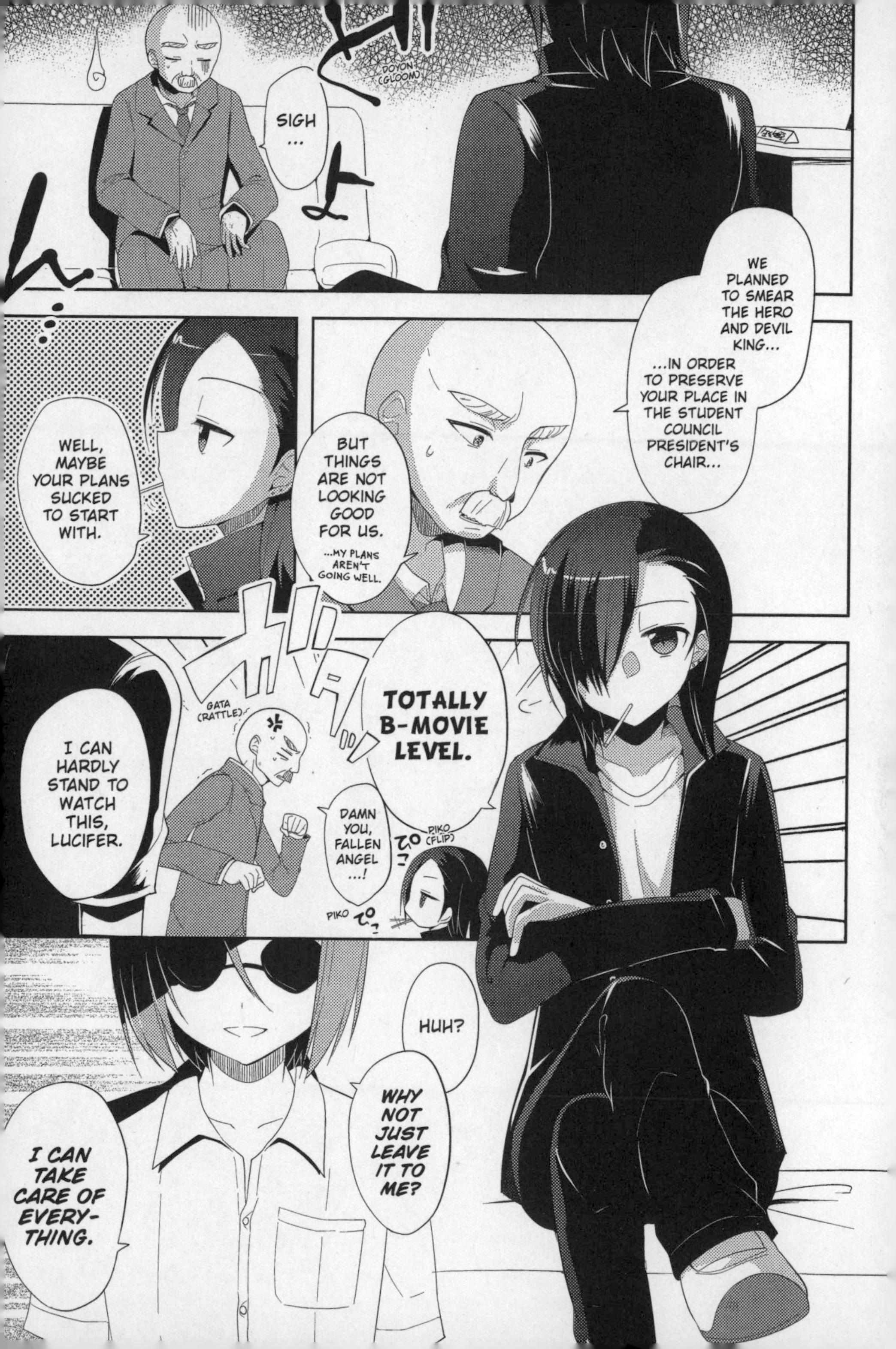
DOYON (GLOOM)
SIGH ...
WE PLANNED TO SMEAR THE HERO AND DEVIL KING...
...IN ORDER TO PRESERVE YOUR PLACE IN THE STUDENT COUNCIL PRESIDENT'S CHAIR...
BUT THINGS ARE NOT LOOKING GOOD FOR US.
...MY PLANS AREN'T GOING WELL.
WELL, MAYBE YOUR PLANS SUCKED TO START WITH.
TOTALLY B-MOVIE LEVEL.
GATA (RATTLE)
DAMN YOU, FALLEN ANGEL ...!
PIKO (FLIP)
PIKO
I CAN HARDLY STAND TO WATCH THIS, LUCIFER.
HUH?
WHY NOT JUST LEAVE IT TO ME?
I CAN TAKE CARE OF EVERYTHING.

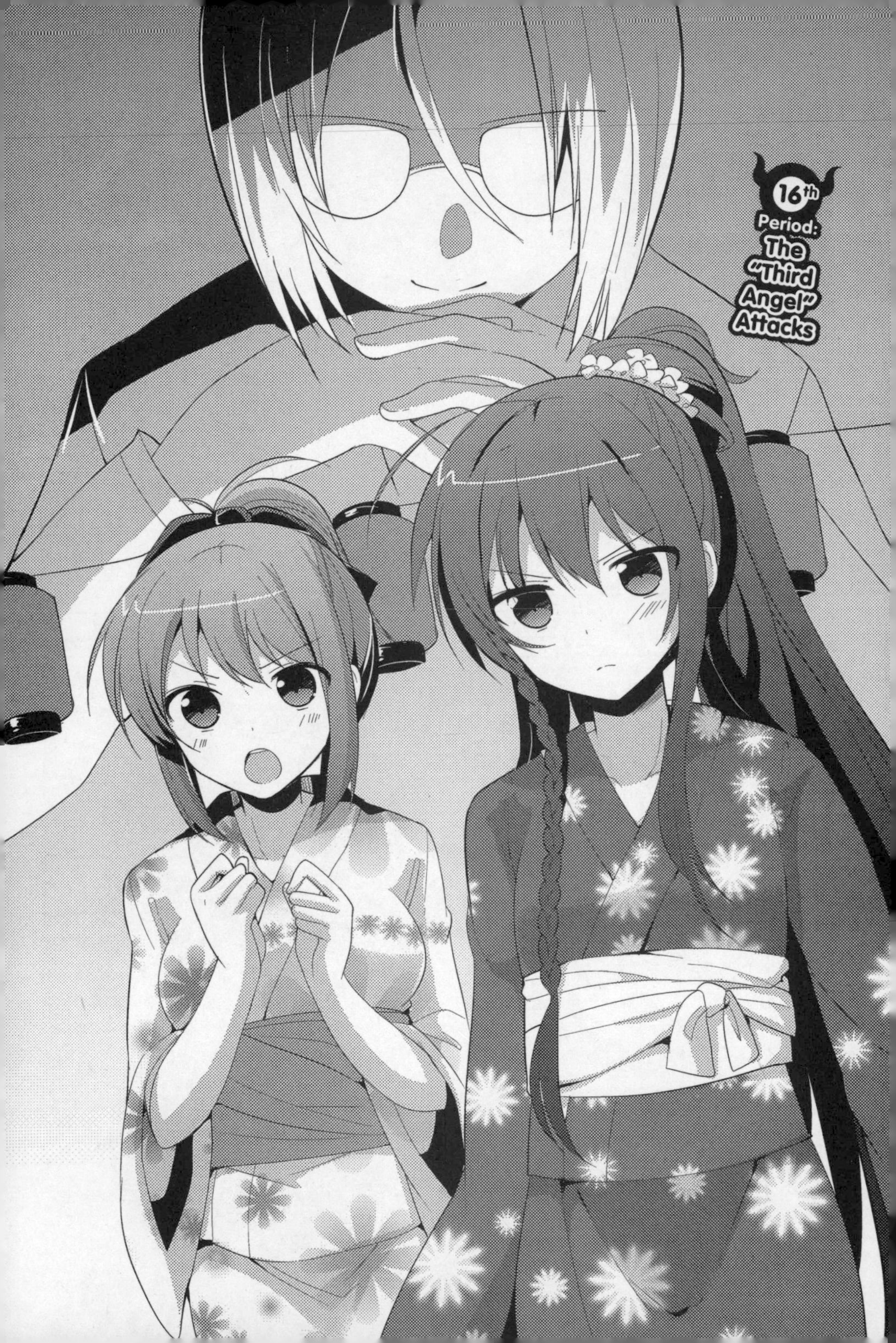
16th
Period:
The "Third Angel" Attacks

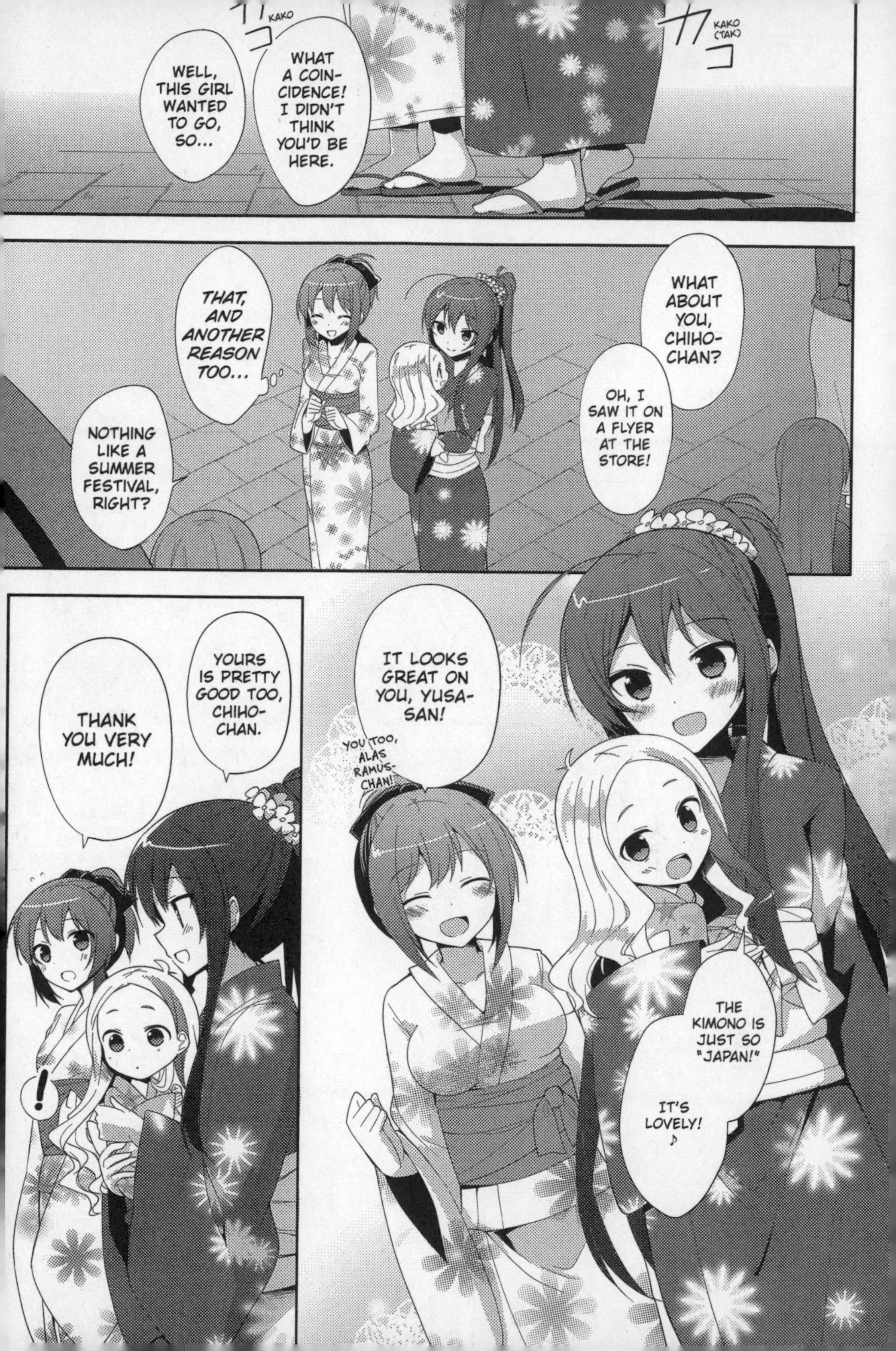
カコ
KAKO (TAK)
WHAT A COINCIDENCE! I DIDN'T THINK YOU'D BE HERE.
WELL, THIS GIRL WANTED TO GO, SO...
カコ
KAKO
WHAT ABOUT YOU, CHIHO-CHAN?
OH, I SAW IT ON A FLYER AT THE STORE!
THAT, AND ANOTHER REASON TOO...
NOTHING LIKE A SUMMER FESTIVAL, RIGHT?
IT LOOKS GREAT ON YOU, YUSA-SAN!
YOU TOO, ALAS RAMUS-CHAN!
THE KIMONO IS JUST SO "JAPAN!"
IT'S LOVELY! ♪
YOURS IS PRETTY GOOD TOO, CHIHO-CHAN.
THANK YOU VERY MUCH!
!

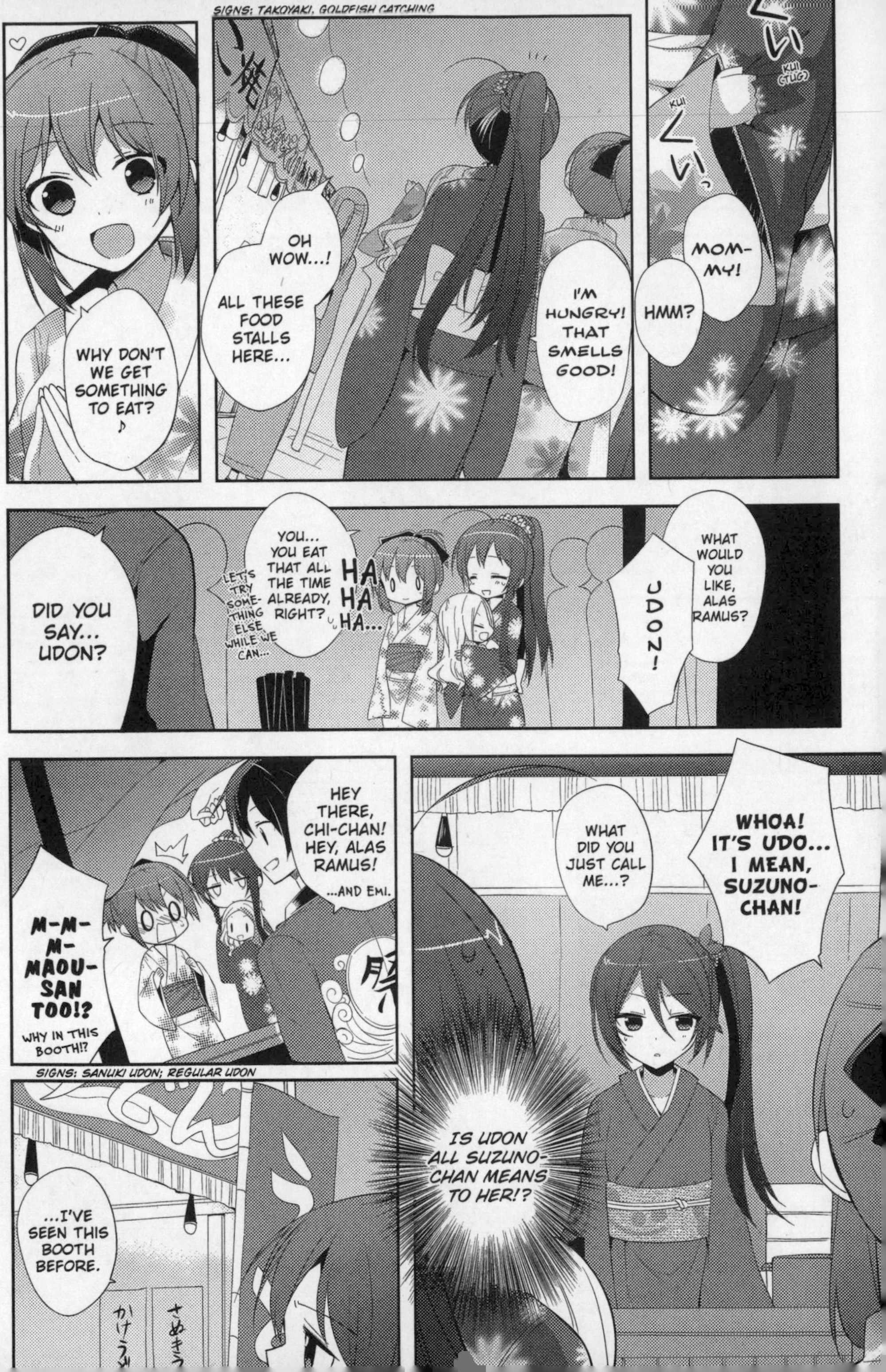
SIGNS: TAKOYAKI, GOLDFISH CATCHING
くい
KUI (TUG)
KUI
くいっ
MOMMY!
HMM?
I'M HUNGRY! THAT SMELLS GOOD!
OH WOW...!
ALL THESE FOOD STALLS HERE...
WHY DON'T WE GET SOMETHING TO EAT? ♪
WHAT WOULD YOU LIKE, ALAS RAMUS?
UDON!
YOU... YOU EAT THAT ALL THE TIME ALREADY, RIGHT?
HA HA HA...
LET'S TRY SOMETHING ELSE WHILE WE CAN...
DID YOU SAY... UDON?
WHOA! IT'S UDO... I MEAN, SUZUNO-CHAN!
WHAT DID YOU JUST CALL ME...?
HEY THERE, CHI-CHAN! HEY, ALAS RAMUS!
...AND EMI.
M-M-M-MAOU-SAN TOO!?
WHY IN THIS BOOTH!?
SIGNS: SANUKI UDON; REGULAR UDON
...I'VE SEEN THIS BOOTH BEFORE.
IS UDON ALL SUZUNO-CHAN MEANS TO HER!?

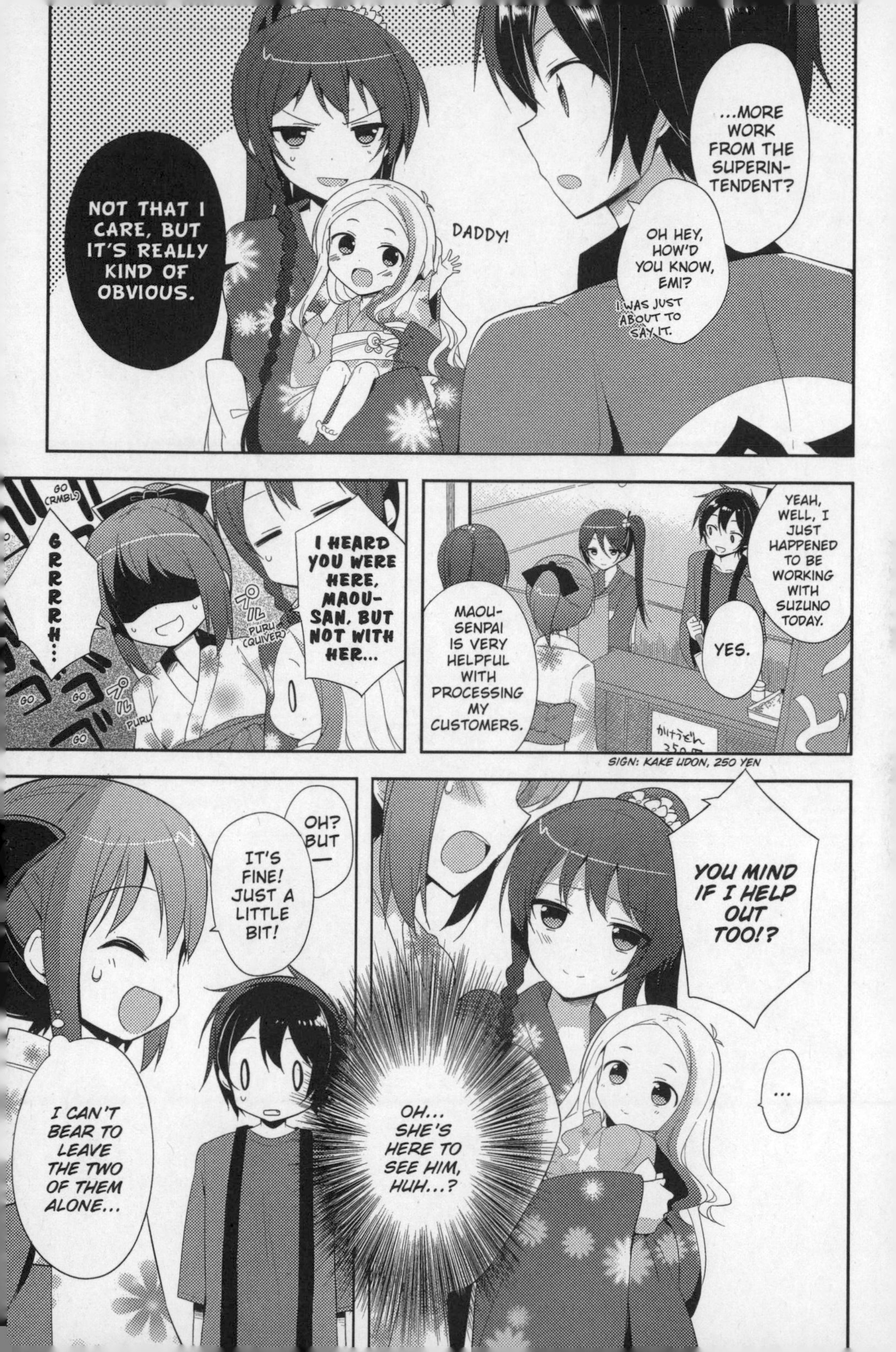

...MORE WORK FROM THE SUPERINTENDENT?
OH HEY, HOW'D YOU KNOW, EMI?
I WAS JUST ABOUT TO SAY IT.
DADDY!
NOT THAT I CARE, BUT IT'S REALLY KIND OF OBVIOUS.
YEAH, WELL, I JUST HAPPENED TO BE WORKING WITH SUZUNO TODAY.
YES.
MAOU-SENPAI IS VERY HELPFUL WITH PROCESSING MY CUSTOMERS.
SIGN: KAKE UDON, 250 YEN
I HEARD YOU WERE HERE, MAOU-SAN, BUT NOT WITH HER...
PURU (QUIVER)
PURU
GRRRRH...
GO (RMBL)
GO
GO
YOU MIND IF I HELP OUT TOO!?
...
OH... SHE'S HERE TO SEE HIM, HUH...?
OH? BUT—
IT'S FINE! JUST A LITTLE BIT!
I CAN'T BEAR TO LEAVE THE TWO OF THEM ALONE...

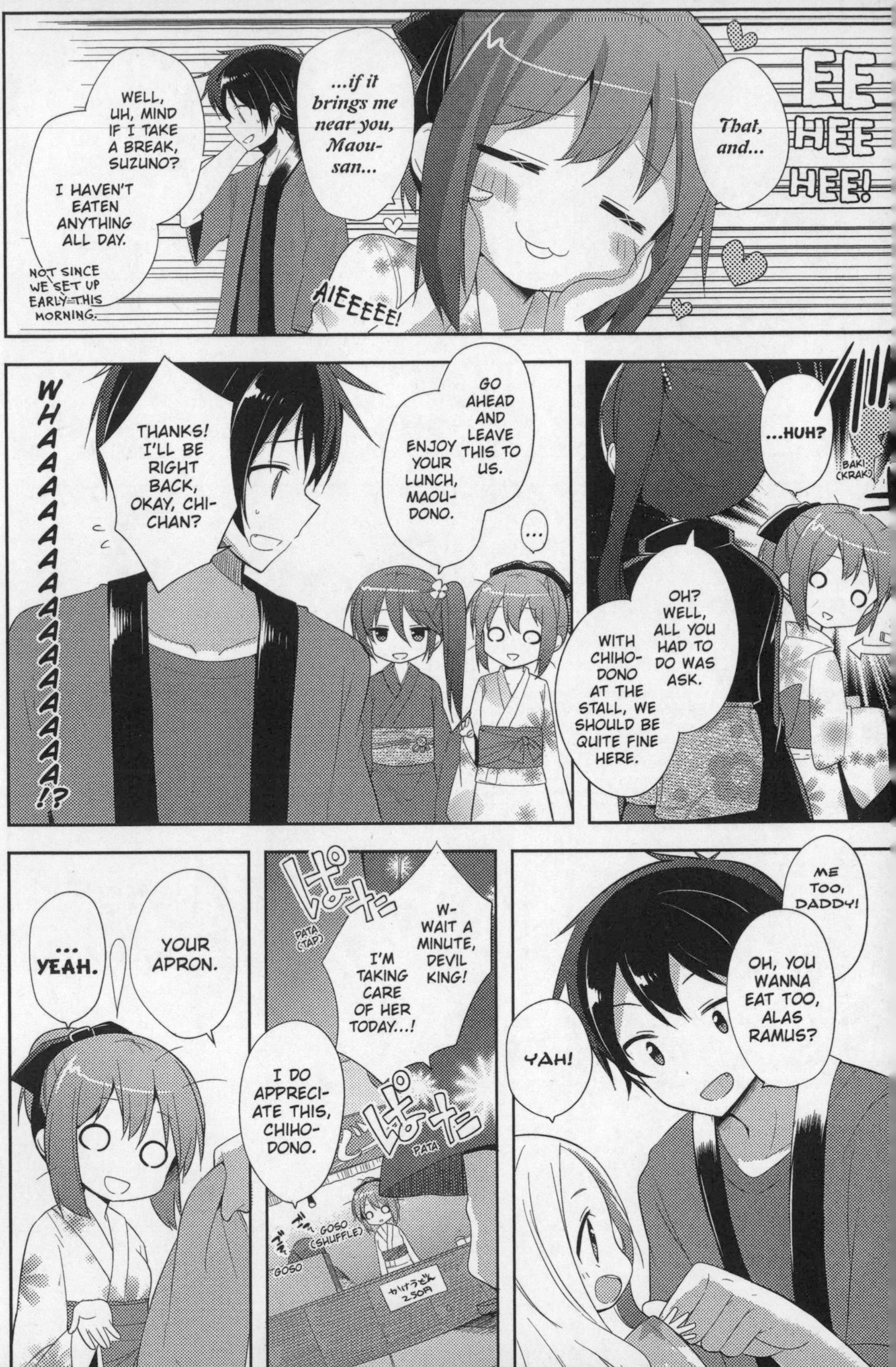
EE HEE HEE!
That, and...
...if it brings me near you, Maou-san...
AIEEEEEE!
WELL, UH, MIND IF I TAKE A BREAK, SUZUNO?
I HAVEN'T EATEN ANYTHING ALL DAY.
NOT SINCE WE SET UP EARLY THIS MORNING.
...HUH?
BAKI (KRAK)
OH? WELL, ALL YOU HAD TO DO WAS ASK.
WITH CHIHO-DONO AT THE STALL, WE SHOULD BE QUITE FINE HERE.
GO AHEAD AND LEAVE THIS TO US.
ENJOY YOUR LUNCH, MAOU-DONO.
...
THANKS! I'LL BE RIGHT BACK, OKAY, CHI-CHAN?
WHAAAAAAAAAAAAAAAAAAAAA!?
ME TOO, DADDY!
OH, YOU WANNA EAT TOO, ALAS RAMUS?
YAH!
W-WAIT A MINUTE, DEVIL KING!
I'M TAKING CARE OF HER TODAY...!
PATA (TAP)
I DO APPRECIATE THIS, CHIHO-DONO.
PATA
GOSO (SHUFFLE)
GOSO
かけうどん 250円
YOUR APRON.
...YEAH.

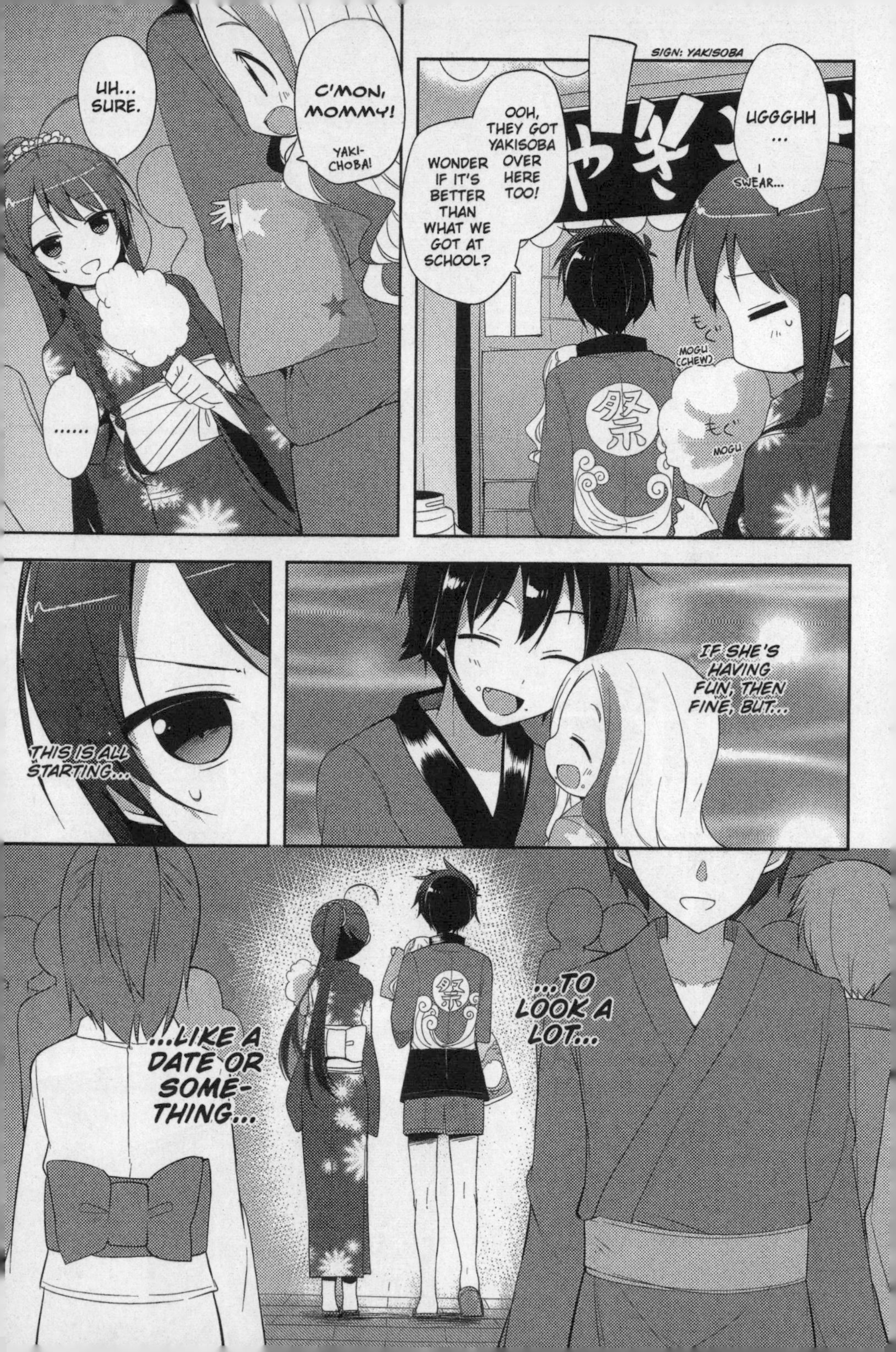
SIGN: YAKISOBA
UGGGHH ...
I SWEAR...
OOH, THEY GOT YAKISOBA OVER HERE TOO!
WONDER IF IT'S BETTER THAN WHAT WE GOT AT SCHOOL?
もぐ MOGU (CHEW)
もぐ MOGU
C'MON, MOMMY!
YAKI-CHOBA!
UH... SURE.
......
IF SHE'S HAVING FUN, THEN FINE, BUT...
THIS IS ALL STARTING...
...TO LOOK A LOT...
...LIKE A DATE OR SOME-THING...

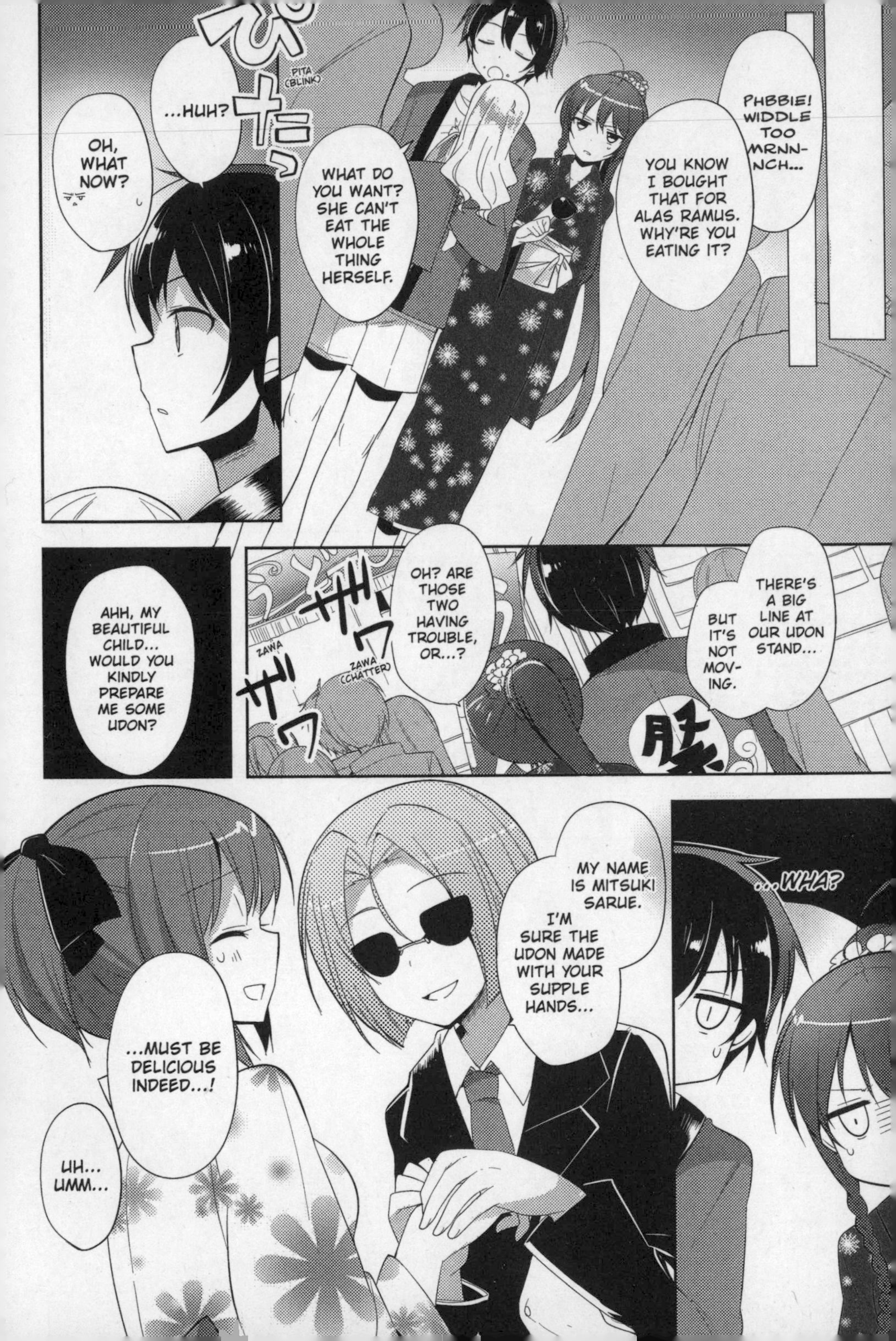
PHBBIE! WIDDLE TOO MRNN-NCH...
YOU KNOW I BOUGHT THAT FOR ALAS RAMUS. WHY'RE YOU EATING IT?
WHAT DO YOU WANT? SHE CAN'T EAT THE WHOLE THING HERSELF.
PITA (BLINK)
...HUH?
OH, WHAT NOW?
THERE'S A BIG LINE AT OUR UDON STAND...
BUT IT'S NOT MOVING.
OH? ARE THOSE TWO HAVING TROUBLE, OR...?
ZAWA (CHATTER)
ZAWA
AHH, MY BEAUTIFUL CHILD... WOULD YOU KINDLY PREPARE ME SOME UDON?
...WHA?
MY NAME IS MITSUKI SARUE.
I'M SURE THE UDON MADE WITH YOUR SUPPLE HANDS...
...MUST BE DELICIOUS INDEED...!
UH... UMM...

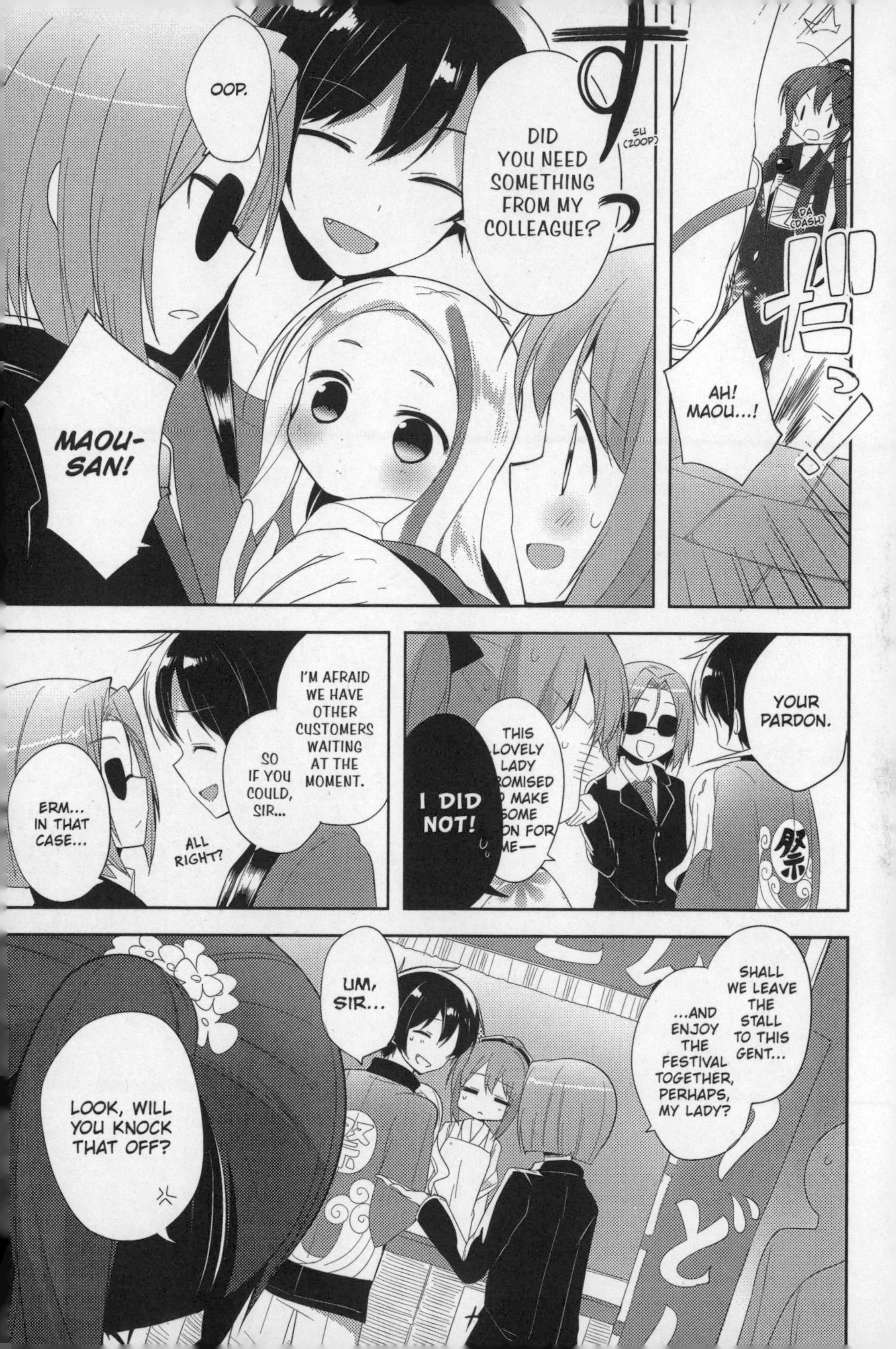
DA (DASH)
AH! MAOU...!
SU (ZOOP)
DID YOU NEED SOMETHING FROM MY COLLEAGUE?
OOP.
MAOU-SAN!
YOUR PARDON.
THIS LOVELY LADY ROMISED MAKE SOME ON FOR ME—
I DID NOT!
I'M AFRAID WE HAVE OTHER CUSTOMERS WAITING AT THE MOMENT.
SO IF YOU COULD, SIR...
ALL RIGHT?
ERM... IN THAT CASE...
SHALL WE LEAVE THE STALL TO THIS GENT...
...AND ENJOY THE FESTIVAL TOGETHER, PERHAPS, MY LADY?
UM, SIR...
LOOK, WILL YOU KNOCK THAT OFF?

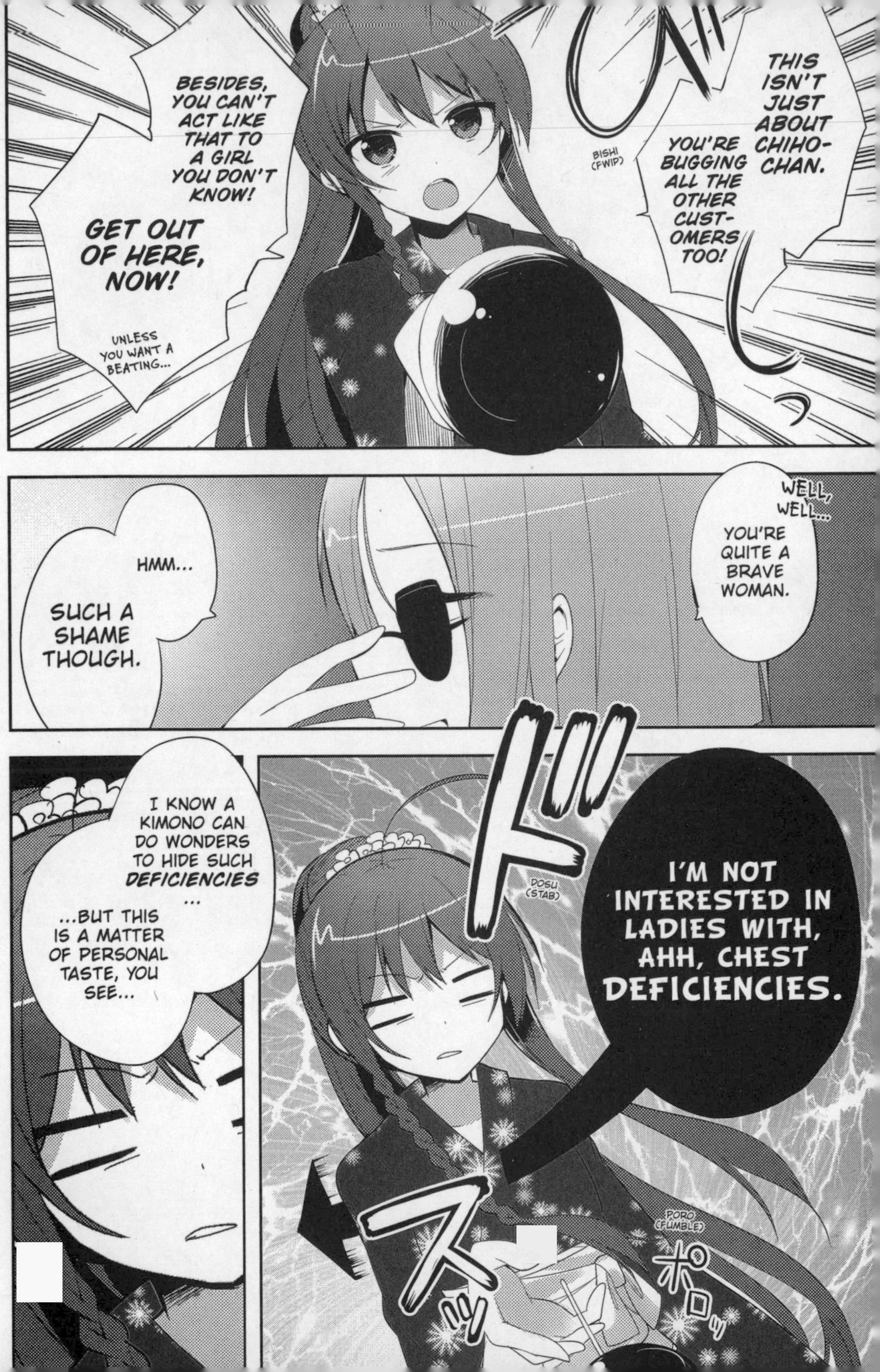
THIS ISN'T JUST ABOUT CHIHO-CHAN.
YOU'RE BUGGING ALL THE OTHER CUST-OMERS TOO!
BISHI (FWIP)
BESIDES, YOU CAN'T ACT LIKE THAT TO A GIRL YOU DON'T KNOW!
GET OUT OF HERE, NOW!
UNLESS YOU WANT A BEATING...
WELL, WELL... YOU'RE QUITE A BRAVE WOMAN.
HMM... SUCH A SHAME THOUGH.
DOSU (STAB)
I'M NOT INTERESTED IN LADIES WITH, AHH, CHEST DEFICIENCIES.
PORO (FUMBLE)
I KNOW A KIMONO CAN DO WONDERS TO HIDE SUCH DEFICIENCIES ...
...BUT THIS IS A MATTER OF PERSONAL TASTE, YOU SEE...

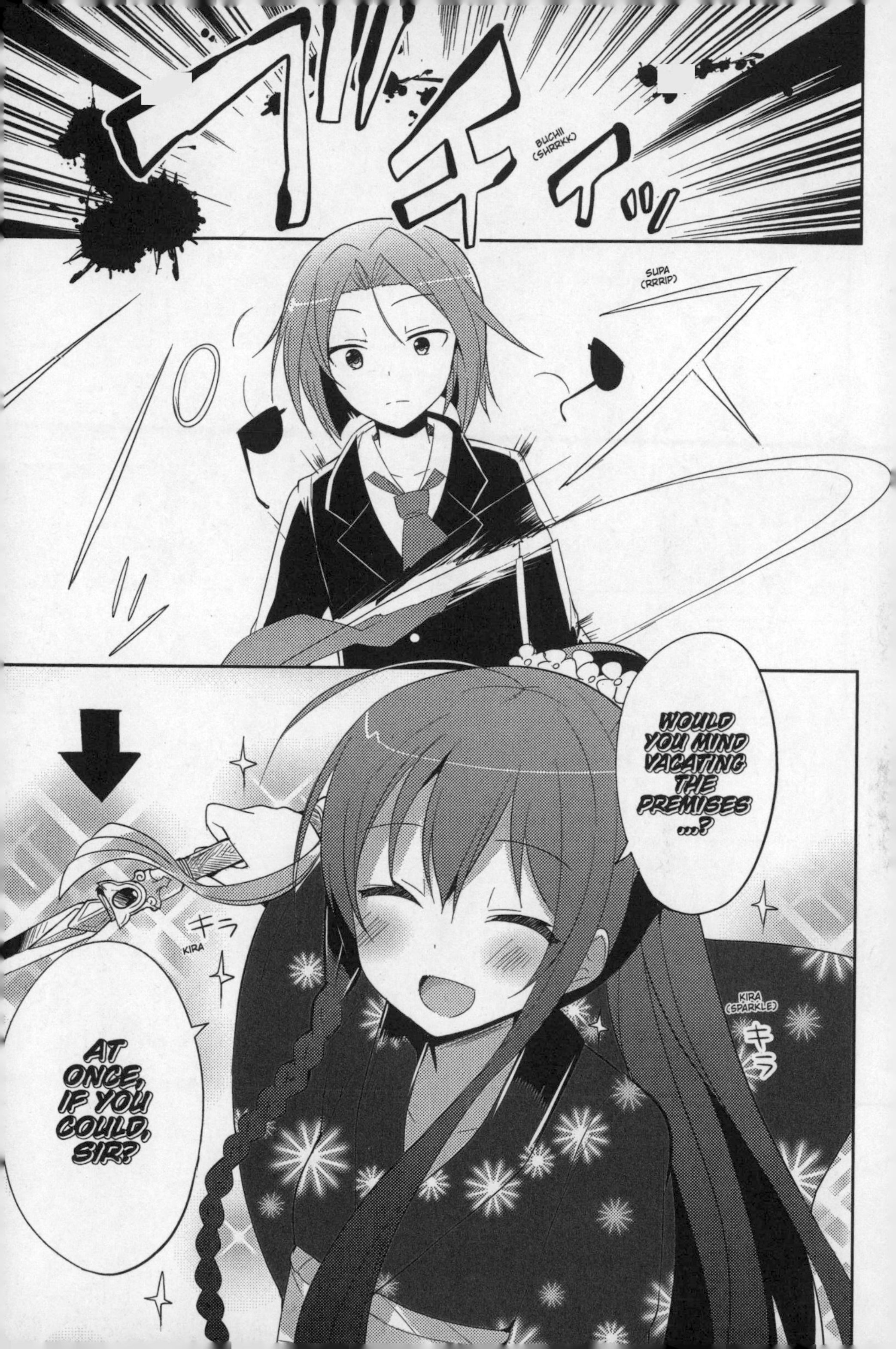
BUCHII (SHRRKK)
SUPA (RRRIP)
WOULD YOU MIND VACATING THE PREMISES ...?
KIRA (SPARKLE)
キラ
キラ
KIRA
AT ONCE, IF YOU COULD, SIR?

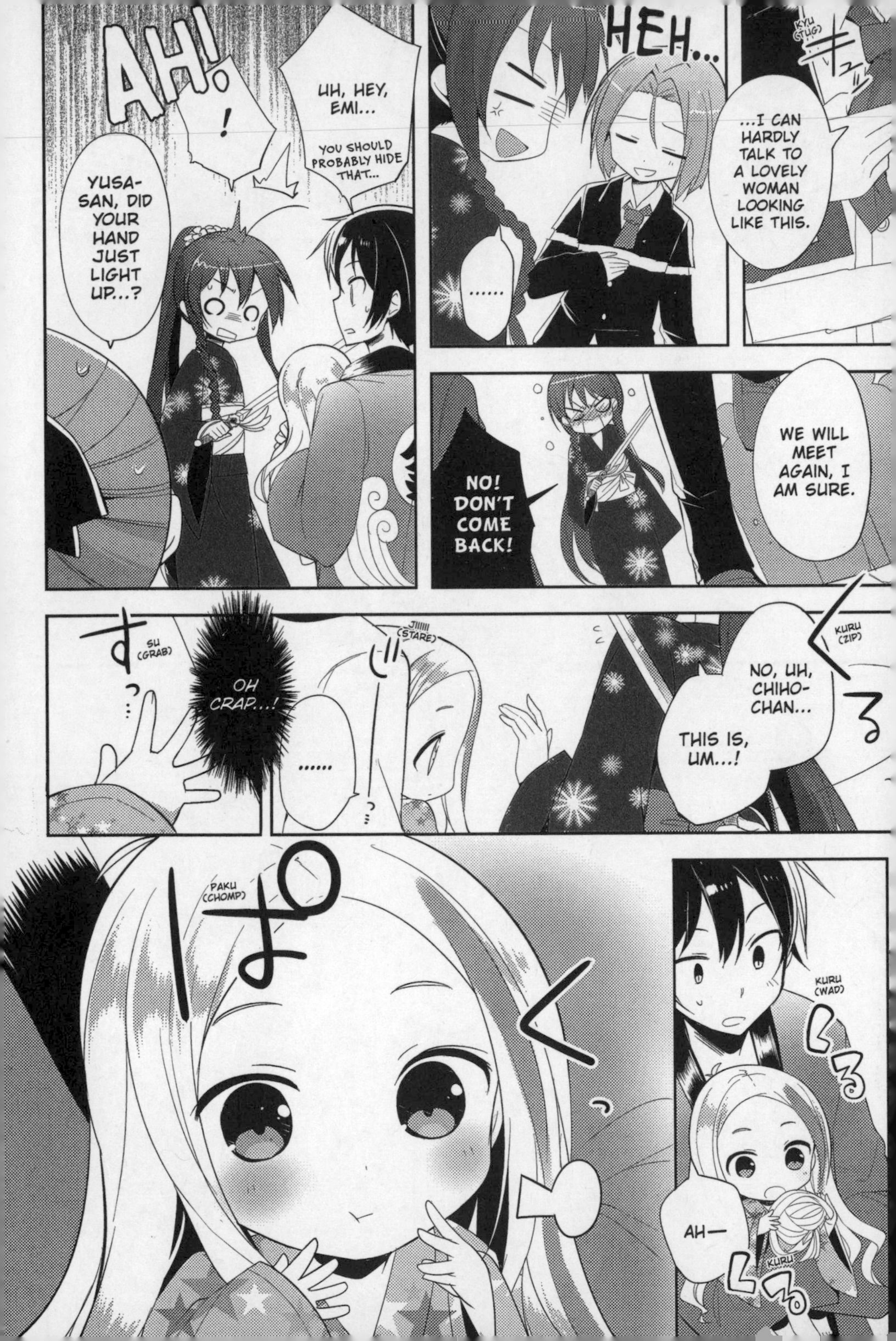
HEH...
KYU (TUG)
...I CAN HARDLY TALK TO A LOVELY WOMAN LOOKING LIKE THIS.
......
WE WILL MEET AGAIN, I AM SURE.
NO! DON'T COME BACK!
UH, HEY, EMI...
YOU SHOULD PROBABLY HIDE THAT...
!
AH!
YUSA-SAN, DID YOUR HAND JUST LIGHT UP...?
KURU (ZIP)
NO, UH, CHIHO-CHAN...
THIS IS, UM...!
JIIIII (STARE)
OH CRAP...!
......
SU (GRAB)
KURU (WAD)
AH—
KURU
PAKU (CHOMP)

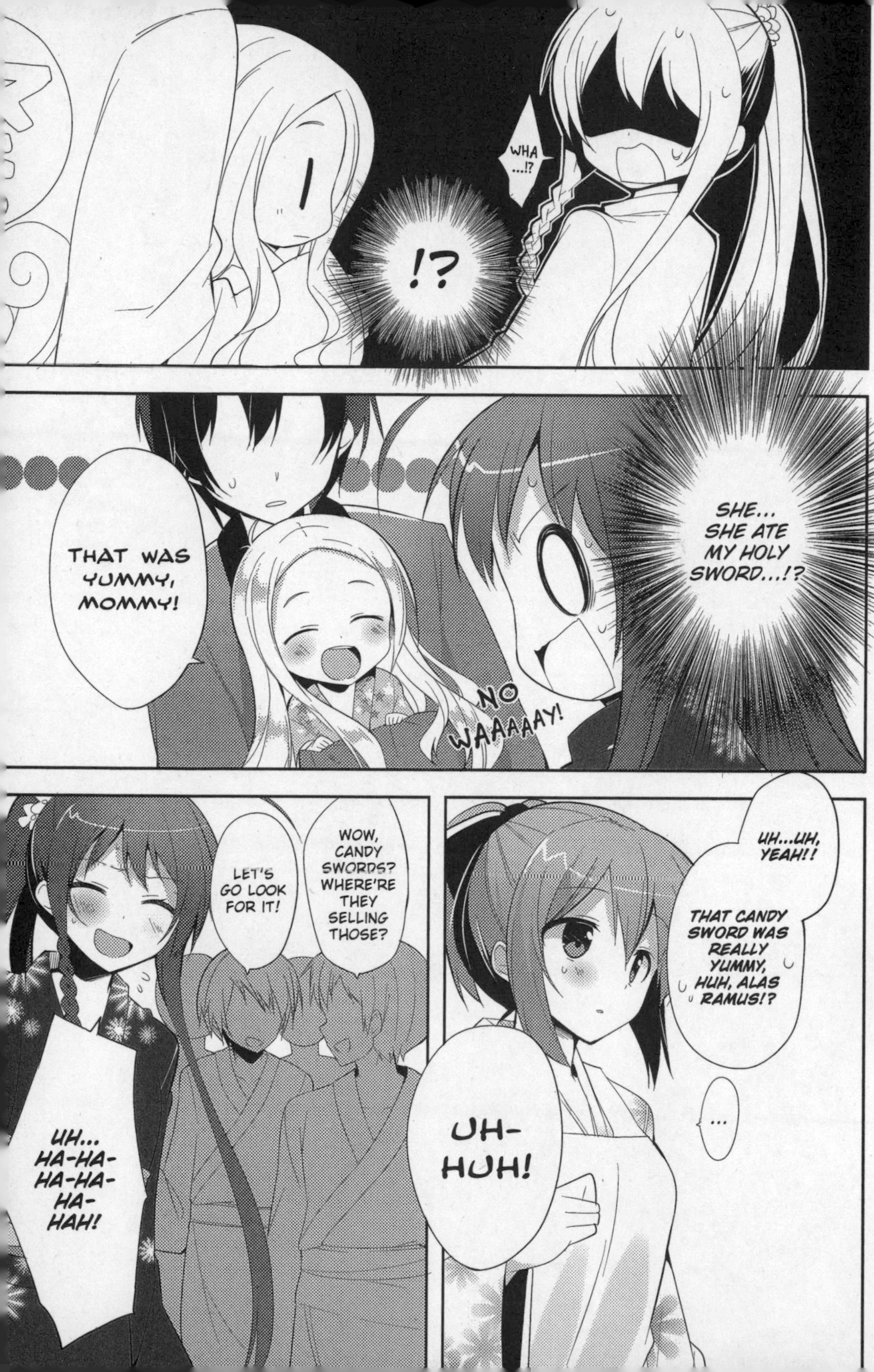
WHA ...!?
!?
SHE... SHE ATE MY HOLY SWORD...!?
THAT WAS YUMMY, MOMMY!
NO WAAAAAY!
UH...UH, YEAH!!
THAT CANDY SWORD WAS REALLY YUMMY, HUH, ALAS RAMUS!?
...
UH-HUH!
WOW, CANDY SWORDS? WHERE'RE THEY SELLING THOSE?
LET'S GO LOOK FOR IT!
UH... HA-HA-HA-HA-HA-HAH!

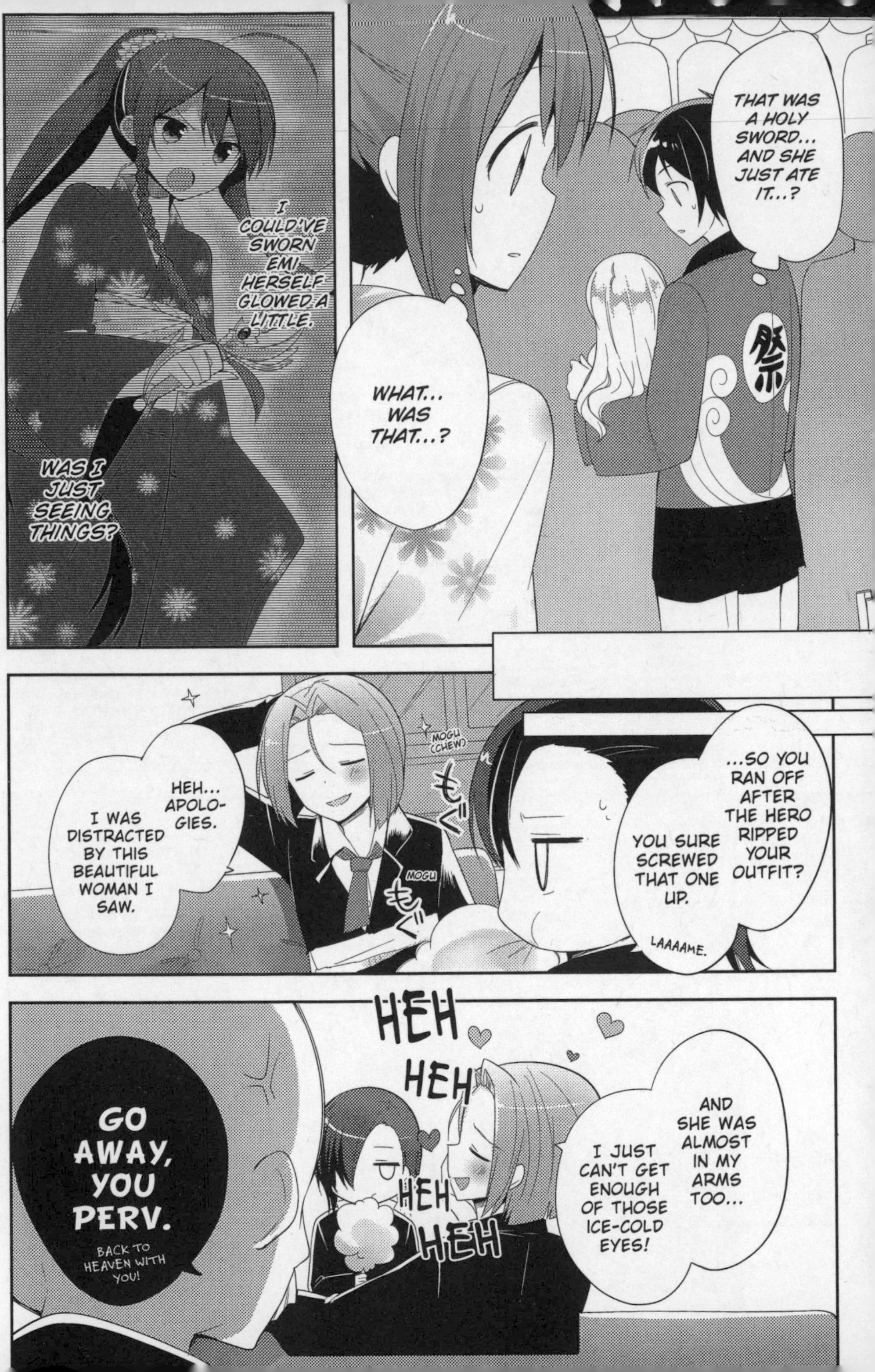
THAT WAS A HOLY SWORD... AND SHE JUST ATE IT...?
WHAT... WAS THAT...?
I COULD'VE SWORN EMI HERSELF GLOWED A LITTLE.
WAS I JUST SEEING THINGS?
...SO YOU RAN OFF AFTER THE HERO RIPPED YOUR OUTFIT?
YOU SURE SCREWED THAT ONE UP.
LAAAAME.
MOGU (CHEW)
MOGU
HEH... APOLOGIES.
I WAS DISTRACTED BY THIS BEAUTIFUL WOMAN I SAW.
AND SHE WAS ALMOST IN MY ARMS TOO...
I JUST CAN'T GET ENOUGH OF THOSE ICE-COLD EYES!
HEH HEH HEH HEH
GO AWAY, YOU PERV.
BACK TO HEAVEN WITH YOU!

THE DEVIL IS A PART-TIMER! HIGH SCHOOL!

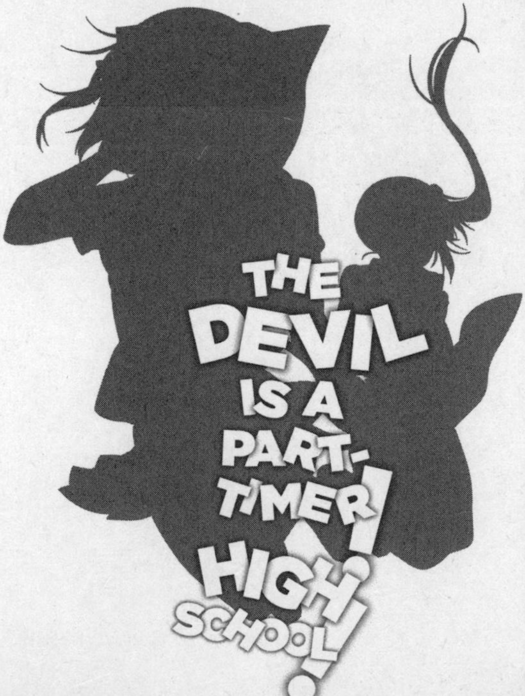
THE DEVIL IS A PART-TIMER!
HIGH SCHOOL!

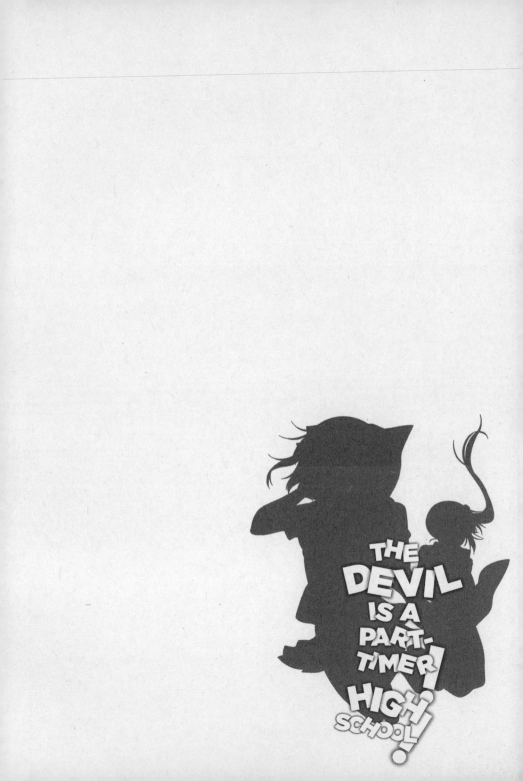

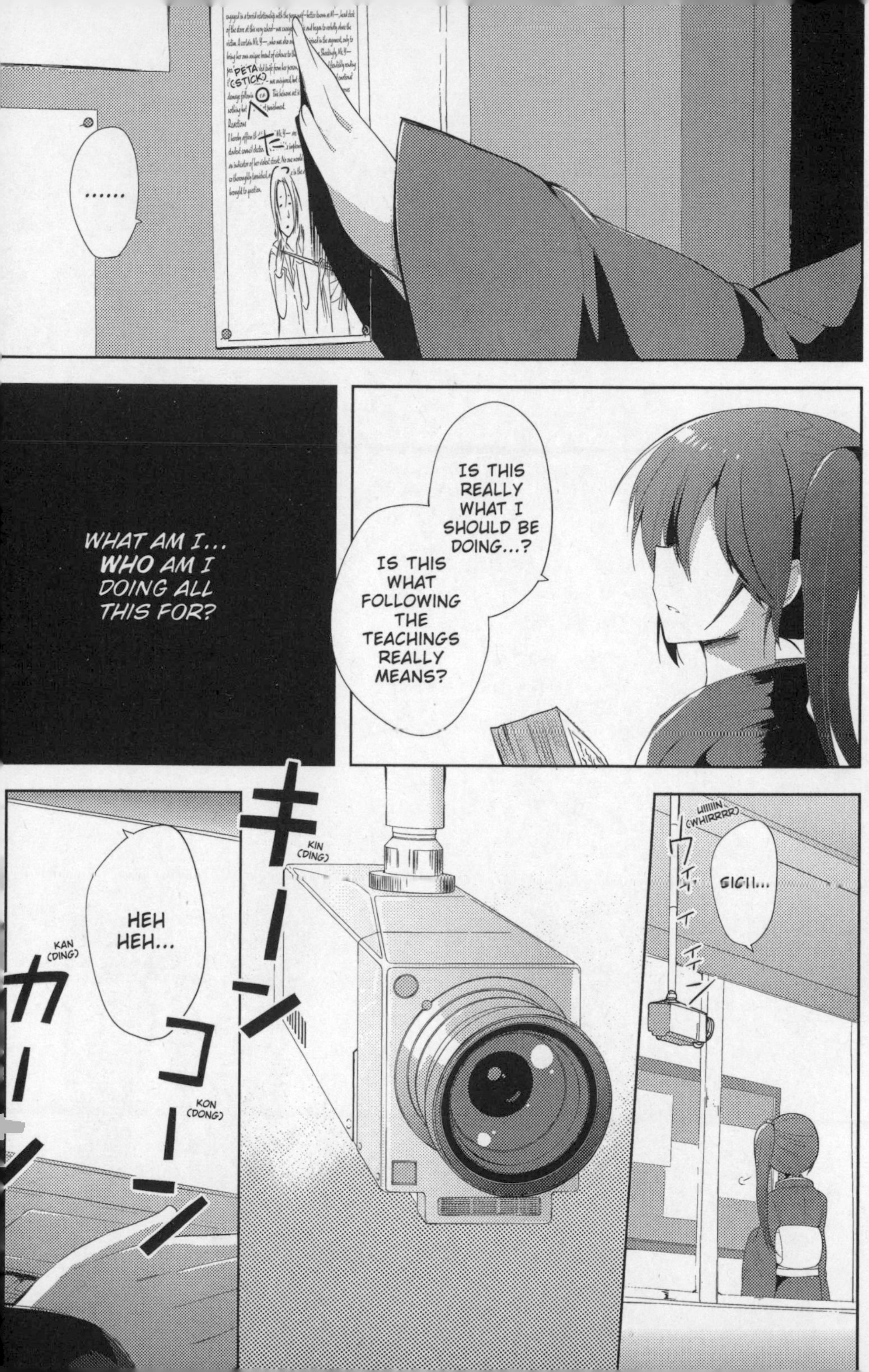
PETA
(STICK)
......
IS THIS REALLY WHAT I SHOULD BE DOING...?
IS THIS WHAT FOLLOWING THE TEACHINGS REALLY MEANS?
WHAT AM I... ***WHO*** AM I DOING ALL THIS FOR?
UIIIIIN (WHIRRRR)
GIGII...
KIN (DING)
HEH HEH...
KAN (DING)
KON (DONG)

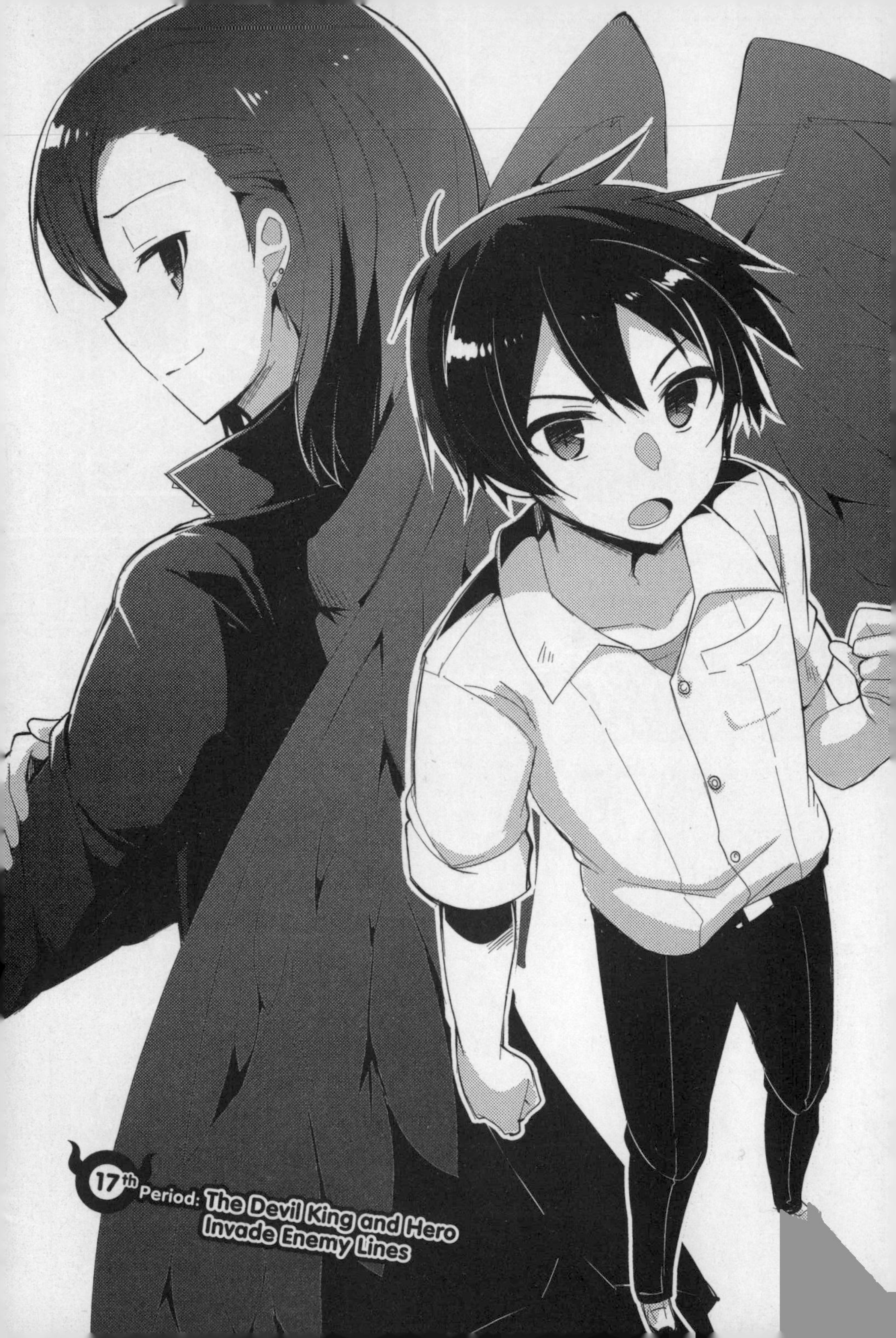
17th Period: The Devil King and Hero Invade Enemy Lines

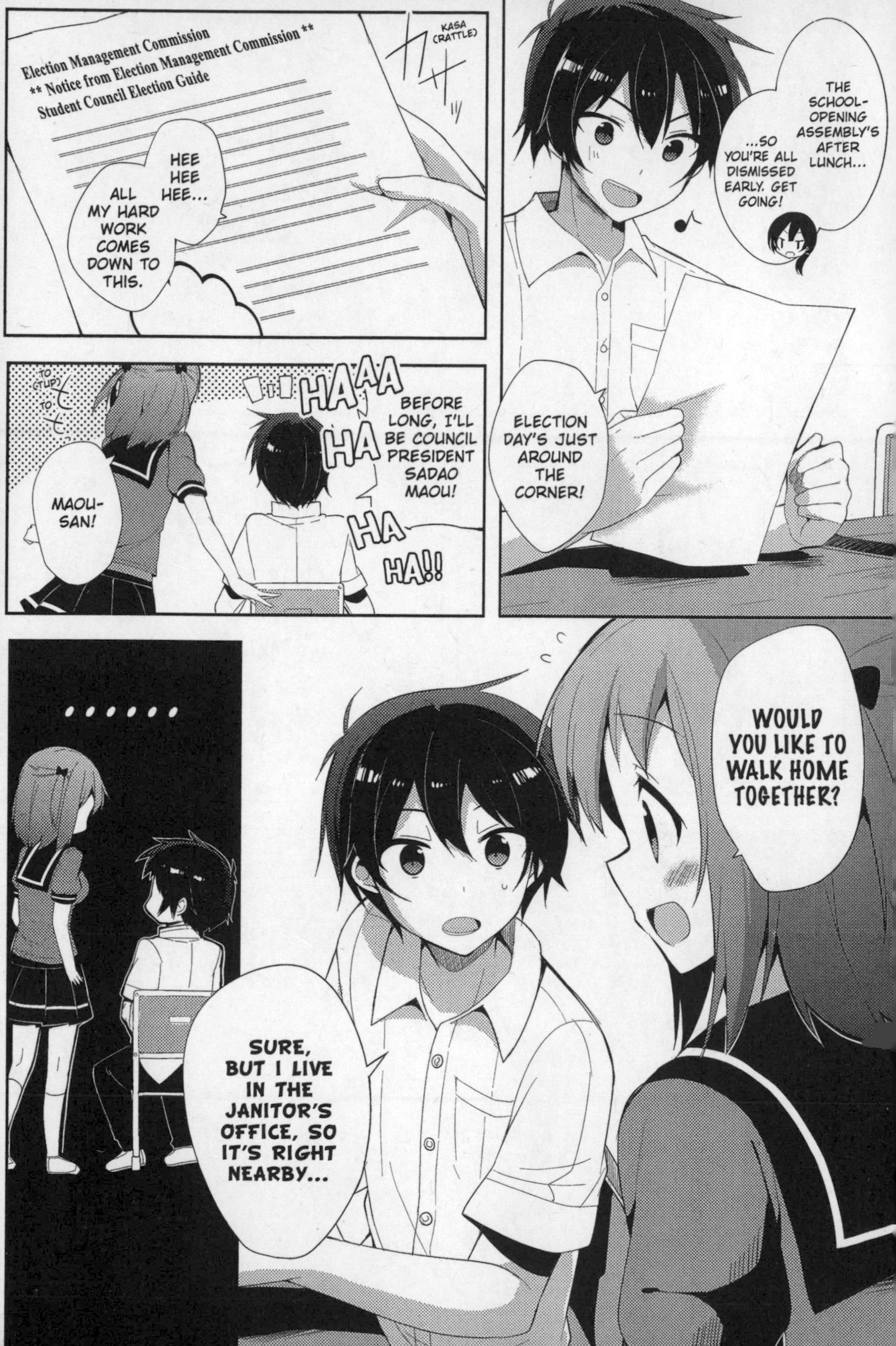
THE SCHOOL-OPENING ASSEMBLY'S AFTER LUNCH...
...SO YOU'RE ALL DISMISSED EARLY. GET GOING!
ELECTION DAY'S JUST AROUND THE CORNER!
Election Management Commission
** Notice from Election Management Commission **
Student Council Election Guide
KASA (RATTLE)
HEE HEE HEE... ALL MY HARD WORK COMES DOWN TO THIS.
HAAA HA HA HA!!
BEFORE LONG, I'LL BE COUNCIL PRESIDENT SADAO MAOU!
TO TO (TUP)
MAOU-SAN!
WOULD YOU LIKE TO WALK HOME TOGETHER?
SURE, BUT I LIVE IN THE JANITOR'S OFFICE, SO IT'S RIGHT NEARBY...
......

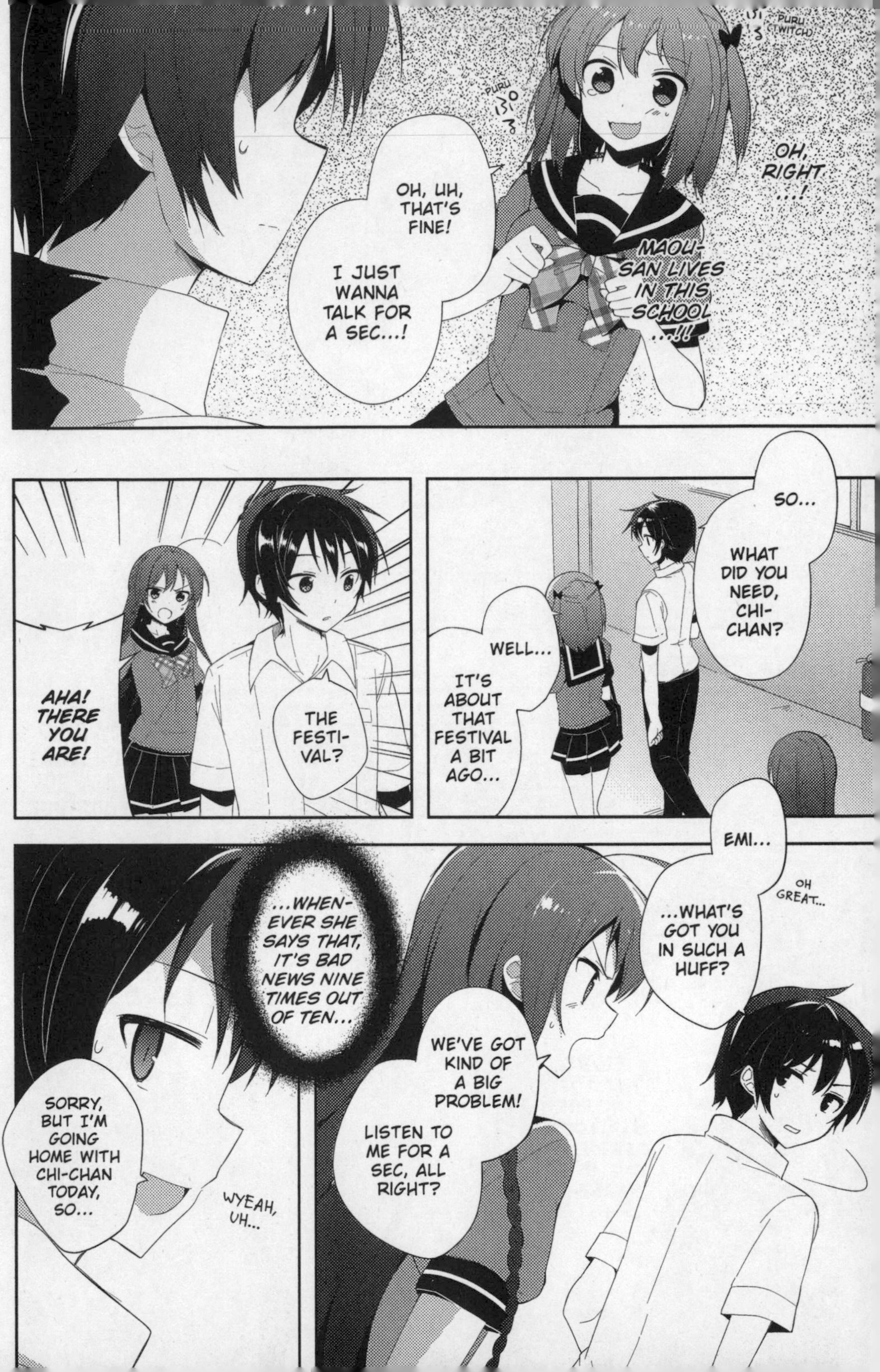

PURU (TWITCH)
OH, RIGHT...!
MAOU-SAN LIVES IN THIS SCHOOL...!!
PURU
OH, UH, THAT'S FINE!
I JUST WANNA TALK FOR A SEC...!
SO...
WHAT DID YOU NEED, CHI-CHAN?
WELL...
IT'S ABOUT THAT FESTIVAL A BIT AGO...
THE FESTI-VAL?
AHA! THERE YOU ARE!
EMI...
OH GREAT...
...WHAT'S GOT YOU IN SUCH A HUFF?
WE'VE GOT KIND OF A BIG PROBLEM!
LISTEN TO ME FOR A SEC, ALL RIGHT?
...WHEN-EVER SHE SAYS THAT, IT'S BAD NEWS NINE TIMES OUT OF TEN...
WYEAH, UH...
SORRY, BUT I'M GOING HOME WITH CHI-CHAN TODAY, SO...

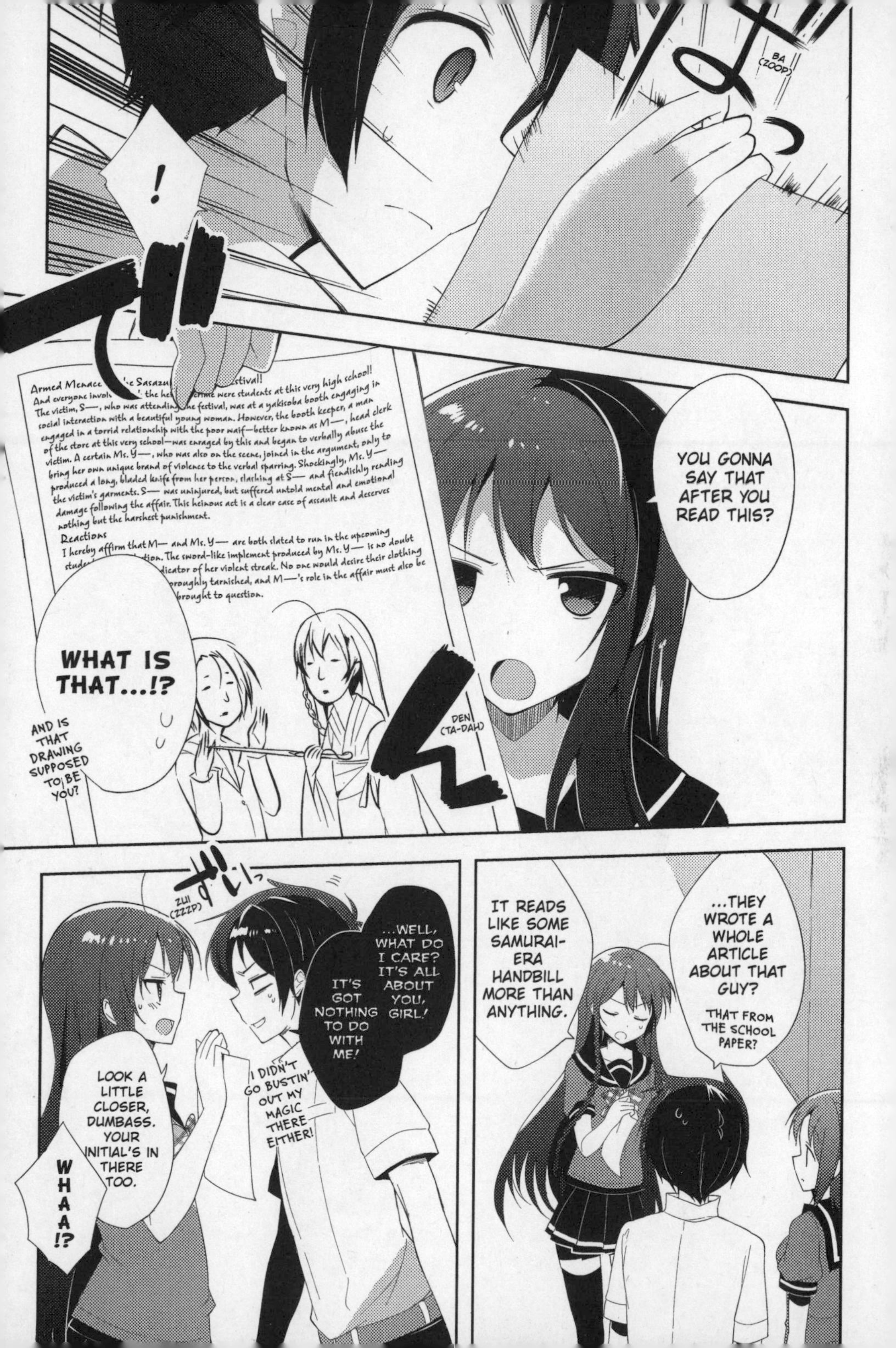
BA (ZOOP)
!
YOU GONNA SAY THAT AFTER YOU READ THIS?
DEN (TA-DAH)
Armed Menace ... Sasazu... estival!
And everyone invol... the he... crime were students at this very high school!
The victim, S—, who was attending ...he festival, was at a yakisoba booth engaging in
social interaction with a beautiful young woman. However, the booth keeper, a man
engaged in a torrid relationship with the poor waif—better known as M—, head clerk
of the store at this very school—was enraged by this and began to verbally abuse the
victim. A certain Ms. Y—, who was also on the scene, joined in the argument, only to
bring her own unique brand of violence to the verbal sparring. Shockingly, Ms. Y—
produced a long, bladed knife from her person, slashing at S— and fiendishly rending
the victim's garments. S— was uninjured, but suffered untold mental and emotional
damage following the affair. This heinous act is a clear case of assault and deserves
nothing but the harshest punishment.
Reactions
I hereby affirm that M— and Ms. Y— are both slated to run in the upcoming
stude... ...tion. The sword-like implement produced by Ms. Y— is no doubt
...dicator of her violent streak. No one would desire their clothing
...oroughly tarnished, and M—'s role in the affair must also be
...brought to question.
WHAT IS THAT...!?
AND IS THAT DRAWING SUPPOSED TO BE YOU?
...THEY WROTE A WHOLE ARTICLE ABOUT THAT GUY?
THAT FROM THE SCHOOL PAPER?
IT READS LIKE SOME SAMURAI-ERA HANDBILL MORE THAN ANYTHING.
ZUI (ZZZP)
...WELL, WHAT DO I CARE? IT'S ALL ABOUT YOU, GIRL!
IT'S GOT NOTHING TO DO WITH ME!
I DIDN'T GO BUSTIN' OUT MY MAGIC THERE EITHER!
LOOK A LITTLE CLOSER, DUMBASS. YOUR INITIAL'S IN THERE TOO.
WHAAA!?

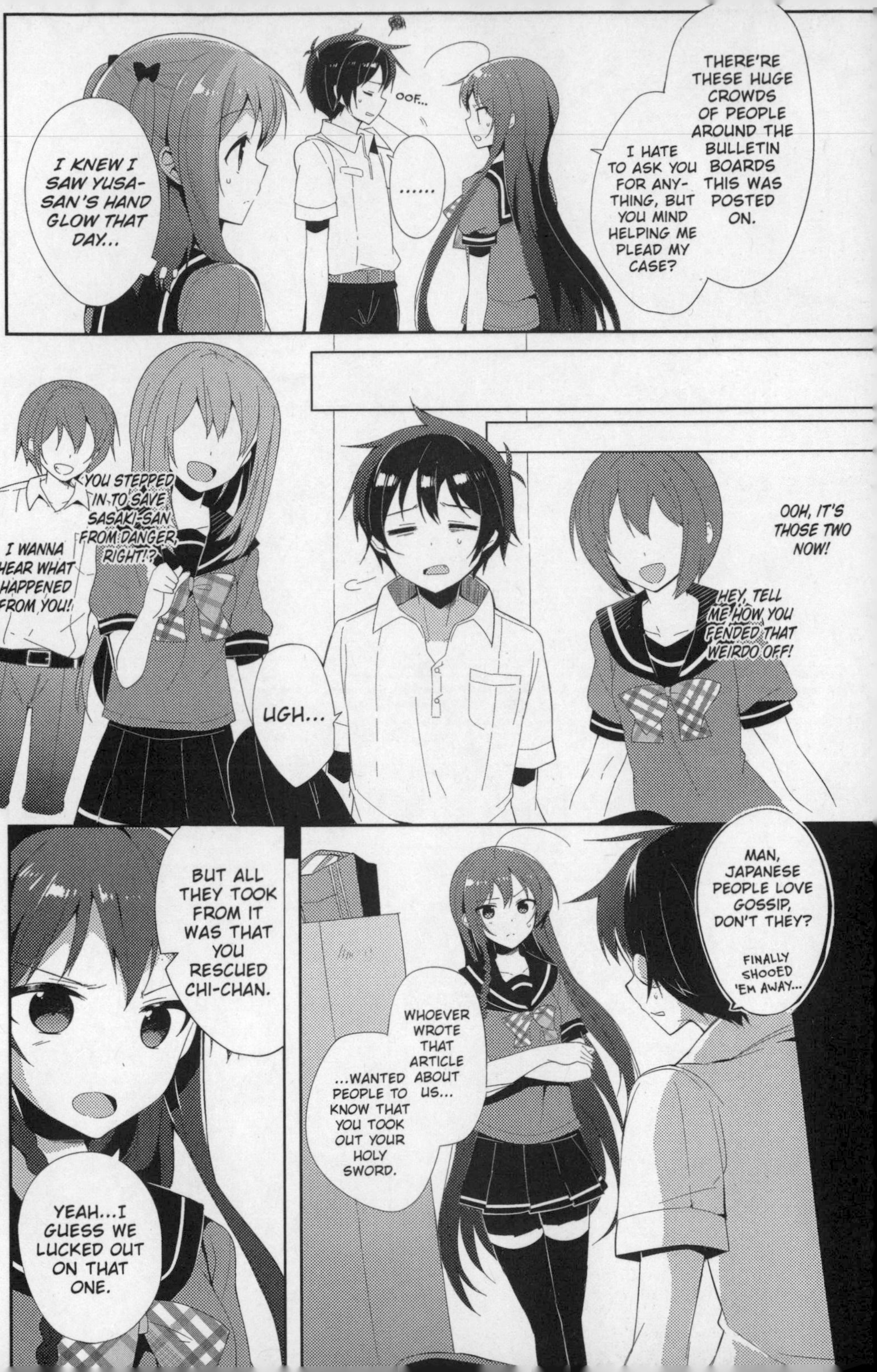
THERE'RE THESE HUGE CROWDS OF PEOPLE AROUND THE BULLETIN BOARDS THIS WAS POSTED ON.
I HATE TO ASK YOU FOR ANY-THING, BUT YOU MIND HELPING ME PLEAD MY CASE?
OOF...
......
I KNEW I SAW YUSA-SAN'S HAND GLOW THAT DAY...
OOH, IT'S THOSE TWO NOW!
HEY, TELL ME HOW YOU FENDED THAT WEIRDO OFF!
UGH...
YOU STEPPED IN TO SAVE SASAKI-SAN FROM DANGER, RIGHT!?
I WANNA HEAR WHAT HAPPENED FROM YOU!
MAN, JAPANESE PEOPLE LOVE GOSSIP, DON'T THEY?
FINALLY SHOOED 'EM AWAY...
WHOEVER WROTE THAT ARTICLE ABOUT US...
...WANTED PEOPLE TO KNOW THAT YOU TOOK OUT YOUR HOLY SWORD.
BUT ALL THEY TOOK FROM IT WAS THAT YOU RESCUED CHI-CHAN.
YEAH...I GUESS WE LUCKED OUT ON THAT ONE.

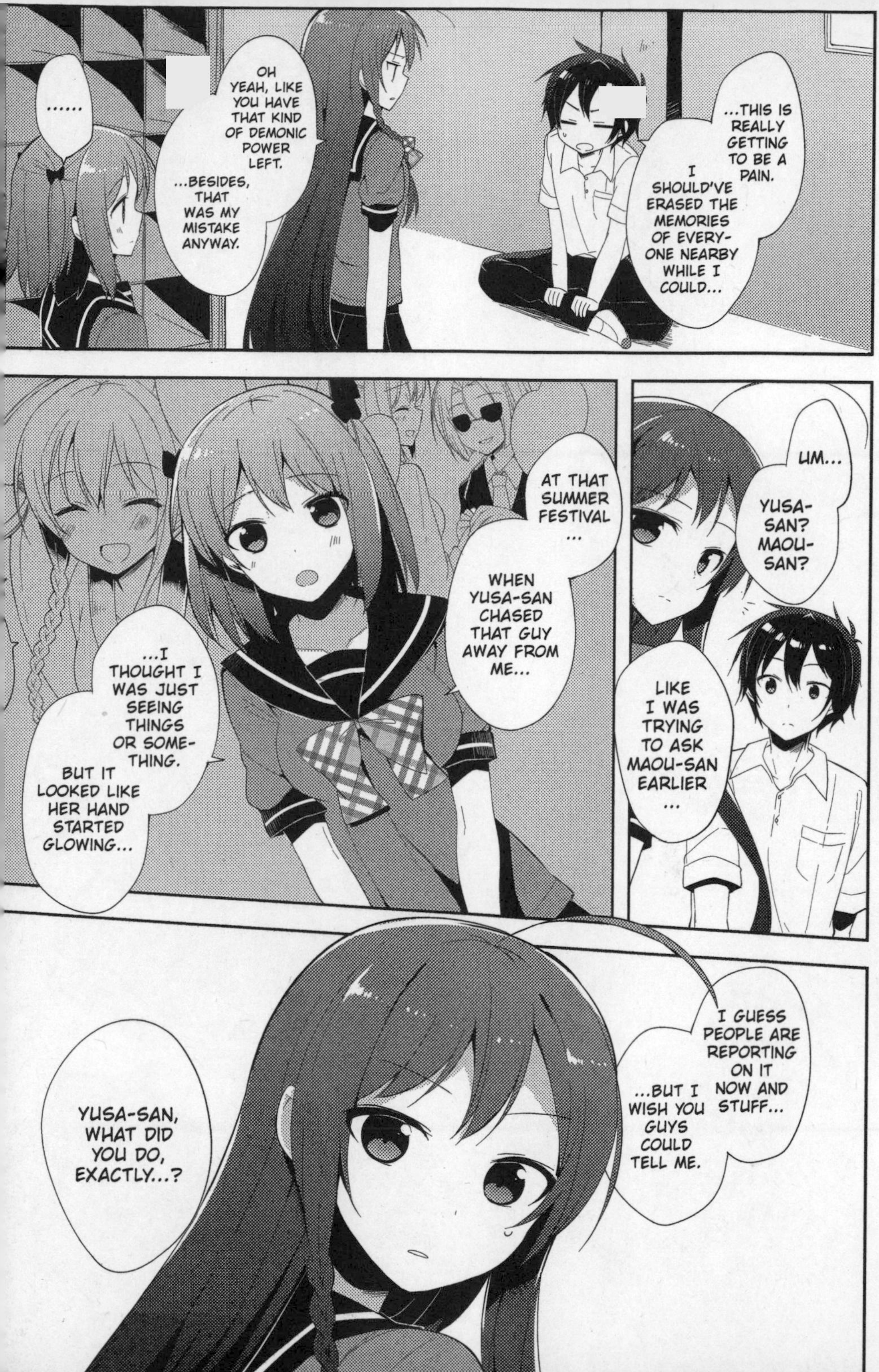
...THIS IS REALLY GETTING TO BE A PAIN.
I SHOULD'VE ERASED THE MEMORIES OF EVERY-ONE NEARBY WHILE I COULD...
OH YEAH, LIKE YOU HAVE THAT KIND OF DEMONIC POWER LEFT.
...BESIDES, THAT WAS MY MISTAKE ANYWAY.
......
UM...
YUSA-SAN? MAOU-SAN?
LIKE I WAS TRYING TO ASK MAOU-SAN EARLIER ...
AT THAT SUMMER FESTIVAL ...
WHEN YUSA-SAN CHASED THAT GUY AWAY FROM ME...
...I THOUGHT I WAS JUST SEEING THINGS OR SOME-THING.
BUT IT LOOKED LIKE HER HAND STARTED GLOWING...
I GUESS PEOPLE ARE REPORTING ON IT NOW AND STUFF...
...BUT I WISH YOU GUYS COULD TELL ME.
YUSA-SAN, WHAT DID YOU DO, EXACTLY...?

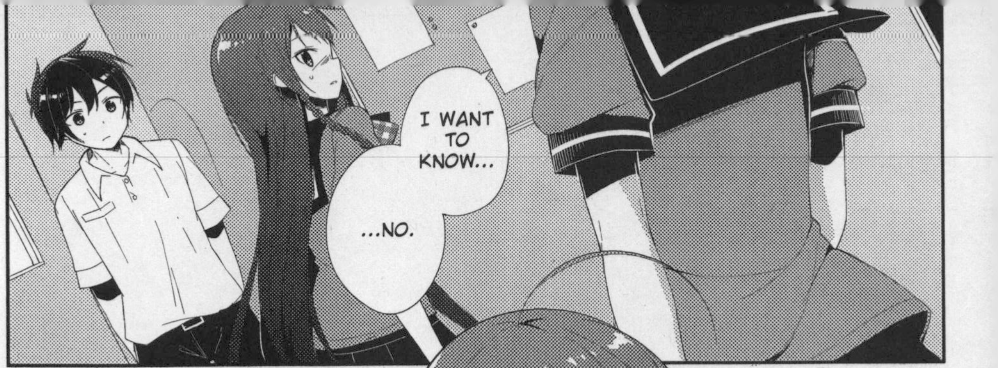
I WANT TO KNOW...
...NO.
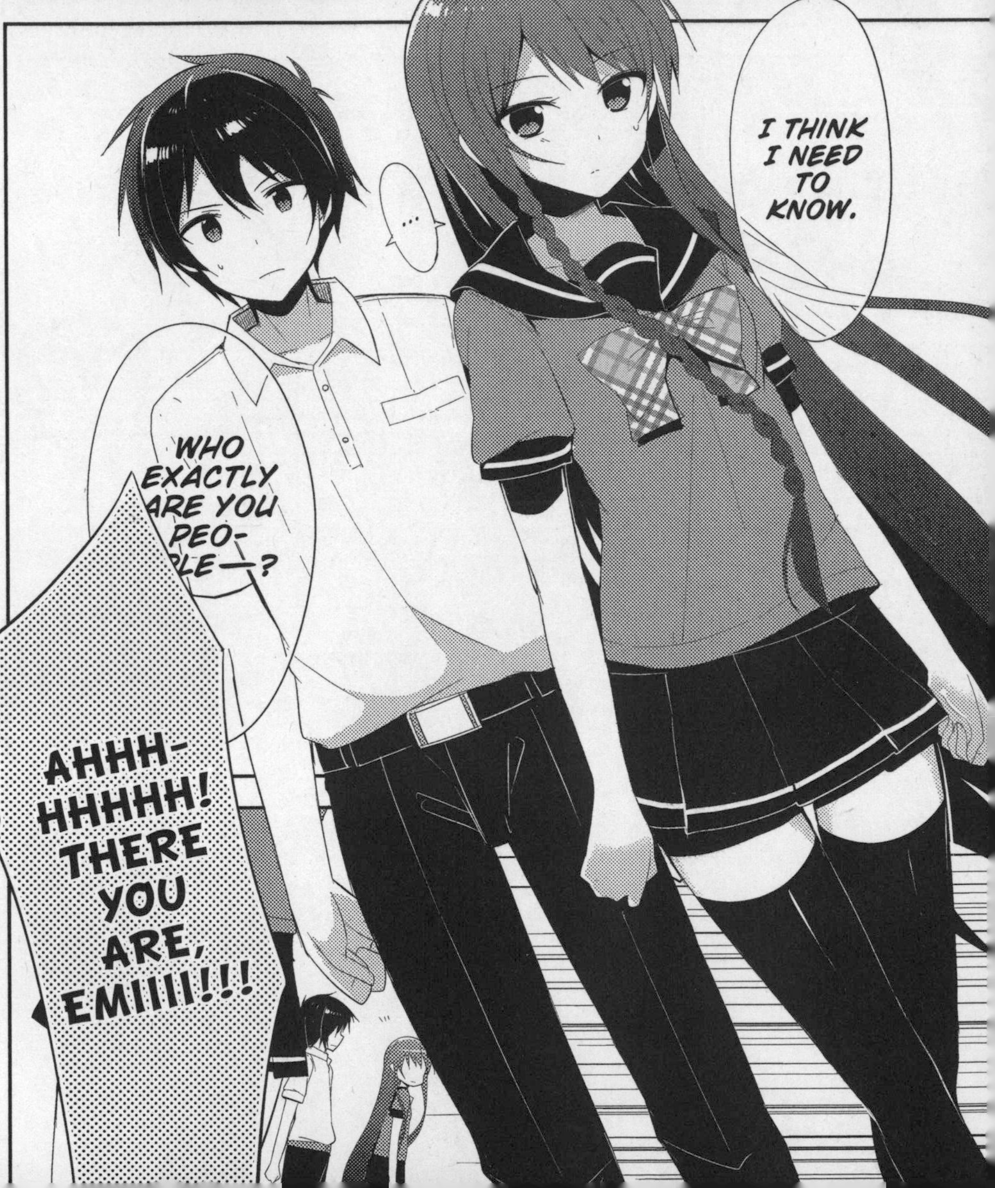
I THINK I NEED TO KNOW.
...
WHO EXACTLY ARE YOU PEO-PLE—?
AHHH-HHHHH! THERE YOU ARE, EMIIII!!!

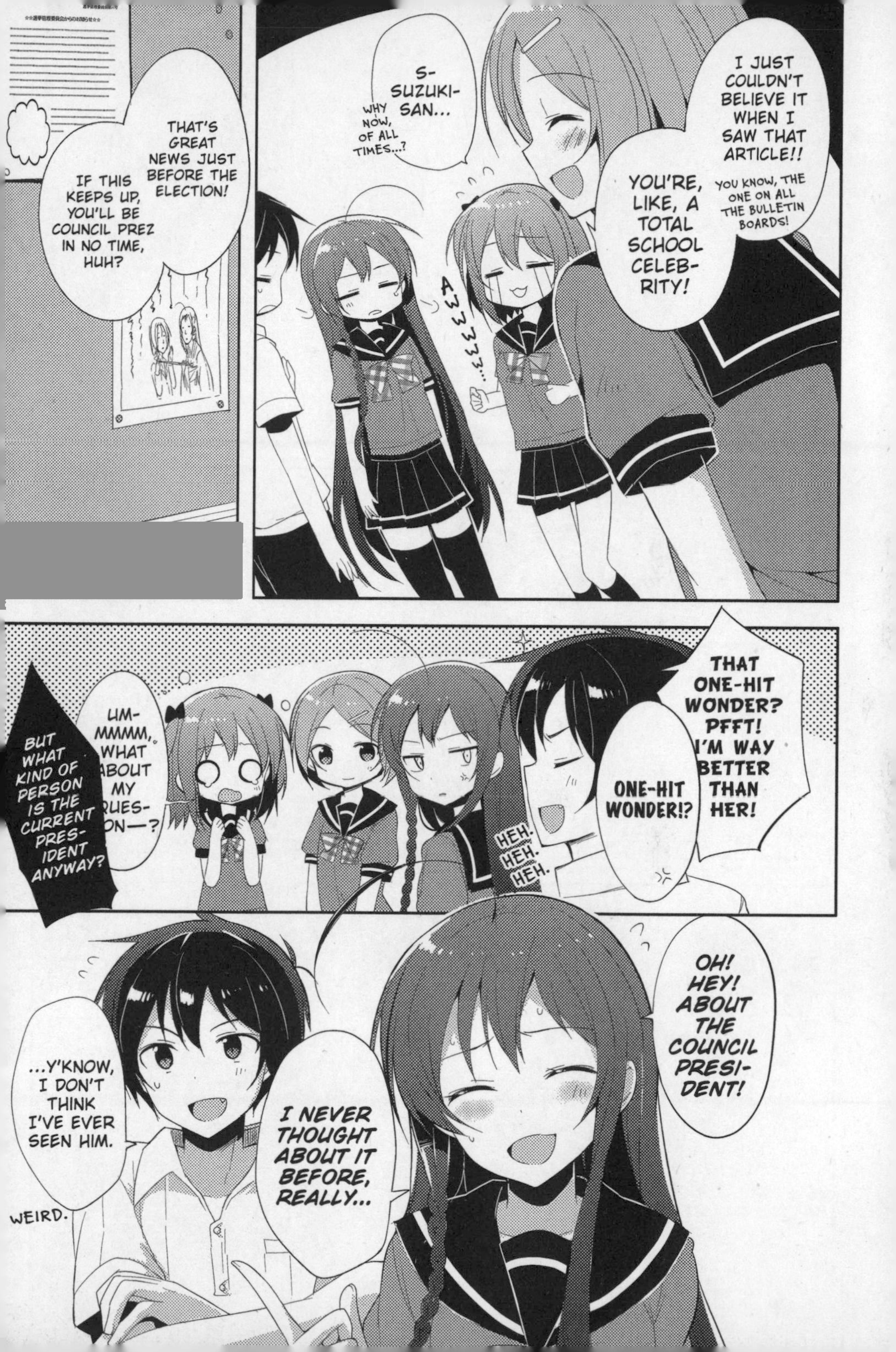
I JUST COULDN'T BELIEVE IT WHEN I SAW THAT ARTICLE!!
YOU KNOW, THE ONE ON ALL THE BULLETIN BOARDS!
YOU'RE, LIKE, A TOTAL SCHOOL CELEB-RITY!
S-SUZUKI-SAN...
WHY NOW, OF ALL TIMES...?
AWWWWW...
THAT'S GREAT NEWS JUST BEFORE THE ELECTION!
IF THIS KEEPS UP, YOU'LL BE COUNCIL PREZ IN NO TIME, HUH?
THAT ONE-HIT WONDER? PFFT! I'M WAY BETTER THAN HER!
ONE-HIT WONDER!?
HEH. HEH. HEH.
UM-MMMM, WHAT ABOUT MY QUES- ON—?
BUT WHAT KIND OF PERSON IS THE CURRENT PRES-IDENT ANYWAY?
OH! HEY! ABOUT THE COUNCIL PRESI-DENT!
I NEVER THOUGHT ABOUT IT BEFORE, REALLY...
...Y'KNOW, I DON'T THINK I'VE EVER SEEN HIM.
WEIRD.

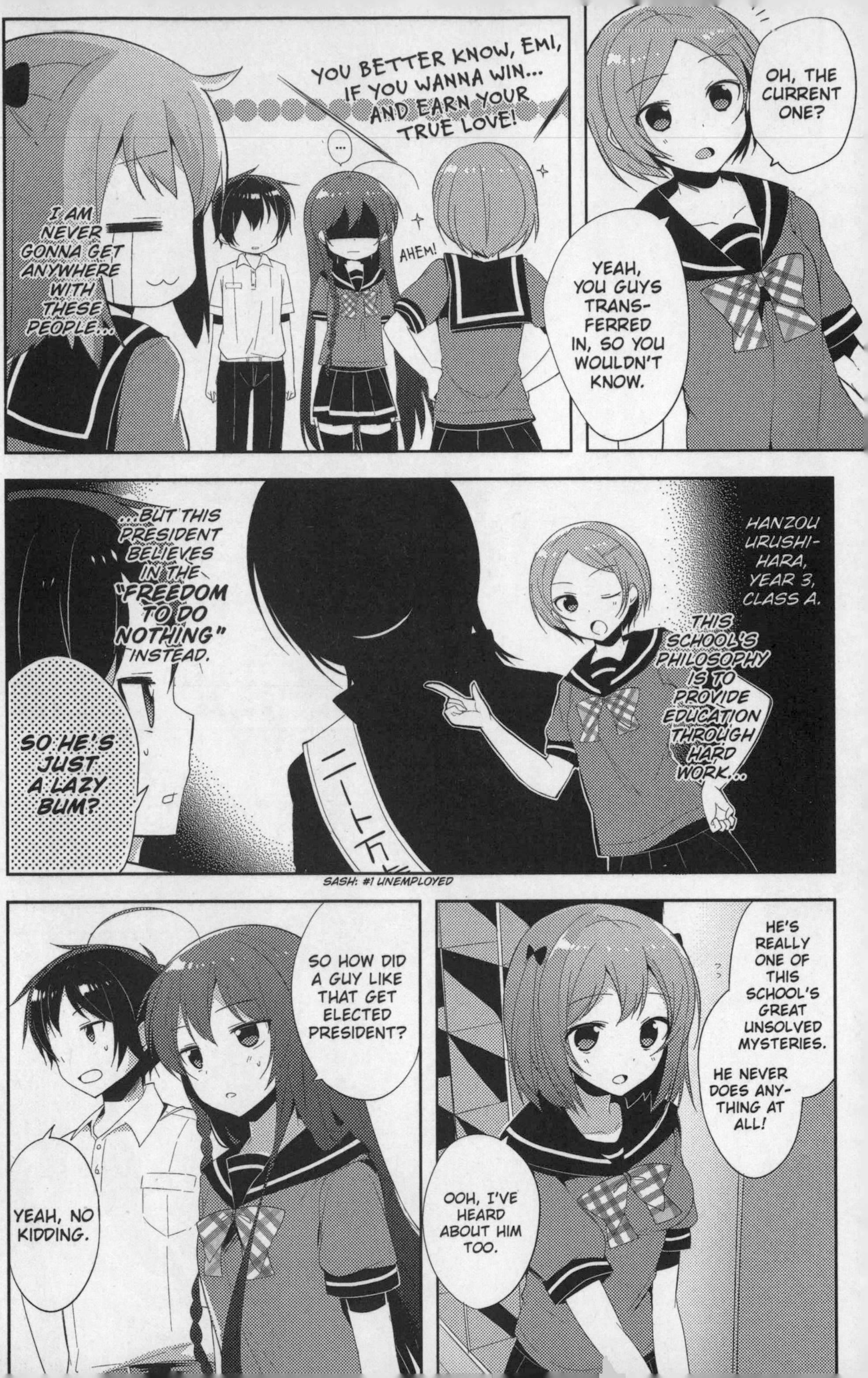
OH, THE CURRENT ONE?
YEAH, YOU GUYS TRANS-FERRED IN, SO YOU WOULDN'T KNOW.
YOU BETTER KNOW, EMI, IF YOU WANNA WIN... AND EARN YOUR TRUE LOVE!
...
AHEM!
I AM NEVER GONNA GET ANYWHERE WITH THESE PEOPLE...
HANZOU URUSHI-HARA, YEAR 3, CLASS A.
THIS SCHOOL'S PHILOSOPHY IS TO PROVIDE EDUCATION THROUGH HARD WORK...
...BUT THIS PRESIDENT BELIEVES IN THE "FREEDOM TO DO NOTHING" INSTEAD.
SO HE'S JUST A LAZY BUM?
SASH: #1 UNEMPLOYED
HE'S REALLY ONE OF THIS SCHOOL'S GREAT UNSOLVED MYSTERIES.
HE NEVER DOES ANY-THING AT ALL!
OOH, I'VE HEARD ABOUT HIM TOO.
SO HOW DID A GUY LIKE THAT GET ELECTED PRESIDENT?
YEAH, NO KIDDING.

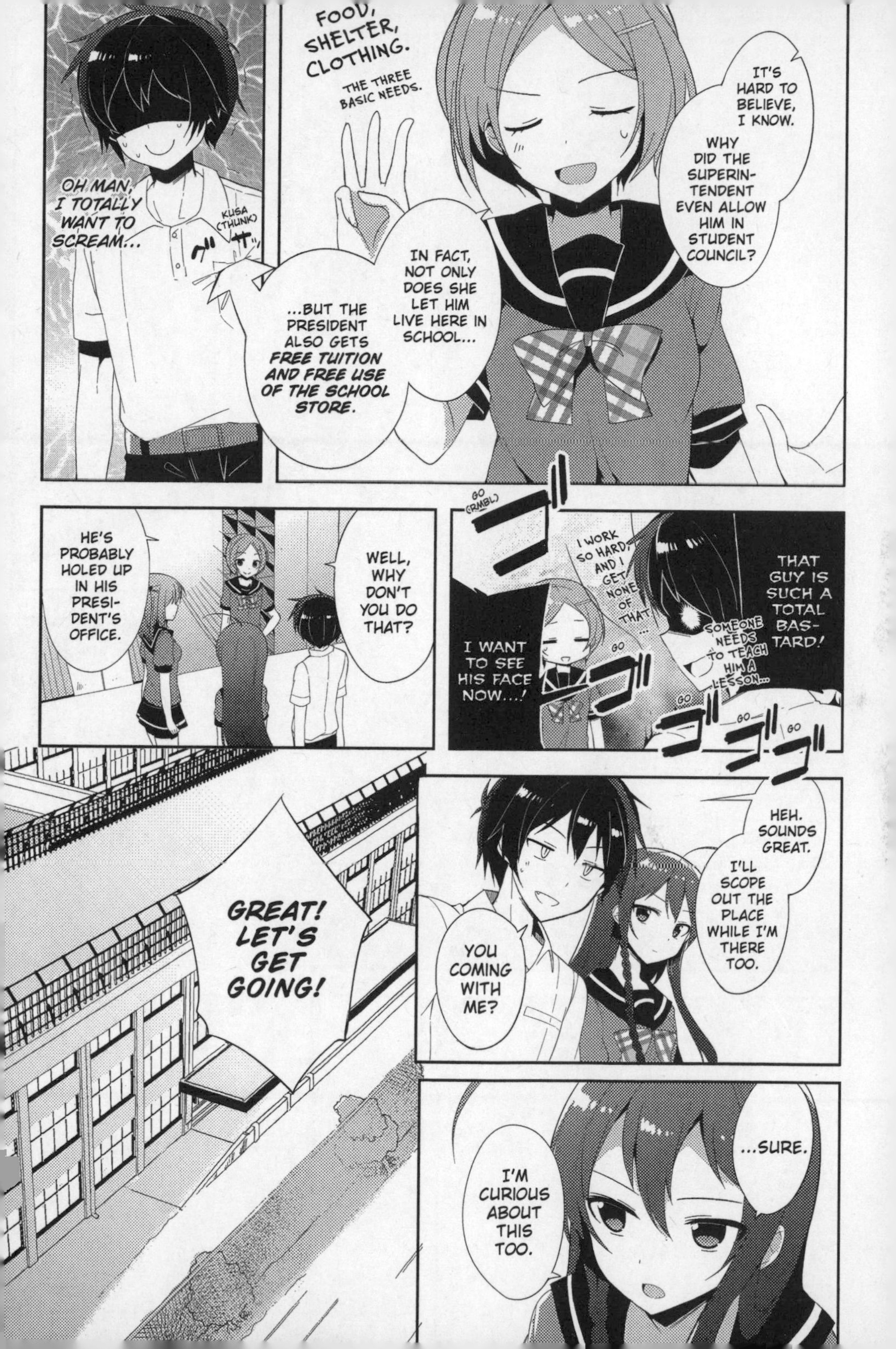

IT'S HARD TO BELIEVE, I KNOW.
WHY DID THE SUPERINTENDENT EVEN ALLOW HIM IN STUDENT COUNCIL?
FOOD, SHELTER, CLOTHING.
THE THREE BASIC NEEDS.
IN FACT, NOT ONLY DOES SHE LET HIM LIVE HERE IN SCHOOL...
...BUT THE PRESIDENT ALSO GETS FREE TUITION AND FREE USE OF THE SCHOOL STORE.
KUSA (THUNK)
OH MAN, I TOTALLY WANT TO SCREAM...
GO (RMBL)
THAT GUY IS SUCH A TOTAL BASTARD!
I WORK SO HARD, AND I GET NONE OF THAT...
SOMEONE NEEDS TO TEACH HIM A LESSON...
I WANT TO SEE HIS FACE NOW...!
GO
GO GO GO
WELL, WHY DON'T YOU DO THAT?
HE'S PROBABLY HOLED UP IN HIS PRESIDENT'S OFFICE.
HEH. SOUNDS GREAT.
I'LL SCOPE OUT THE PLACE WHILE I'M THERE TOO.
YOU COMING WITH ME?
...SURE.
I'M CURIOUS ABOUT THIS TOO.
GREAT! LET'S GET GOING!

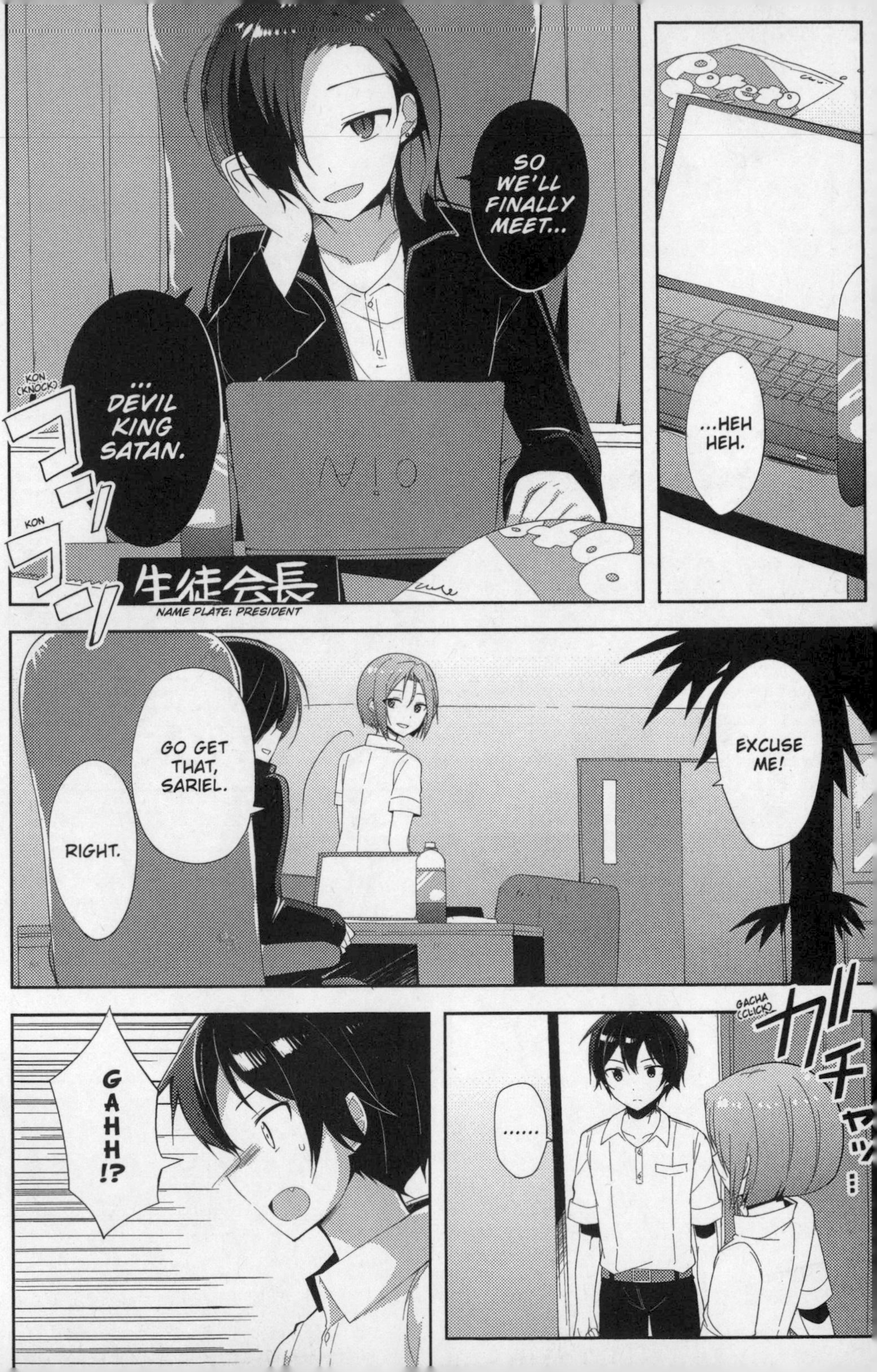
...HEH HEH.
SO WE'LL FINALLY MEET...
...DEVIL KING SATAN.
KON (KNOCK)
コン
KON
コン
生徒会長
NAME PLATE: PRESIDENT
EXCUSE ME!
GO GET THAT, SARIEL.
RIGHT.
GACHA (CLICK)
ガチャッ...
......
GAHH!?

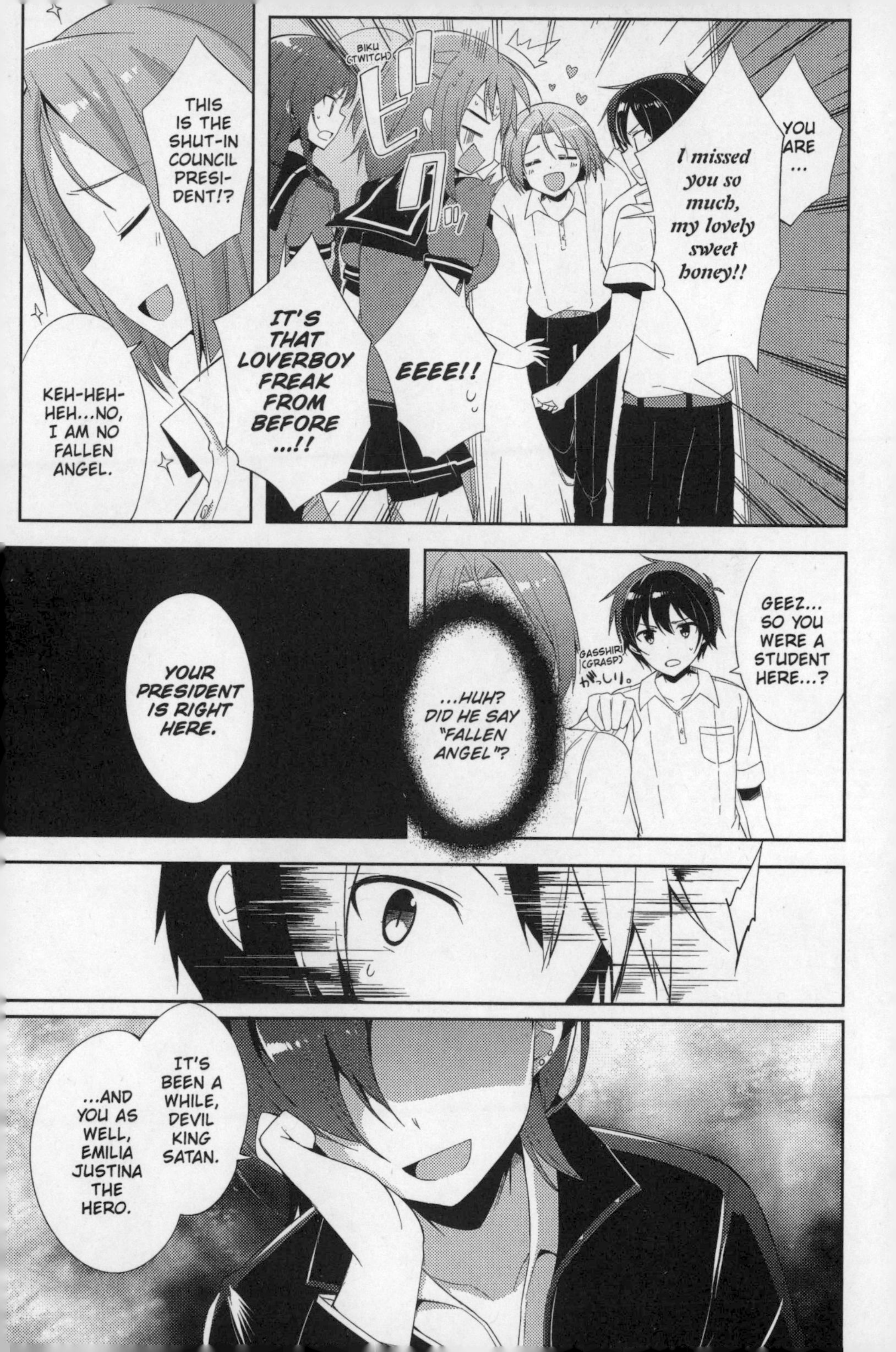
YOU ARE ...
I missed you so much, my lovely sweet honey!!
BIKU (TWITCH)
ビクッ
EEEE!!
IT'S THAT LOVERBOY FREAK FROM BEFORE ...!!
THIS IS THE SHUT-IN COUNCIL PRESIDENT!?
KEH-HEH-HEH...NO, I AM NO FALLEN ANGEL.
GEEZ... SO YOU WERE A STUDENT HERE...?
GASSHIRI (GRASP)
がっしり。
...HUH? DID HE SAY "FALLEN ANGEL"?
YOUR PRESIDENT IS RIGHT HERE.
IT'S BEEN A WHILE, DEVIL KING SATAN.
...AND YOU AS WELL, EMILIA JUSTINA THE HERO.

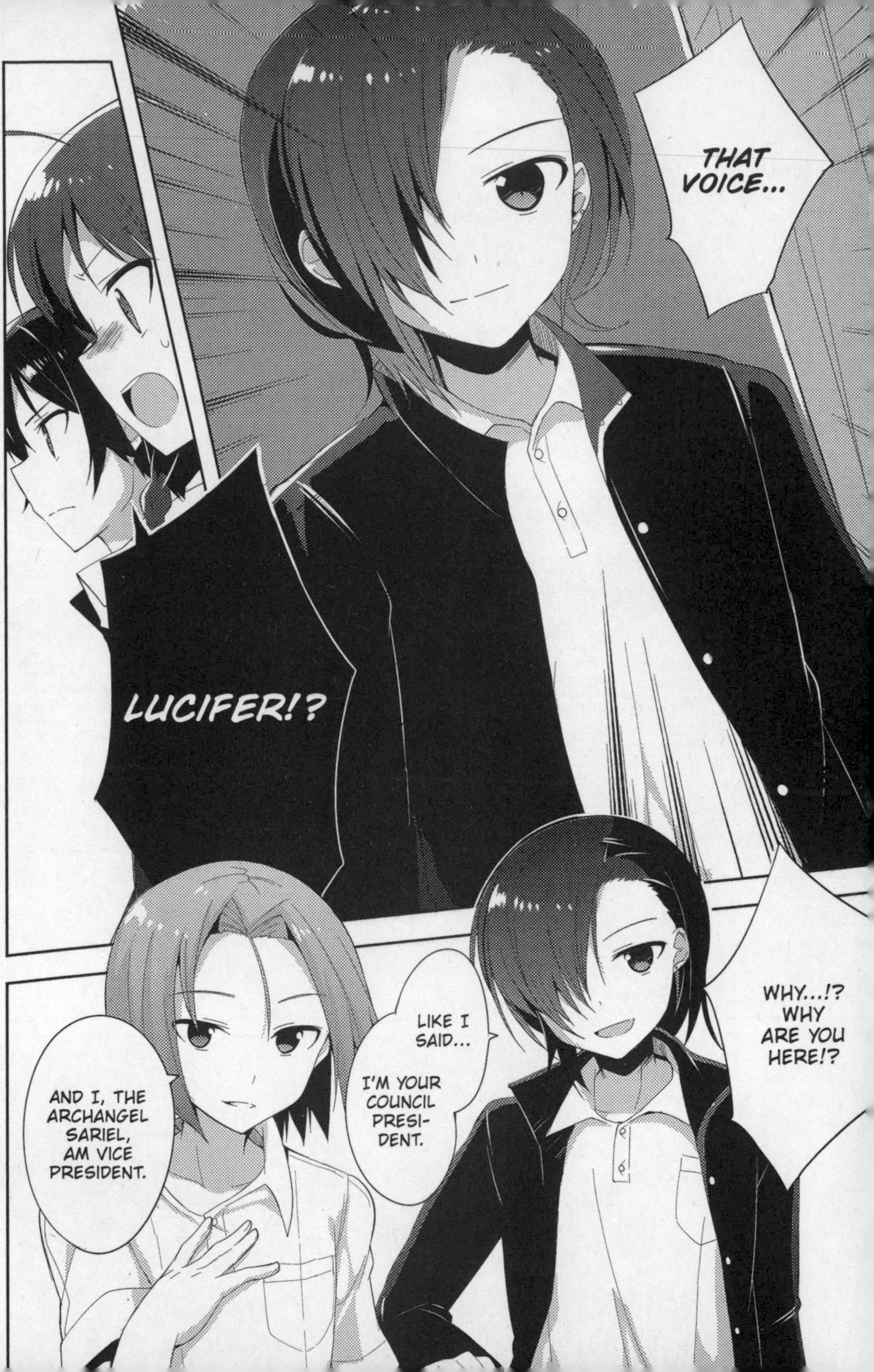
THAT VOICE...
LUCIFER!?
WHY...!? WHY ARE YOU HERE!?
LIKE I SAID...
I'M YOUR COUNCIL PRESI-DENT.
AND I, THE ARCHANGEL SARIEL, AM VICE PRESIDENT.

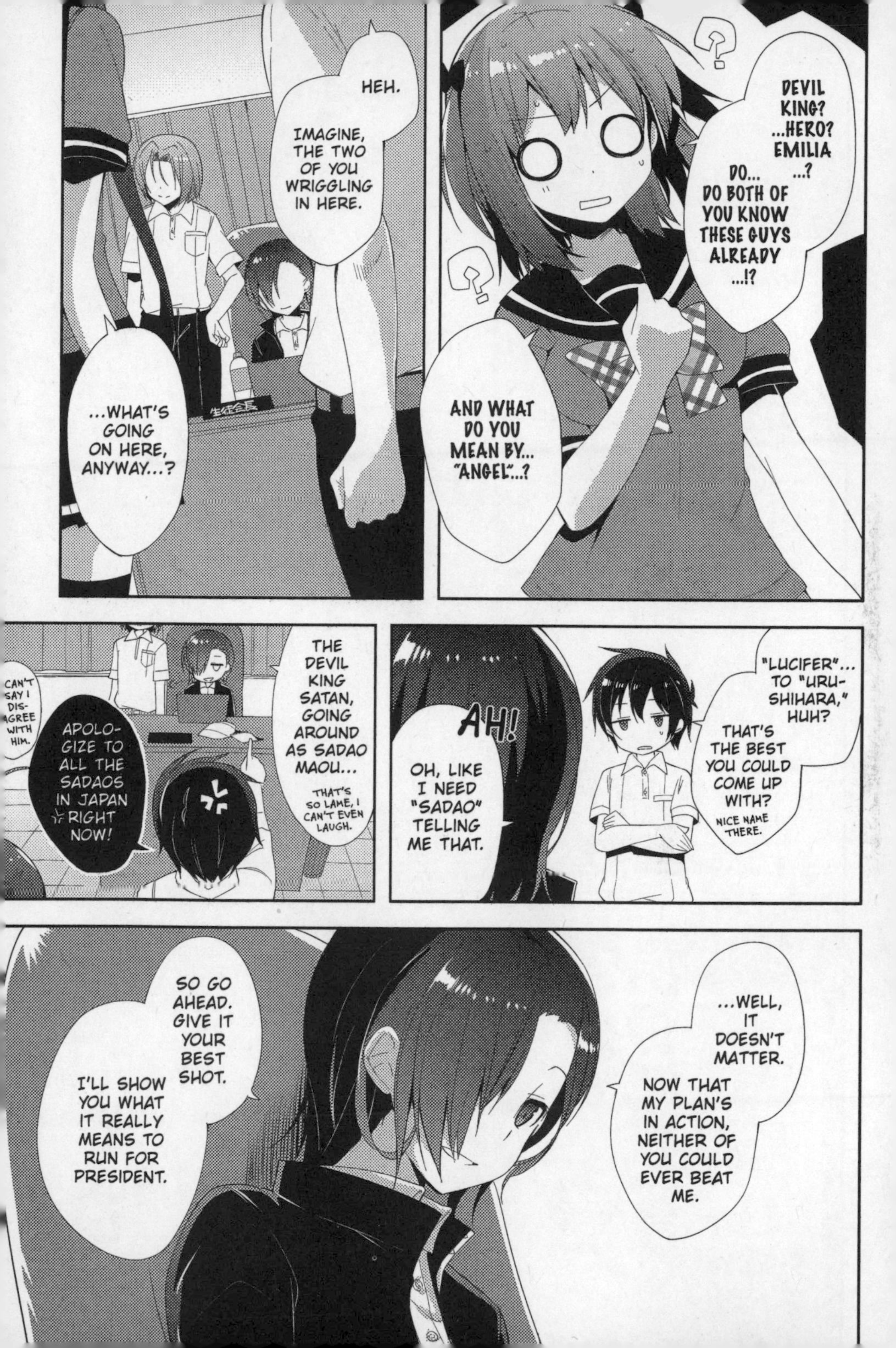
DEVIL KING? ...HERO? EMILIA ...?
DO... DO BOTH OF YOU KNOW THESE GUYS ALREADY ...!?
AND WHAT DO YOU MEAN BY... "ANGEL"...?
HEH.
IMAGINE, THE TWO OF YOU WRIGGLING IN HERE.
生徒会長
...WHAT'S GOING ON HERE, ANYWAY...?
"LUCIFER"... TO "URU-SHIHARA," HUH?
THAT'S THE BEST YOU COULD COME UP WITH?
NICE NAME THERE.
AH!
OH, LIKE I NEED "SADAO" TELLING ME THAT.
THE DEVIL KING SATAN, GOING AROUND AS SADAO MAOU...
THAT'S SO LAME, I CAN'T EVEN LAUGH.
APOLOGIZE TO ALL THE SADAOS IN JAPAN RIGHT NOW!
CAN'T SAY I DISAGREE WITH HIM.
...WELL, IT DOESN'T MATTER.
NOW THAT MY PLAN'S IN ACTION, NEITHER OF YOU COULD EVER BEAT ME.
SO GO AHEAD. GIVE IT YOUR BEST SHOT.
I'LL SHOW YOU WHAT IT REALLY MEANS TO RUN FOR PRESIDENT.

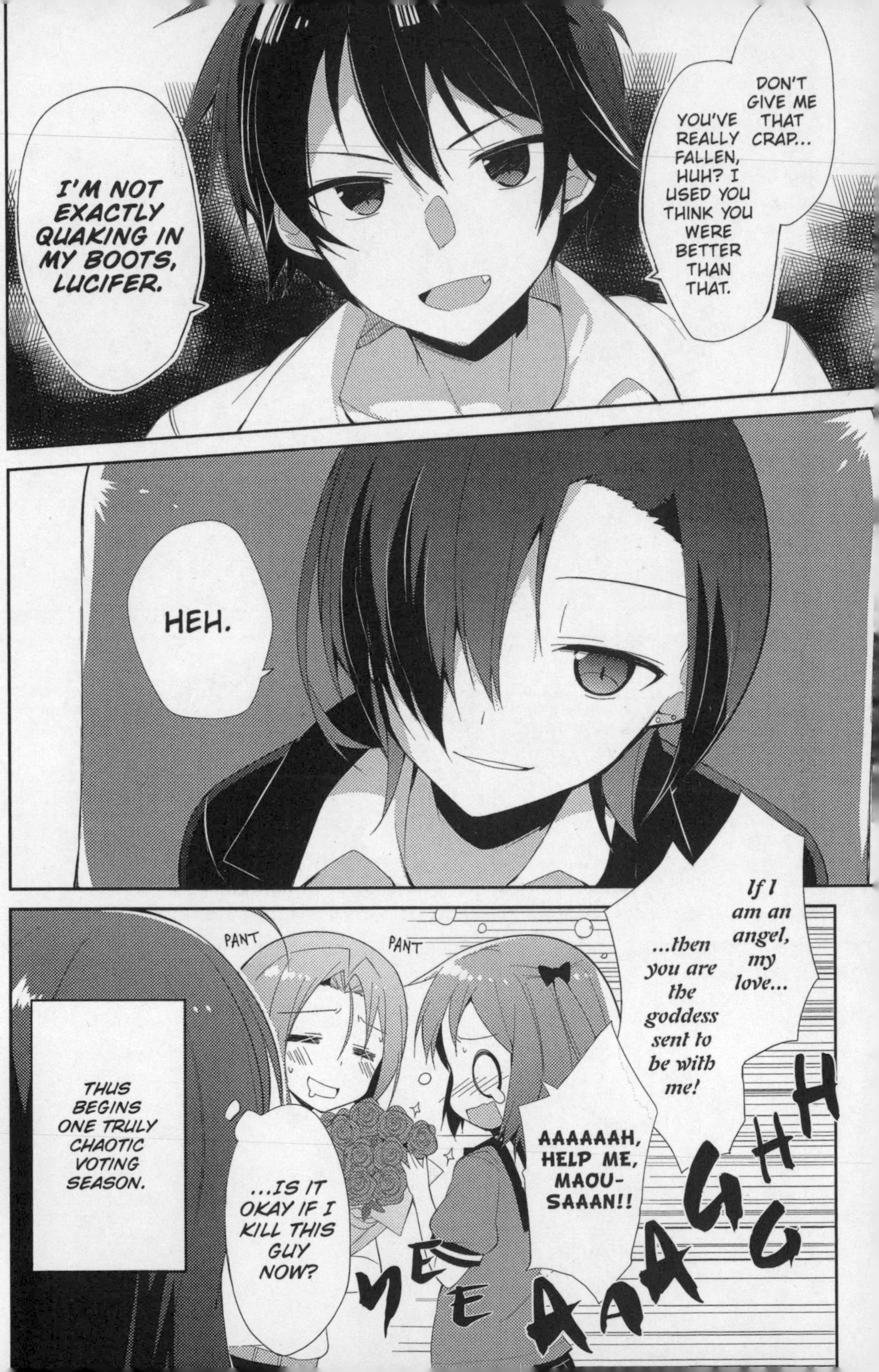
DON'T GIVE ME THAT CRAP...
YOU'VE REALLY FALLEN, HUH? I USED YOU THINK YOU WERE BETTER THAN THAT.
I'M NOT EXACTLY QUAKING IN MY BOOTS, LUCIFER.
HEH.
If I am an angel, my love...
...then you are the goddess sent to be with me!
AAAAAAH, HELP ME, MAOU-SAAAN!!
PANT
PANT
...IS IT OKAY IF I KILL THIS GUY NOW?
THUS BEGINS ONE TRULY CHAOTIC VOTING SEASON.

THE DEVIL IS A PART-TIMER! HIGH SCHOOL!

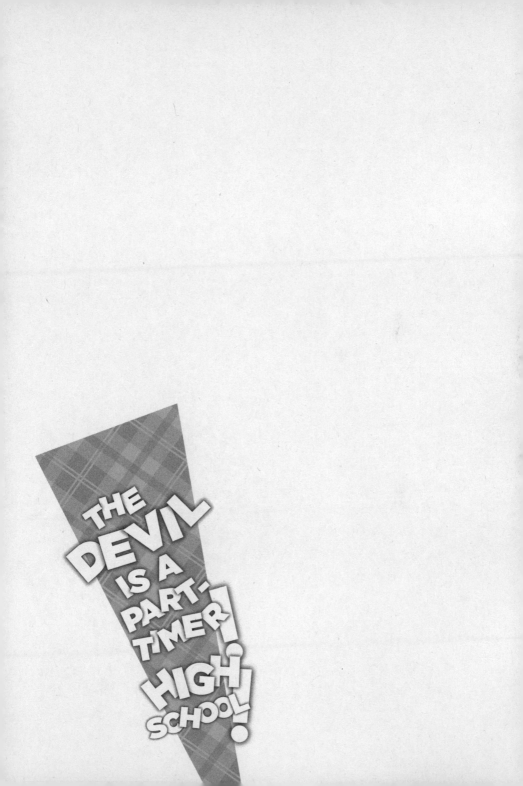

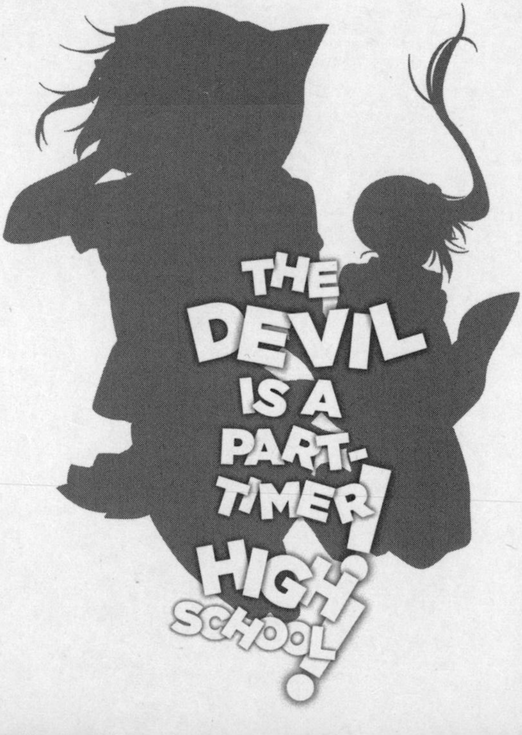
THE DEVIL IS A PART-TIMER! HIGH SCHOOL!

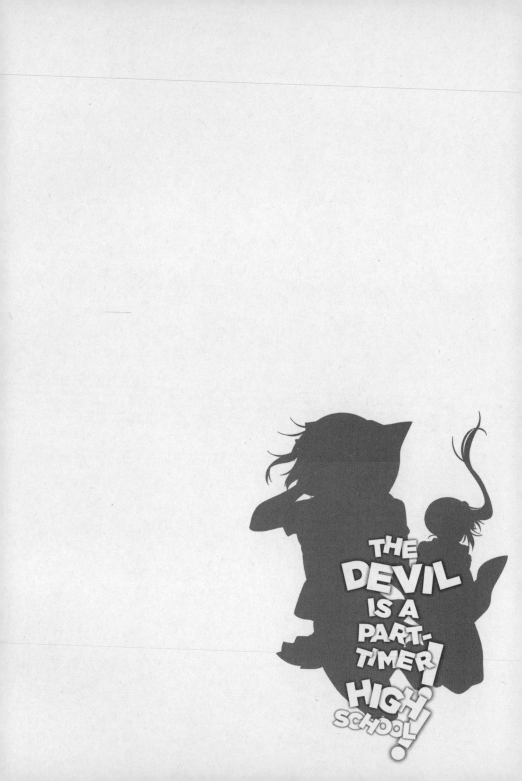

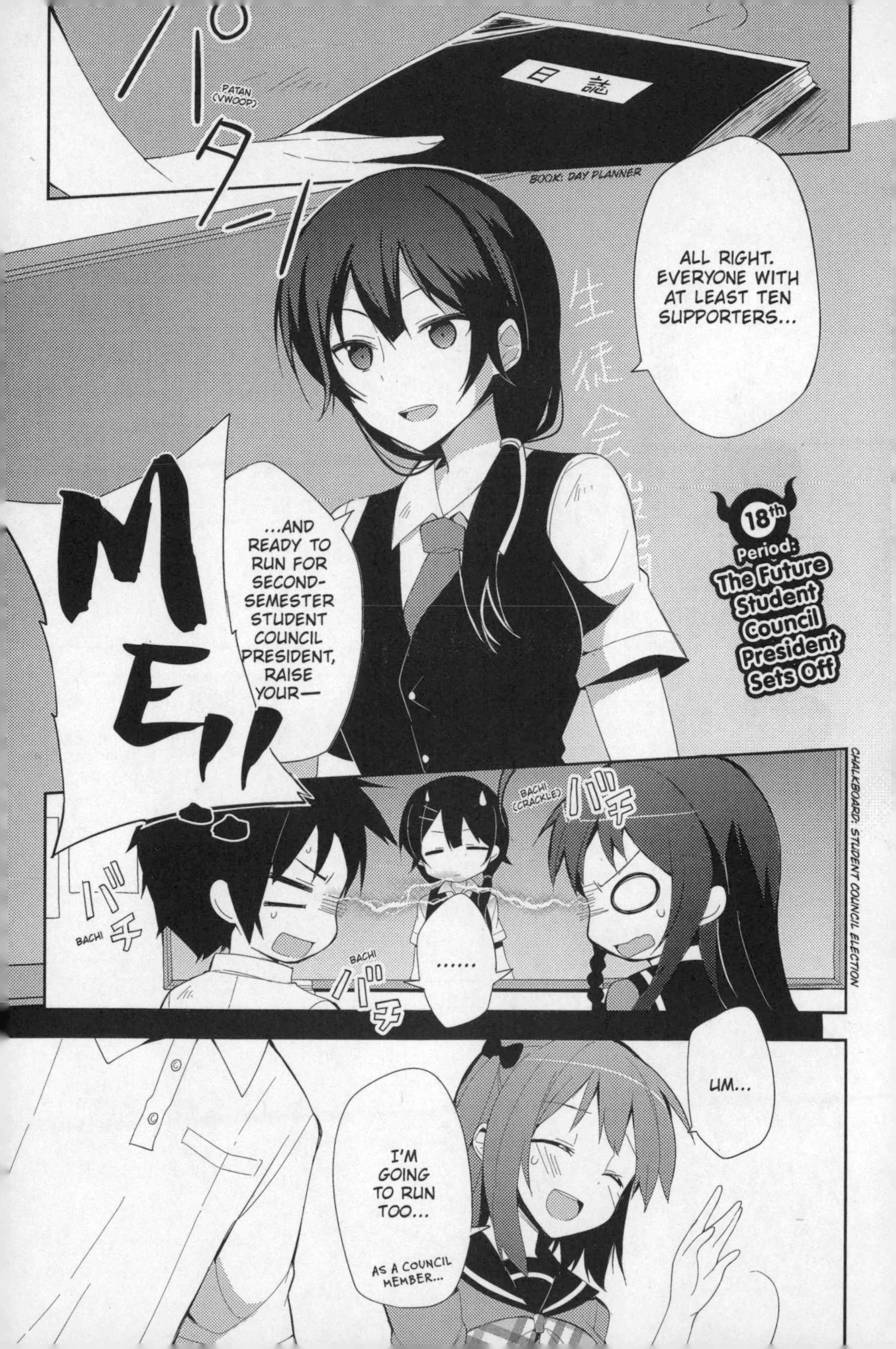

18th Period: The Future Student Council President Sets Off
日誌
PATAN (VWOOP)
BOOK: DAY PLANNER
ALL RIGHT. EVERYONE WITH AT LEAST TEN SUPPORTERS...
...AND READY TO RUN FOR SECOND-SEMESTER STUDENT COUNCIL PRESIDENT, RAISE YOUR—
ME!!
CHALKBOARD: STUDENT COUNCIL ELECTION
BACHI (CRACKLE)
BACHI
BACHI
......
UM...
I'M GOING TO RUN TOO...
AS A COUNCIL MEMBER...

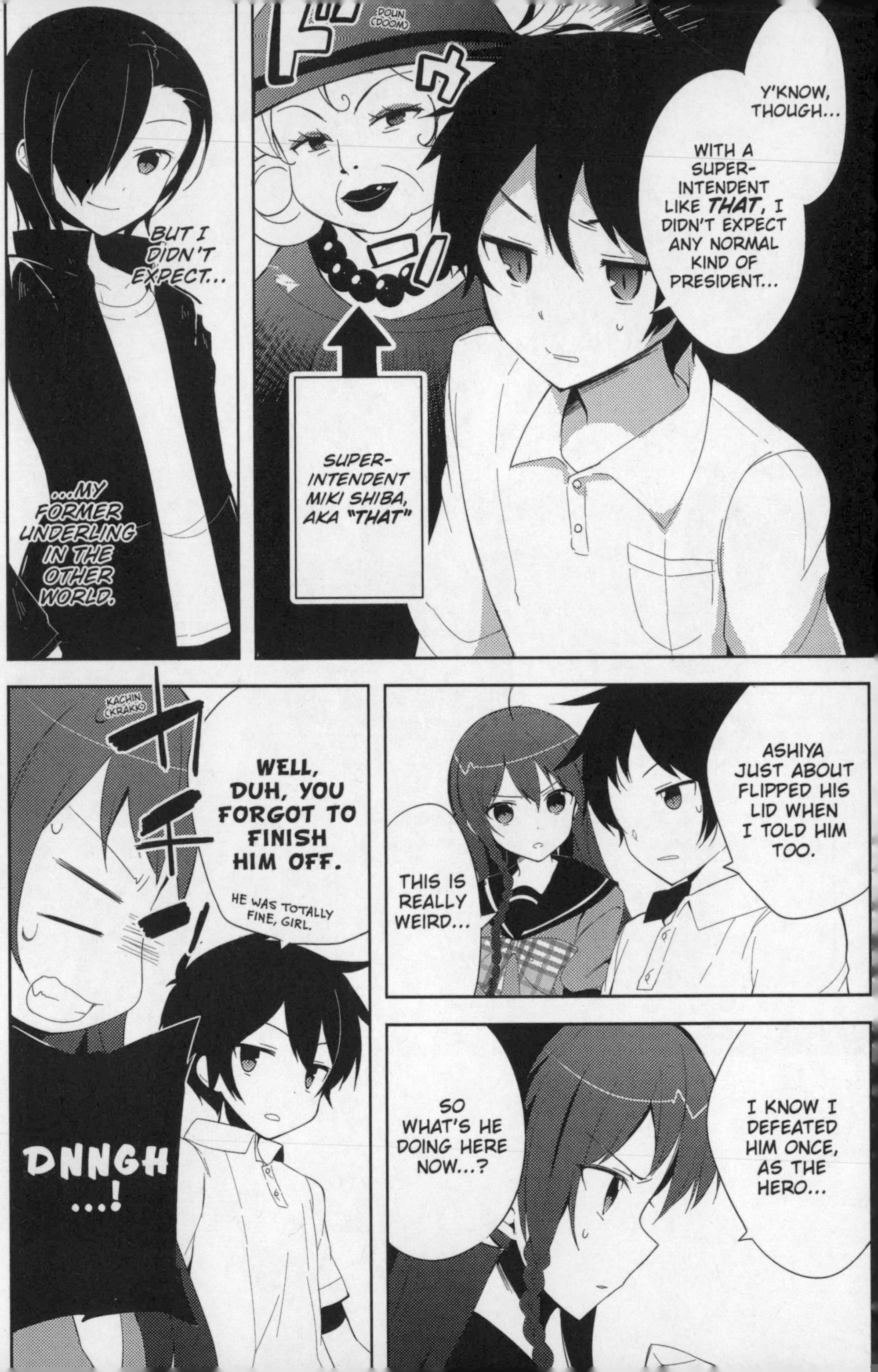
Y'KNOW, THOUGH...
WITH A SUPER-INTENDENT LIKE *THAT*, I DIDN'T EXPECT ANY NORMAL KIND OF PRESIDENT...
DOUN (DOOM)
SUPER-INTENDENT MIKI SHIBA, AKA "*THAT*"
BUT I DIDN'T EXPECT...
...MY FORMER UNDERLING IN THE OTHER WORLD.
ASHIYA JUST ABOUT FLIPPED HIS LID WHEN I TOLD HIM TOO.
THIS IS REALLY WEIRD...
I KNOW I DEFEATED HIM ONCE, AS THE HERO...
SO WHAT'S HE DOING HERE NOW...?
KACHIN (KRAKK)
WELL, DUH, YOU FORGOT TO FINISH HIM OFF.
HE WAS TOTALLY FINE, GIRL.
DNNGH ...!

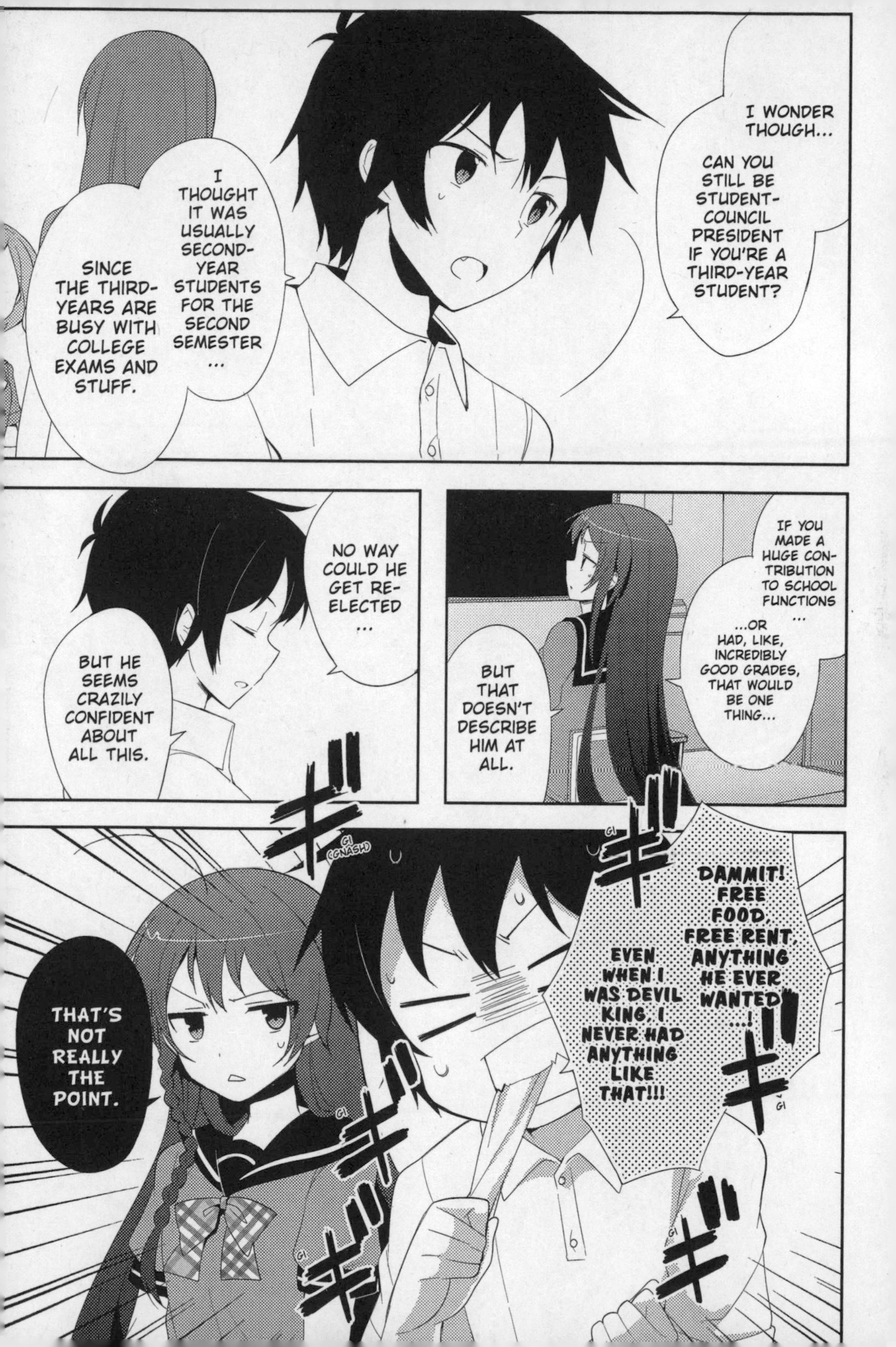
I WONDER THOUGH... CAN YOU STILL BE STUDENT-COUNCIL PRESIDENT IF YOU'RE A THIRD-YEAR STUDENT?
I THOUGHT IT WAS USUALLY SECOND-YEAR STUDENTS FOR THE SECOND SEMESTER...
SINCE THE THIRD-YEARS ARE BUSY WITH COLLEGE EXAMS AND STUFF.
IF YOU MADE A HUGE CON-TRIBUTION TO SCHOOL FUNCTIONS... ...OR HAD, LIKE, INCREDIBLY GOOD GRADES, THAT WOULD BE ONE THING...
BUT THAT DOESN'T DESCRIBE HIM AT ALL.
NO WAY COULD HE GET RE-ELECTED...
BUT HE SEEMS CRAZILY CONFIDENT ABOUT ALL THIS.
GI
DAMMIT! FREE FOOD, FREE RENT, ANYTHING HE EVER WANTED...!
EVEN WHEN I WAS DEVIL KING, I NEVER HAD ANYTHING LIKE THAT!!!
GI (GNASH)
GI
THAT'S NOT REALLY THE POINT.
GI
GI
GI

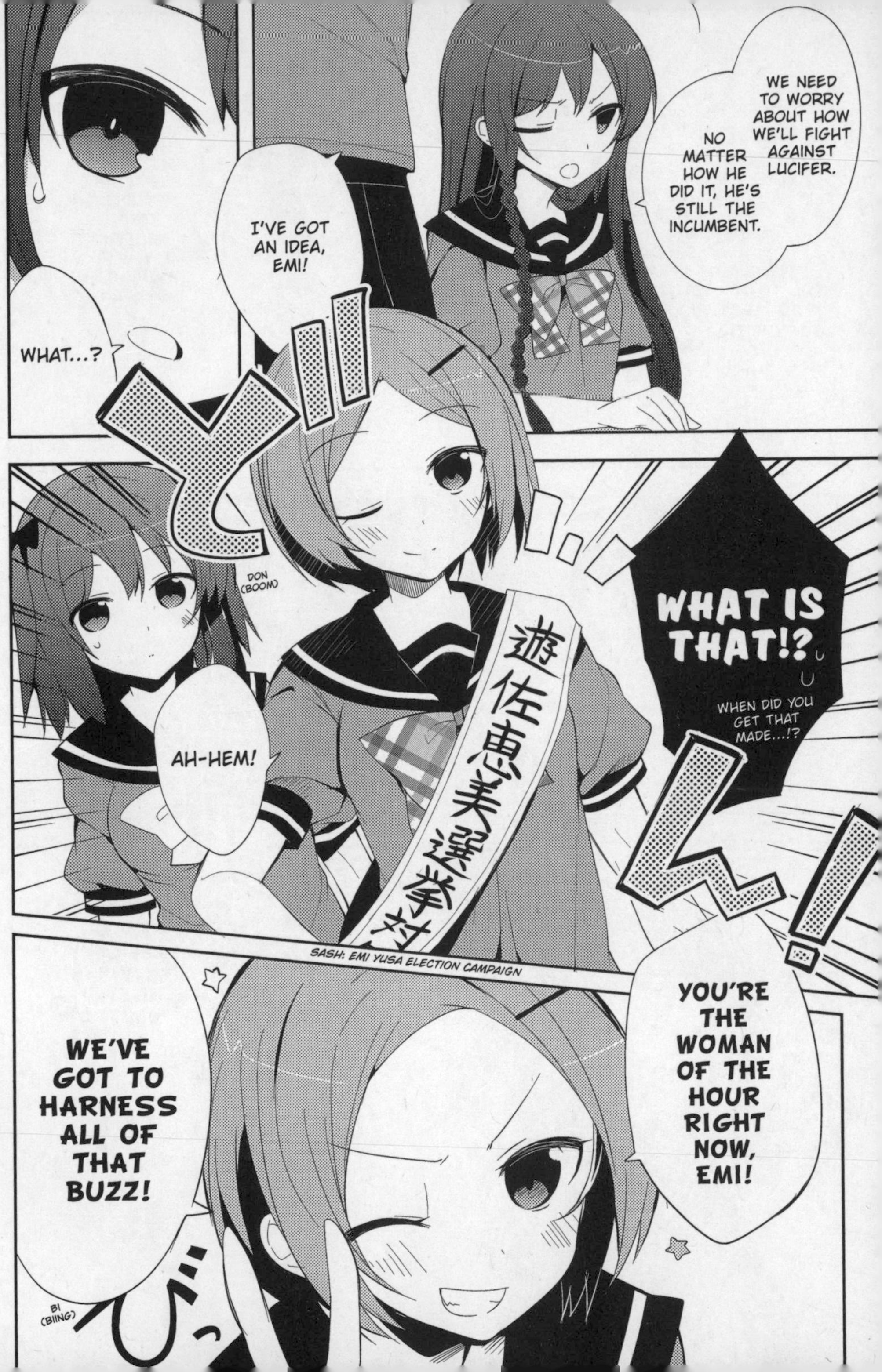
WE NEED TO WORRY ABOUT HOW WE'LL FIGHT AGAINST LUCIFER.
NO MATTER HOW HE DID IT, HE'S STILL THE INCUMBENT.
I'VE GOT AN IDEA, EMI!
WHAT...?
WHAT IS THAT!?
WHEN DID YOU GET THAT MADE...!?
DON (BOOM)
遊佐恵美選挙対
AH-HEM!
SASH: EMI YUSA ELECTION CAMPAIGN
YOU'RE THE WOMAN OF THE HOUR RIGHT NOW, EMI!
WE'VE GOT TO HARNESS ALL OF THAT BUZZ!
BI (BIING)

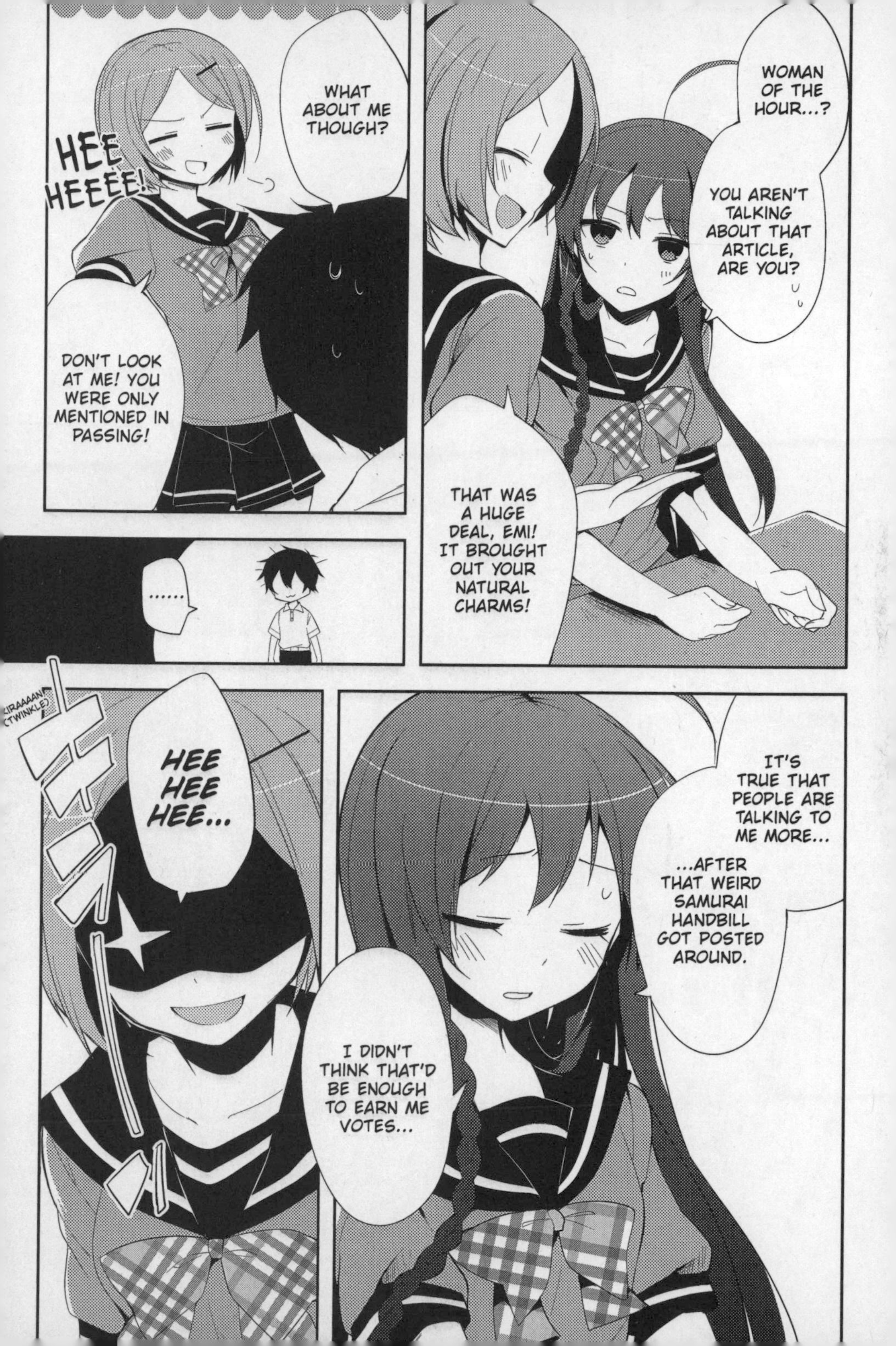
WOMAN OF THE HOUR...?
YOU AREN'T TALKING ABOUT THAT ARTICLE, ARE YOU?
THAT WAS A HUGE DEAL, EMI! IT BROUGHT OUT YOUR NATURAL CHARMS!
WHAT ABOUT ME THOUGH?
HEE HEEEEE!
DON'T LOOK AT ME! YOU WERE ONLY MENTIONED IN PASSING!
......
IT'S TRUE THAT PEOPLE ARE TALKING TO ME MORE...
...AFTER THAT WEIRD SAMURAI HANDBILL GOT POSTED AROUND.
I DIDN'T THINK THAT'D BE ENOUGH TO EARN ME VOTES...
KIRAAAAAN (TWINKLE)
HEE HEE HEE...

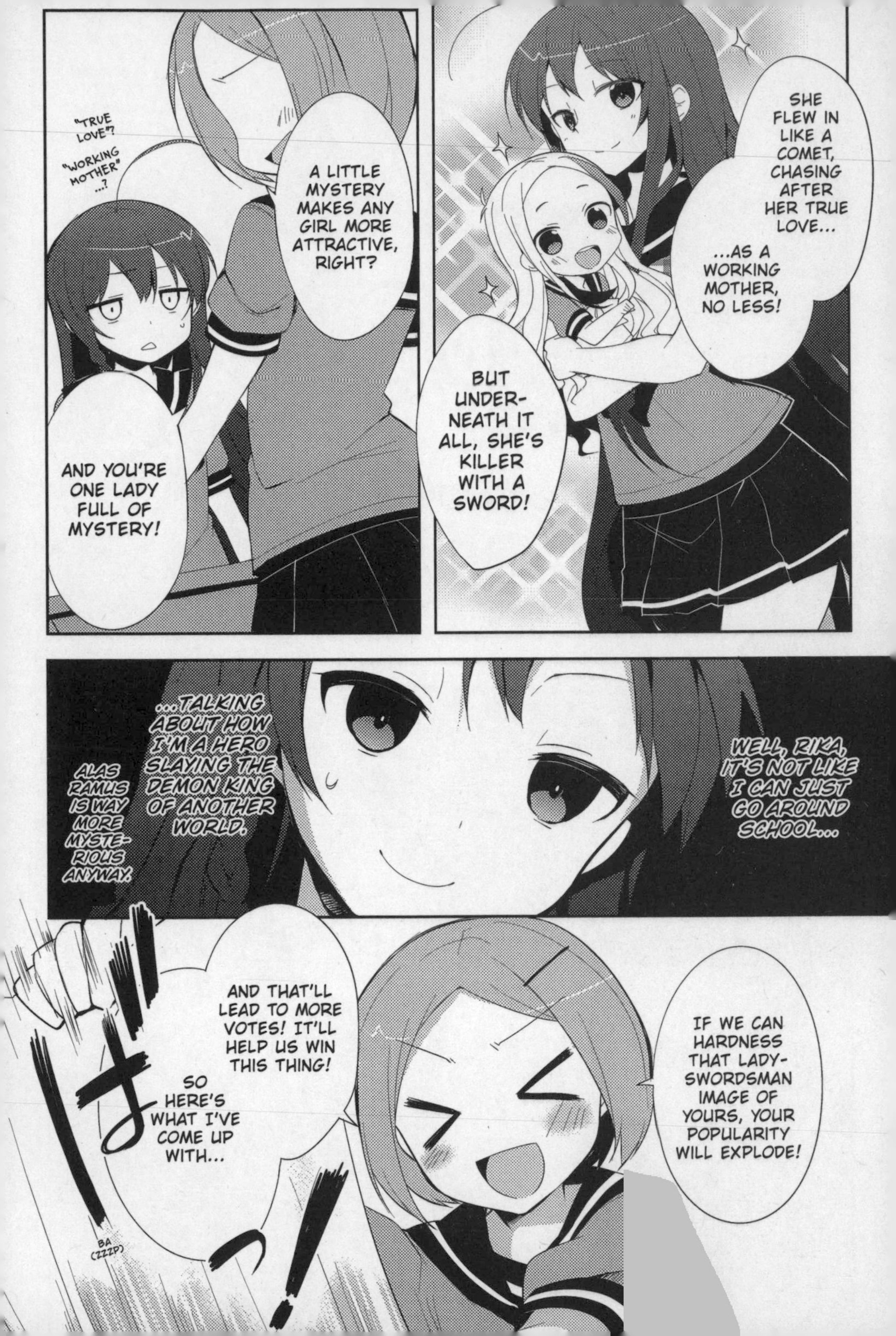
SHE FLEW IN LIKE A COMET, CHASING AFTER HER TRUE LOVE...
...AS A WORKING MOTHER, NO LESS!
BUT UNDERNEATH IT ALL, SHE'S KILLER WITH A SWORD!
A LITTLE MYSTERY MAKES ANY GIRL MORE ATTRACTIVE, RIGHT?
"TRUE LOVE"? "WORKING MOTHER" ...?
AND YOU'RE ONE LADY FULL OF MYSTERY!
WELL, RIKA, IT'S NOT LIKE I CAN JUST GO AROUND SCHOOL...
...TALKING ABOUT HOW I'M A HERO SLAYING THE DEMON KING OF ANOTHER WORLD.
ALAS RAMUS IS WAY MORE MYSTE-RIOUS ANYWAY.
IF WE CAN HARDNESS THAT LADY-SWORDSMAN IMAGE OF YOURS, YOUR POPULARITY WILL EXPLODE!
AND THAT'LL LEAD TO MORE VOTES! IT'LL HELP US WIN THIS THING!
SO HERE'S WHAT I'VE COME UP WITH...
BA (ZZZP)

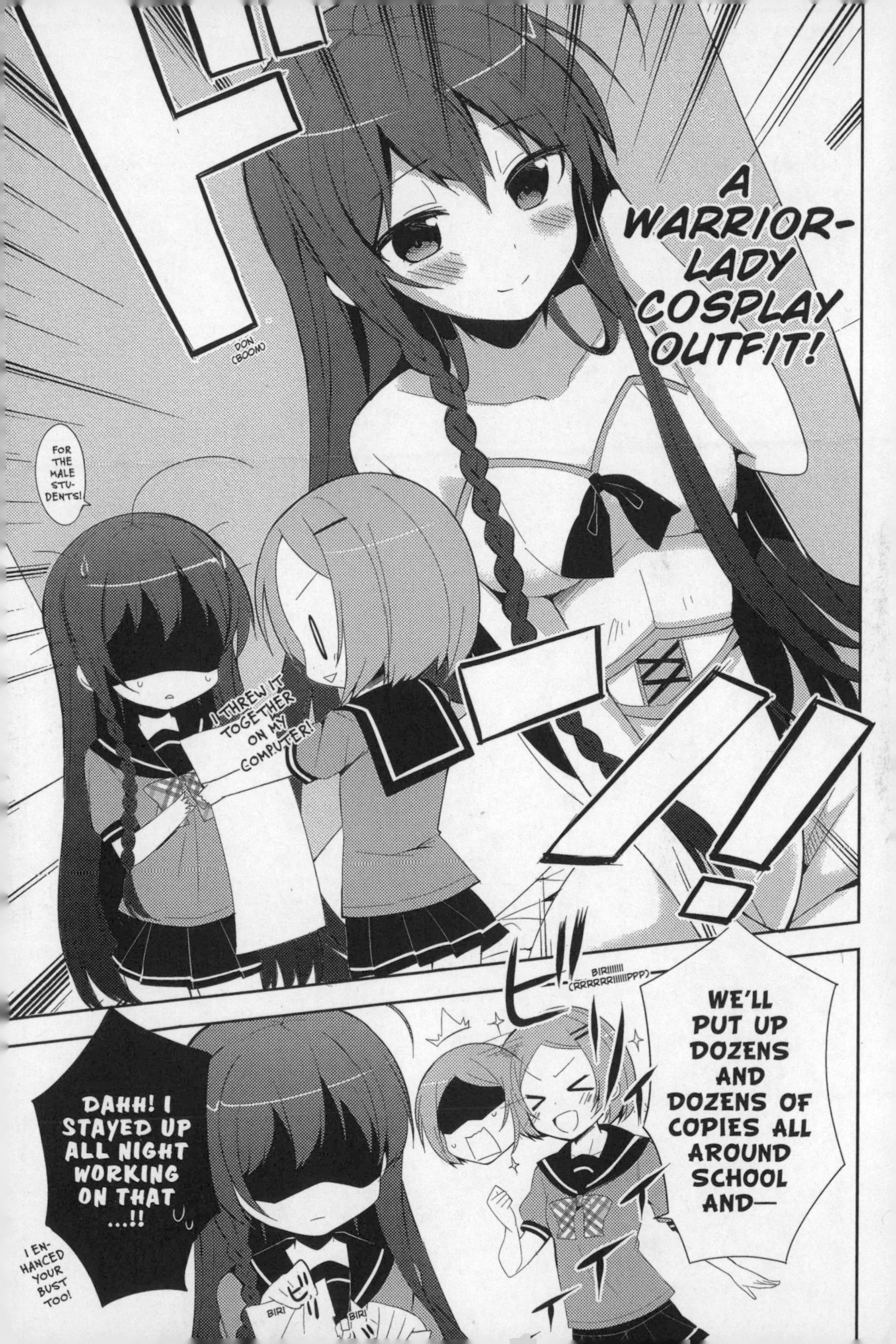
A WARRIOR-LADY COSPLAY OUTFIT!
DON (BOOM)
FOR THE MALE STUDENTS!
I THREW IT TOGETHER ON MY COMPUTER!
BIRIIIIIIII (RRRRRRIIIIIIIPPP)
WE'LL PUT UP DOZENS AND DOZENS OF COPIES ALL AROUND SCHOOL AND—
DAHH! I STAYED UP ALL NIGHT WORKING ON THAT ...!!
I ENHANCED YOUR BUST TOO!
BIRI
BIRI

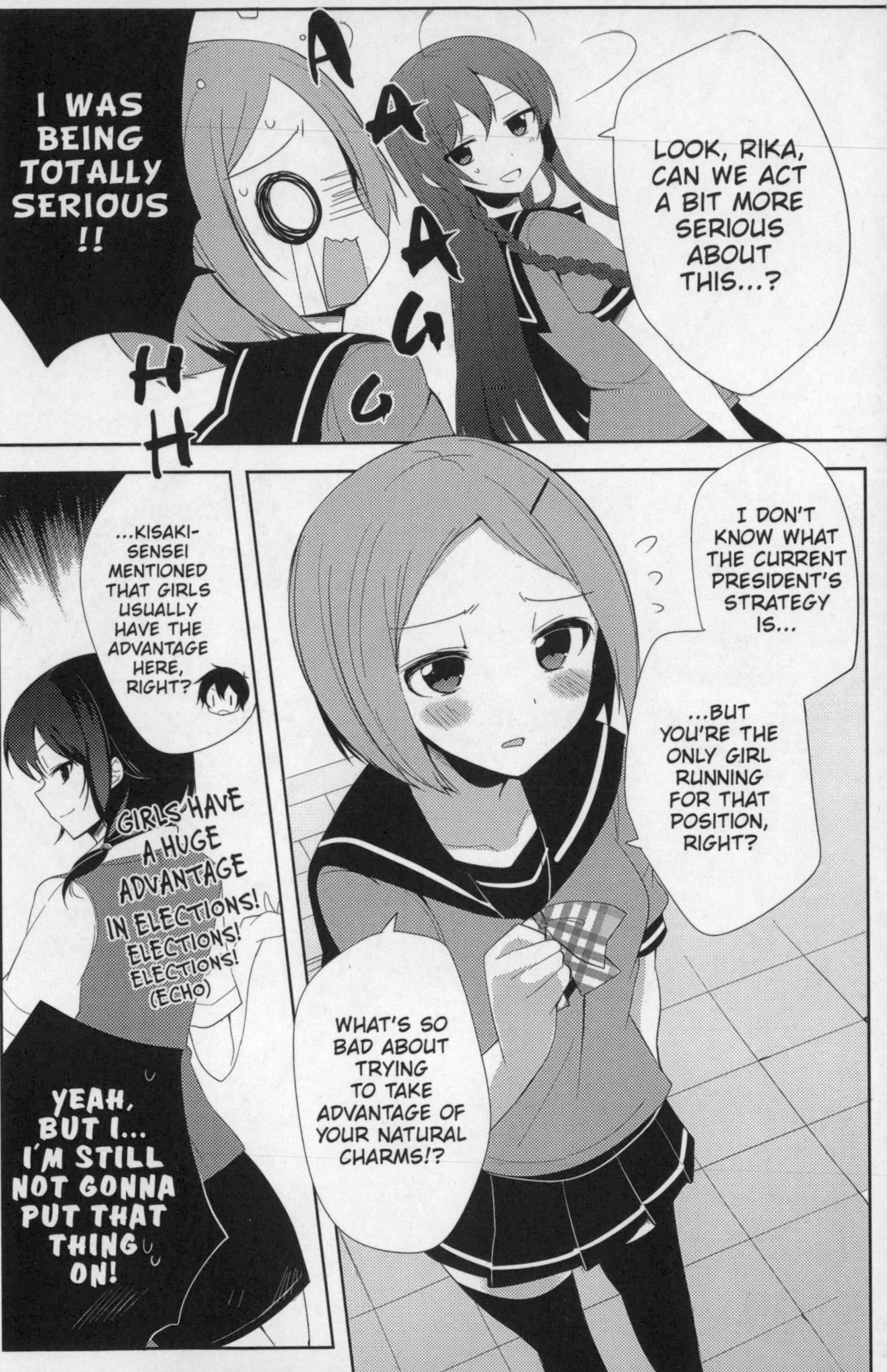
LOOK, RIKA, CAN WE ACT A BIT MORE SERIOUS ABOUT THIS...?
AAAGGHH
I WAS BEING TOTALLY SERIOUS!!
I DON'T KNOW WHAT THE CURRENT PRESIDENT'S STRATEGY IS...
...BUT YOU'RE THE ONLY GIRL RUNNING FOR THAT POSITION, RIGHT?
WHAT'S SO BAD ABOUT TRYING TO TAKE ADVANTAGE OF YOUR NATURAL CHARMS!?
...KISAKI-SENSEI MENTIONED THAT GIRLS USUALLY HAVE THE ADVANTAGE HERE, RIGHT?
GIRLS HAVE A HUGE ADVANTAGE IN ELECTIONS! ELECTIONS! ELECTIONS! (ECHO)
YEAH, BUT I... I'M STILL NOT GONNA PUT THAT THING ON!

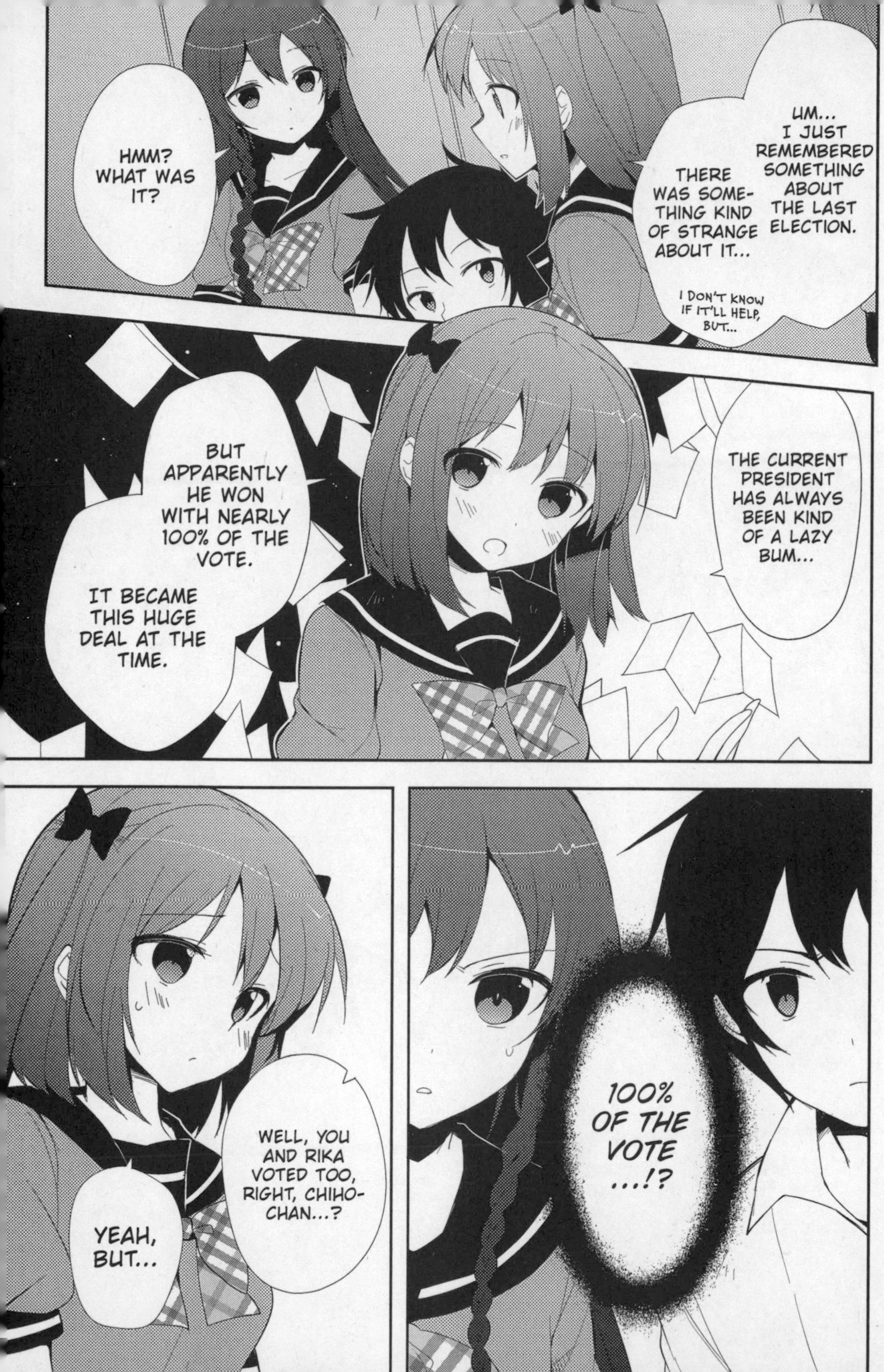
UM... I JUST REMEMBERED SOMETHING ABOUT THE LAST ELECTION.
THERE WAS SOME-THING KIND OF STRANGE ABOUT IT...
I DON'T KNOW IF IT'LL HELP, BUT...
HMM? WHAT WAS IT?
THE CURRENT PRESIDENT HAS ALWAYS BEEN KIND OF A LAZY BUM...
BUT APPARENTLY HE WON WITH NEARLY 100% OF THE VOTE.
IT BECAME THIS HUGE DEAL AT THE TIME.
100% OF THE VOTE ...!?
WELL, YOU AND RIKA VOTED TOO, RIGHT, CHIHO-CHAN...?
YEAH, BUT...

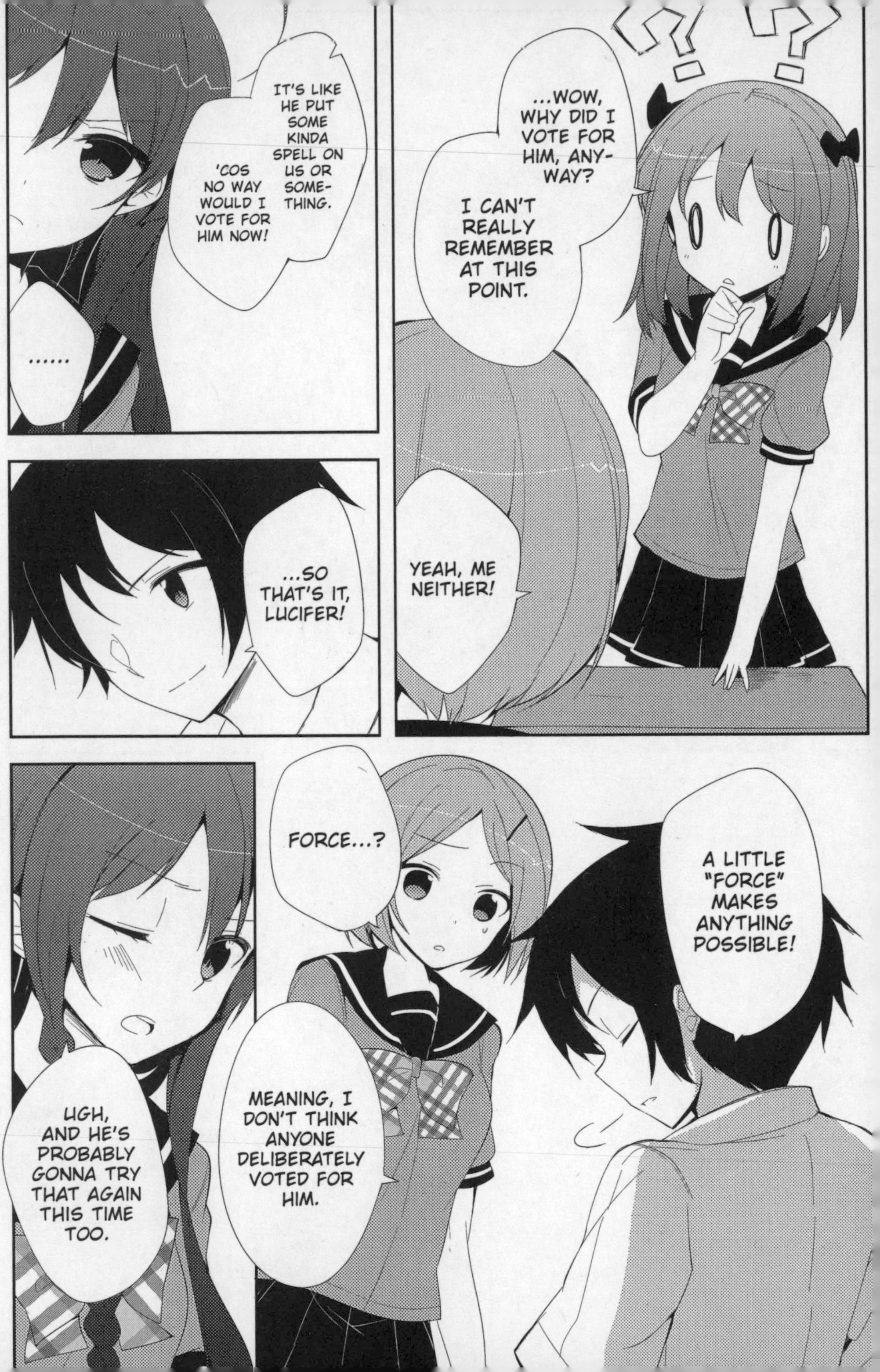
...WOW, WHY DID I VOTE FOR HIM, ANYWAY?
I CAN'T REALLY REMEMBER AT THIS POINT.
YEAH, ME NEITHER!
IT'S LIKE HE PUT SOME KINDA SPELL ON US OR SOMETHING.
'COS NO WAY WOULD I VOTE FOR HIM NOW!
......
...SO THAT'S IT, LUCIFER!
A LITTLE "FORCE" MAKES ANYTHING POSSIBLE!
FORCE...?
MEANING, I DON'T THINK ANYONE DELIBERATELY VOTED FOR HIM.
UGH, AND HE'S PROBABLY GONNA TRY THAT AGAIN THIS TIME TOO.

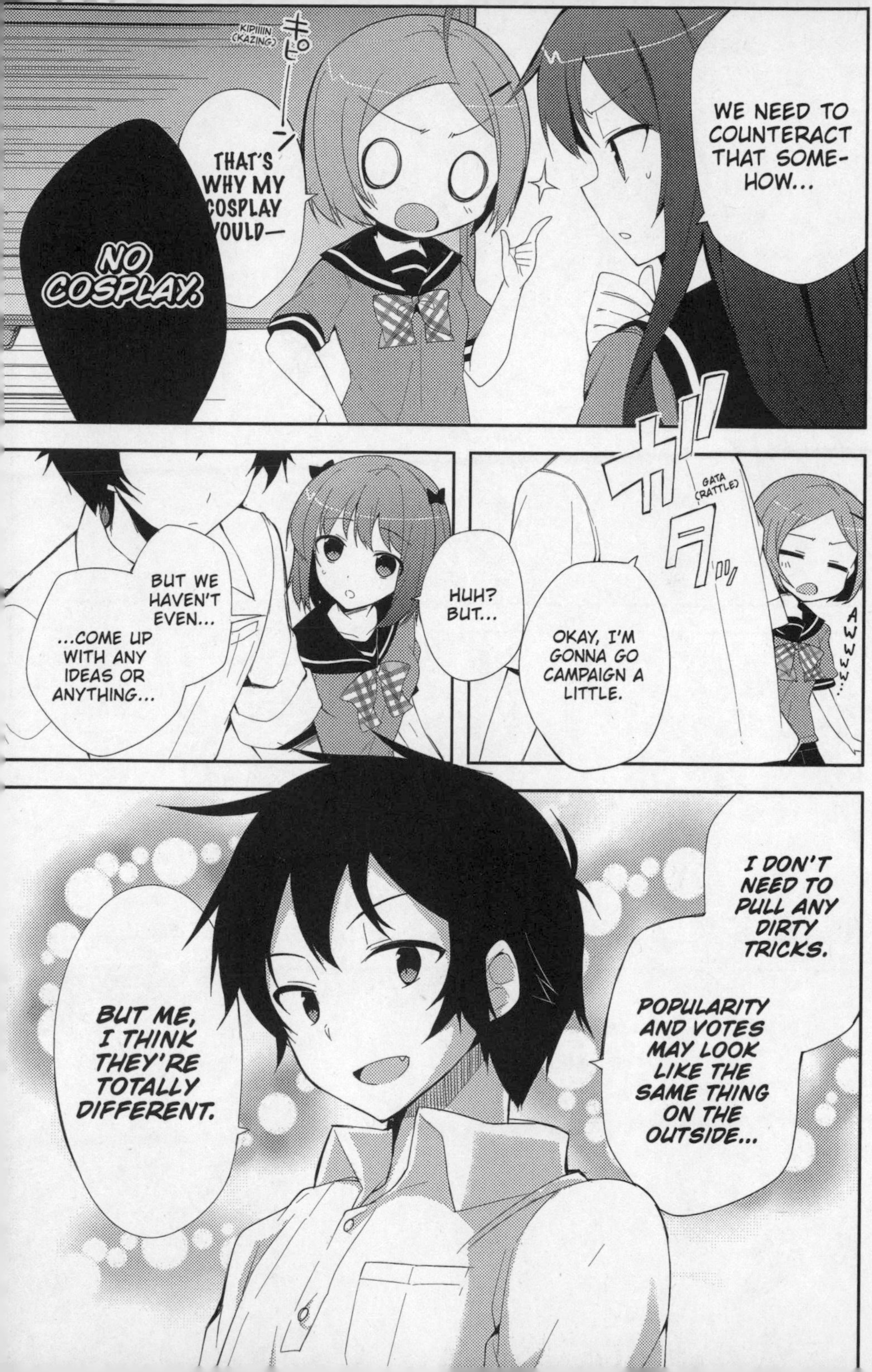
WE NEED TO COUNTERACT THAT SOME-HOW...
KIPIIIN (KAZING)
THAT'S WHY MY COSPLAY WOULD—
NO COSPLAY.
GATA (RATTLE)
AWWWWW...
OKAY, I'M GONNA GO CAMPAIGN A LITTLE.
HUH? BUT...
BUT WE HAVEN'T EVEN...
...COME UP WITH ANY IDEAS OR ANYTHING...
I DON'T NEED TO PULL ANY DIRTY TRICKS.
POPULARITY AND VOTES MAY LOOK LIKE THE SAME THING ON THE OUTSIDE...
BUT ME, I THINK THEY'RE TOTALLY DIFFERENT.

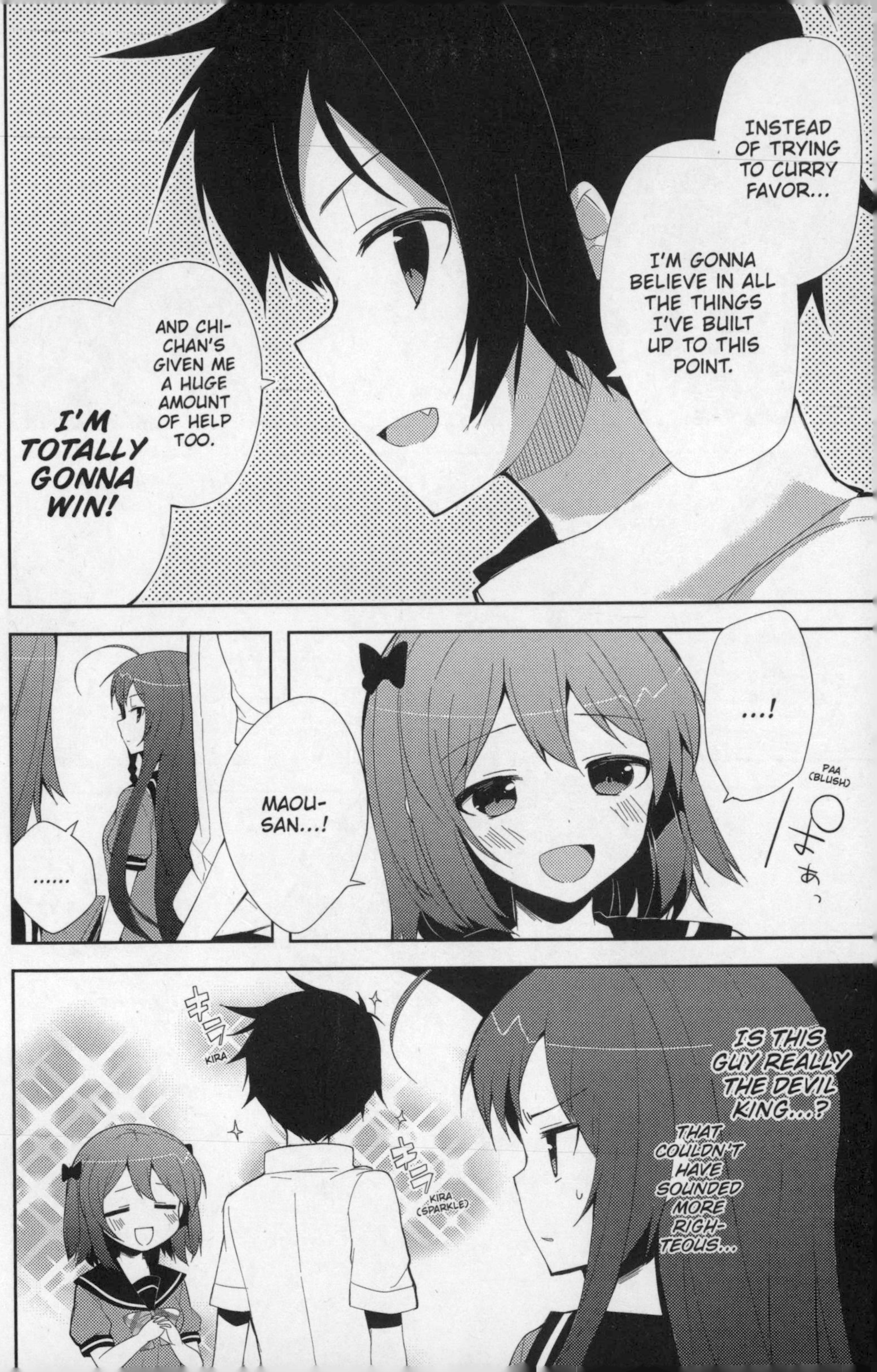
INSTEAD OF TRYING TO CURRY FAVOR...
I'M GONNA BELIEVE IN ALL THE THINGS I'VE BUILT UP TO THIS POINT.
AND CHI-CHAN'S GIVEN ME A HUGE AMOUNT OF HELP TOO.
I'M TOTALLY GONNA WIN!
...!
PAA (BLUSH)
MAOU-SAN...!
......
IS THIS GUY REALLY THE DEVIL KING...?
THAT COULDN'T HAVE SOUNDED MORE RIGH-TEOUS...
KIRA (SPARKLE)
KIRA

THE DEVIL IS A PART-TIMER! HIGH SCHOOL!

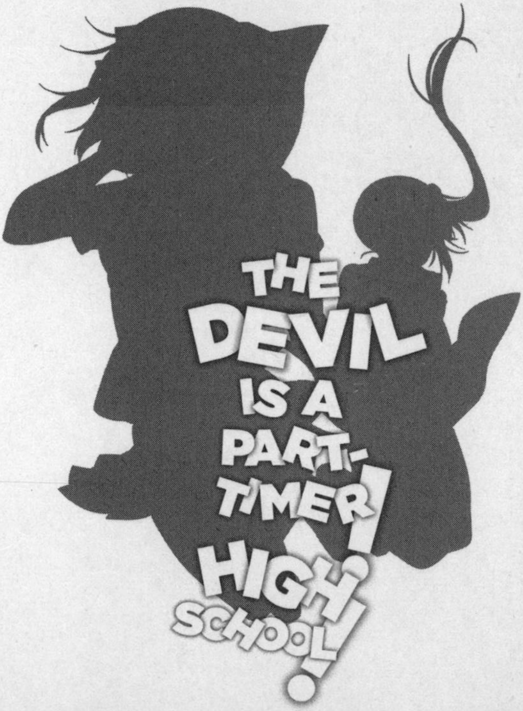
THE DEVIL IS A PART-TIMER! HIGH SCHOOL!

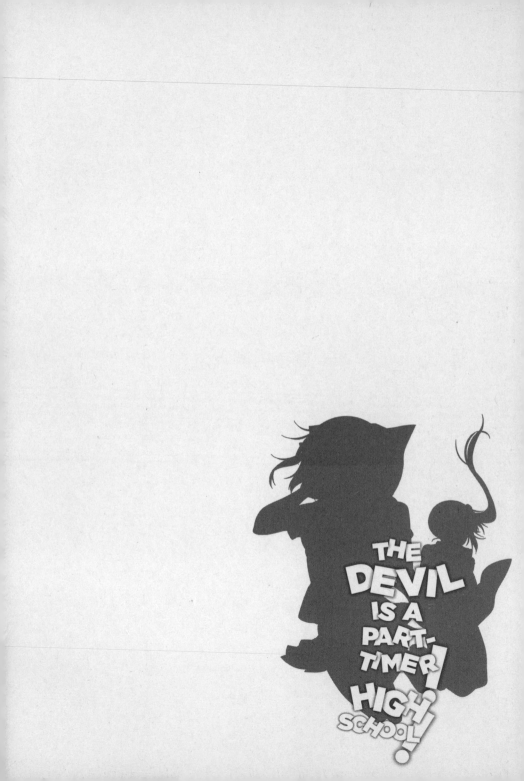

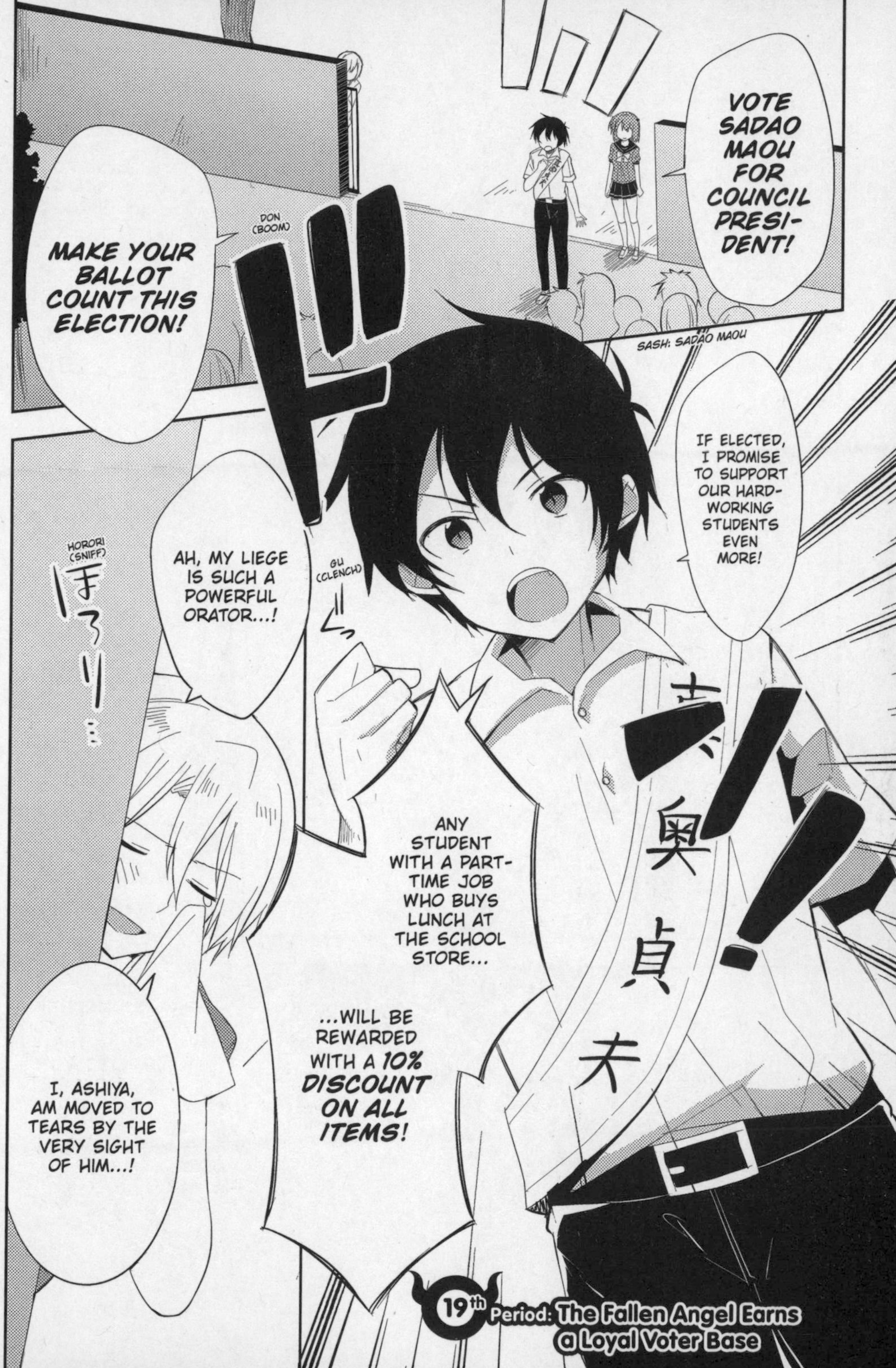
VOTE SADAO MAOU FOR COUNCIL PRESIDENT!
DON (BOOM)
MAKE YOUR BALLOT COUNT THIS ELECTION!
SASH: SADAO MAOU
IF ELECTED, I PROMISE TO SUPPORT OUR HARD-WORKING STUDENTS EVEN MORE!
ANY STUDENT WITH A PART-TIME JOB WHO BUYS LUNCH AT THE SCHOOL STORE...
...WILL BE REWARDED WITH A 10% DISCOUNT ON ALL ITEMS!
GU (CLENCH)
AH, MY LIEGE IS SUCH A POWERFUL ORATOR...!
HORORI (SNIFF)
I, ASHIYA, AM MOVED TO TEARS BY THE VERY SIGHT OF HIM...!
19th Period: The Fallen Angel Earns a Loyal Voter Base

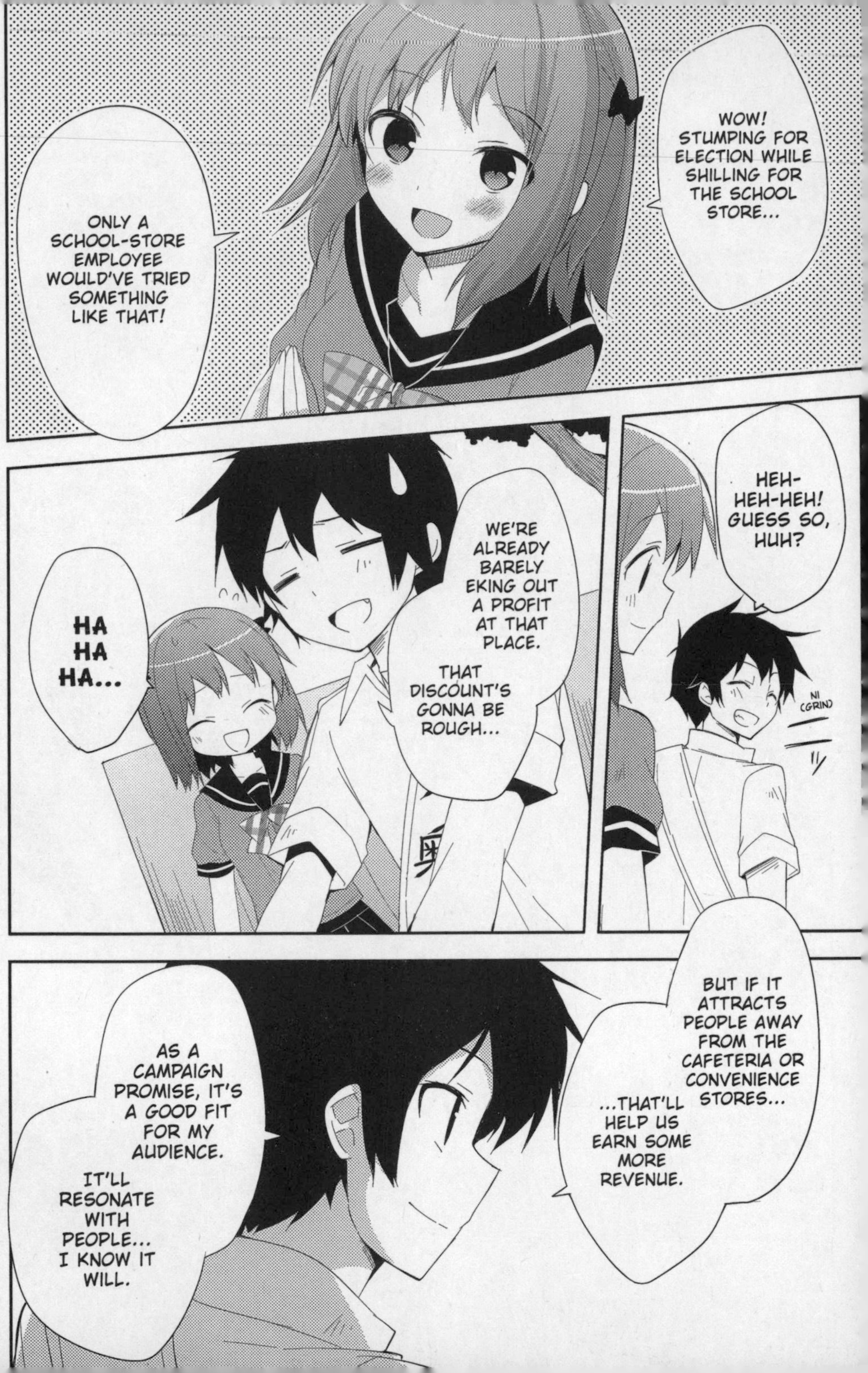
WOW! STUMPING FOR ELECTION WHILE SHILLING FOR THE SCHOOL STORE...
ONLY A SCHOOL-STORE EMPLOYEE WOULD'VE TRIED SOMETHING LIKE THAT!
HEH-HEH-HEH! GUESS SO, HUH?
NI (GRIN)
WE'RE ALREADY BARELY EKING OUT A PROFIT AT THAT PLACE.
THAT DISCOUNT'S GONNA BE ROUGH...
HA HA HA...
BUT IF IT ATTRACTS PEOPLE AWAY FROM THE CAFETERIA OR CONVENIENCE STORES...
...THAT'LL HELP US EARN SOME MORE REVENUE.
AS A CAMPAIGN PROMISE, IT'S A GOOD FIT FOR MY AUDIENCE.
IT'LL RESONATE WITH PEOPLE... I KNOW IT WILL.

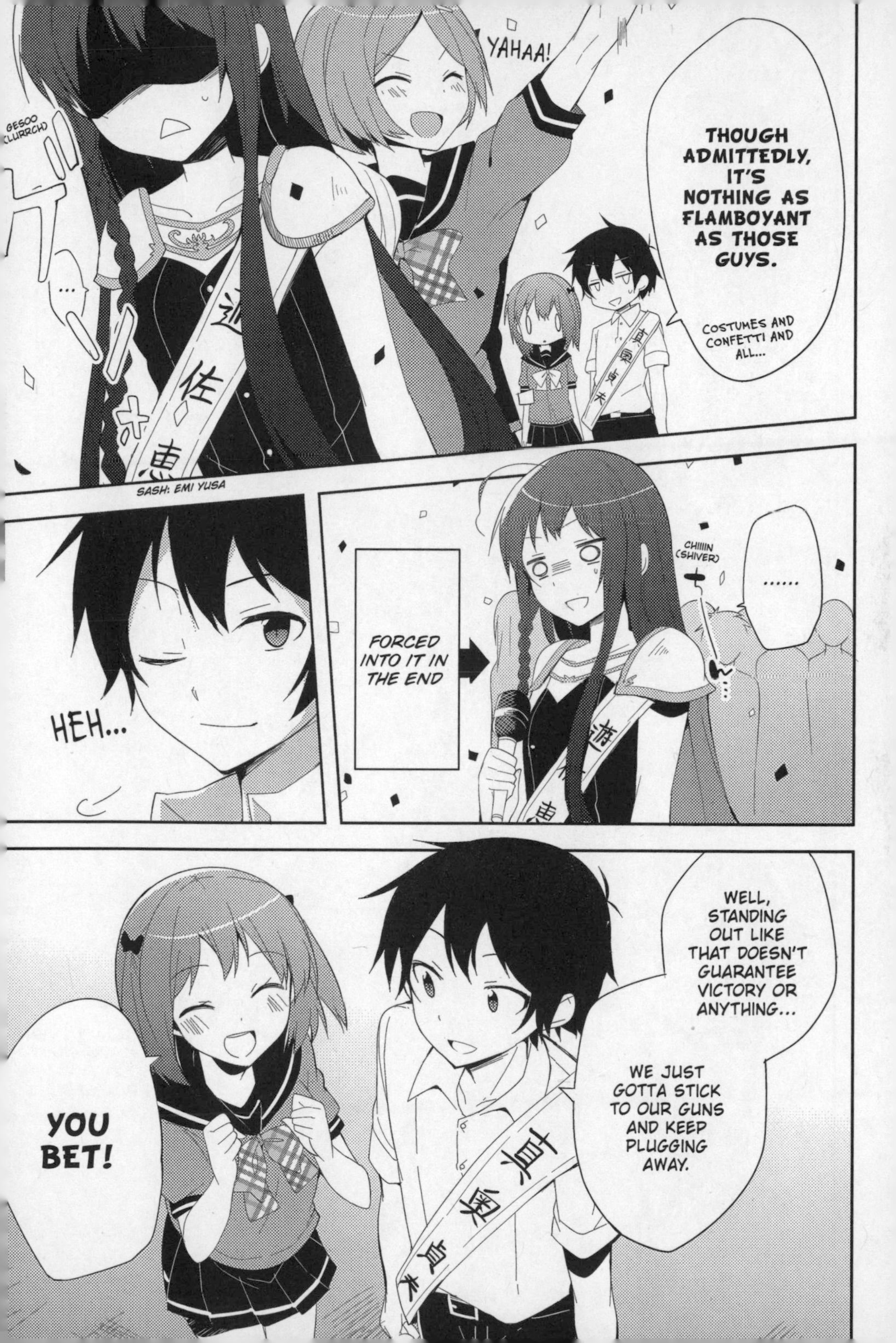
YAHAA!
THOUGH ADMITTEDLY, IT'S NOTHING AS FLAMBOYANT AS THOSE GUYS.
COSTUMES AND CONFETTI AND ALL...
GESOO (CLURRCH)
...
SASH: EMI YUSA
CHIIIN (SHIVER)
......
FORCED INTO IT IN THE END
HEH...
WELL, STANDING OUT LIKE THAT DOESN'T GUARANTEE VICTORY OR ANYTHING...
WE JUST GOTTA STICK TO OUR GUNS AND KEEP PLUGGING AWAY.
YOU BET!

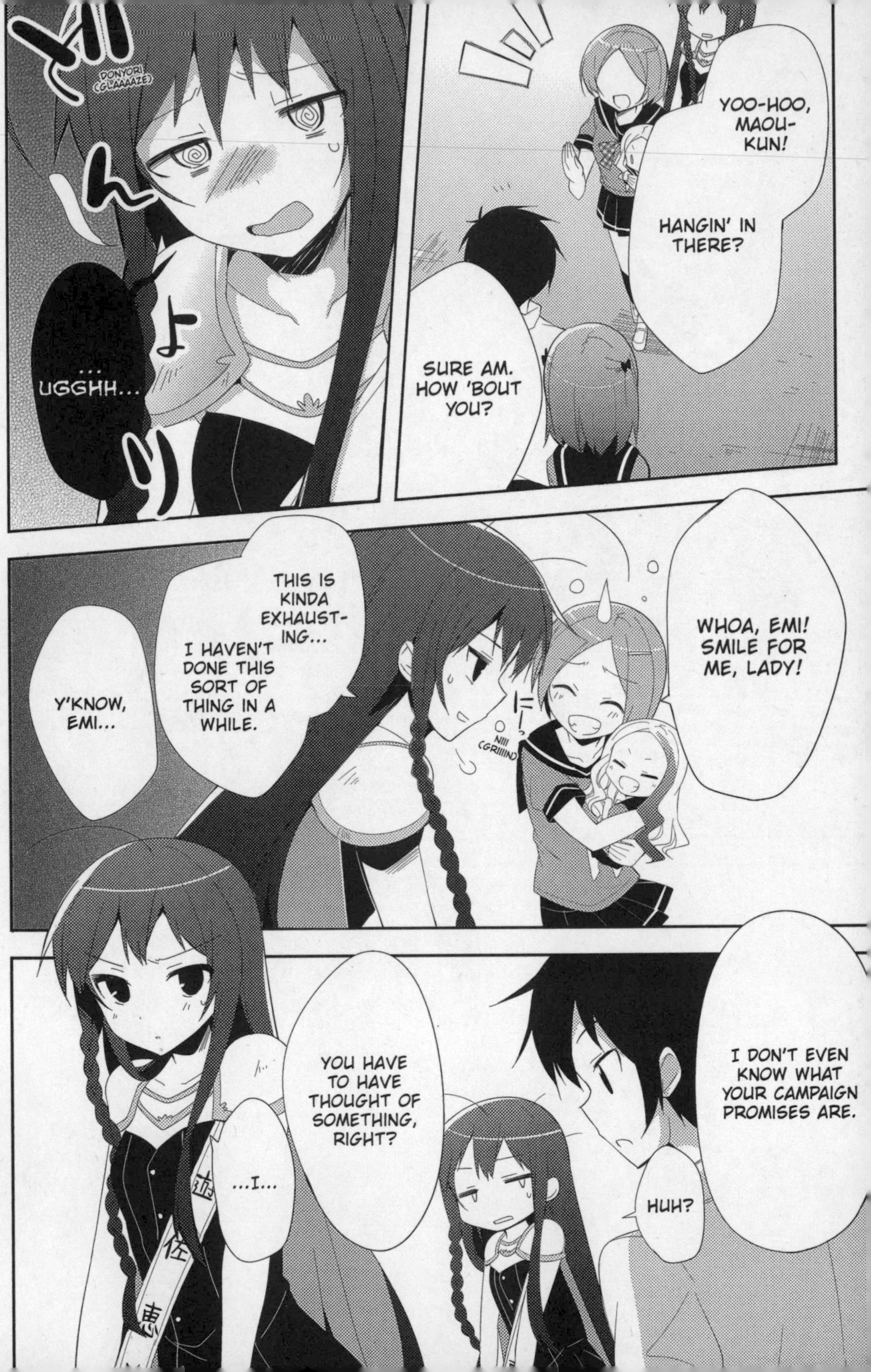
YOO-HOO, MAOU-KUN!
HANGIN' IN THERE?
SURE AM. HOW 'BOUT YOU?
DONYORI (GLAAAAZE)
...UGGHH...
WHOA, EMI! SMILE FOR ME, LADY!
NIII (GRIIIN)
THIS IS KINDA EXHAUSTING...
I HAVEN'T DONE THIS SORT OF THING IN A WHILE.
Y'KNOW, EMI...
I DON'T EVEN KNOW WHAT YOUR CAMPAIGN PROMISES ARE.
HUH?
YOU HAVE TO HAVE THOUGHT OF SOMETHING, RIGHT?
...I...

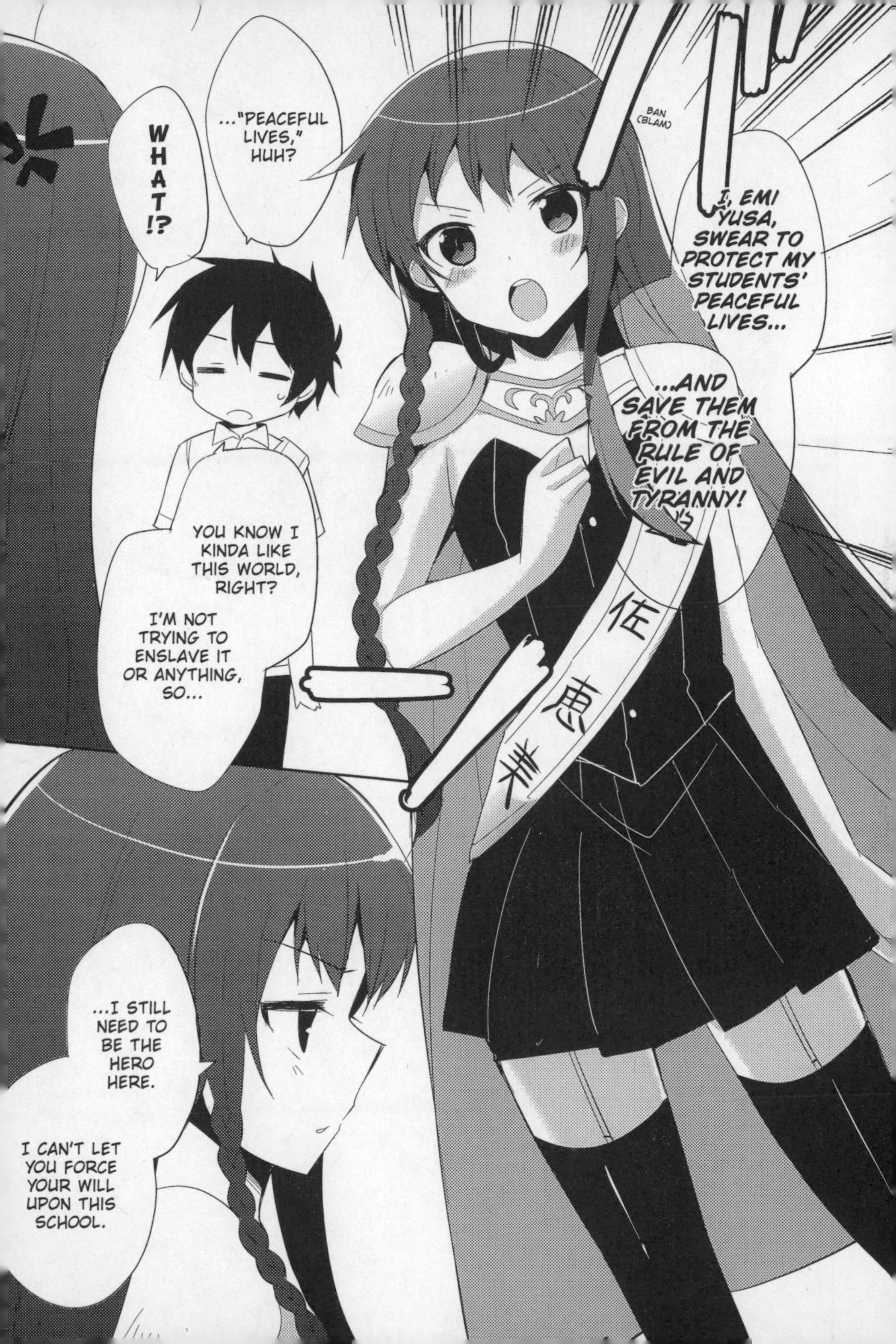
BAN (BLAM)
I, EMI YUSA, SWEAR TO PROTECT MY STUDENTS' PEACEFUL LIVES...
...AND SAVE THEM FROM THE RULE OF EVIL AND TYRANNY!
佐恵美
..."PEACEFUL LIVES," HUH?
WHAT!?
YOU KNOW I KINDA LIKE THIS WORLD, RIGHT?
I'M NOT TRYING TO ENSLAVE IT OR ANYTHING, SO...
...I STILL NEED TO BE THE HERO HERE.
I CAN'T LET YOU FORCE YOUR WILL UPON THIS SCHOOL.

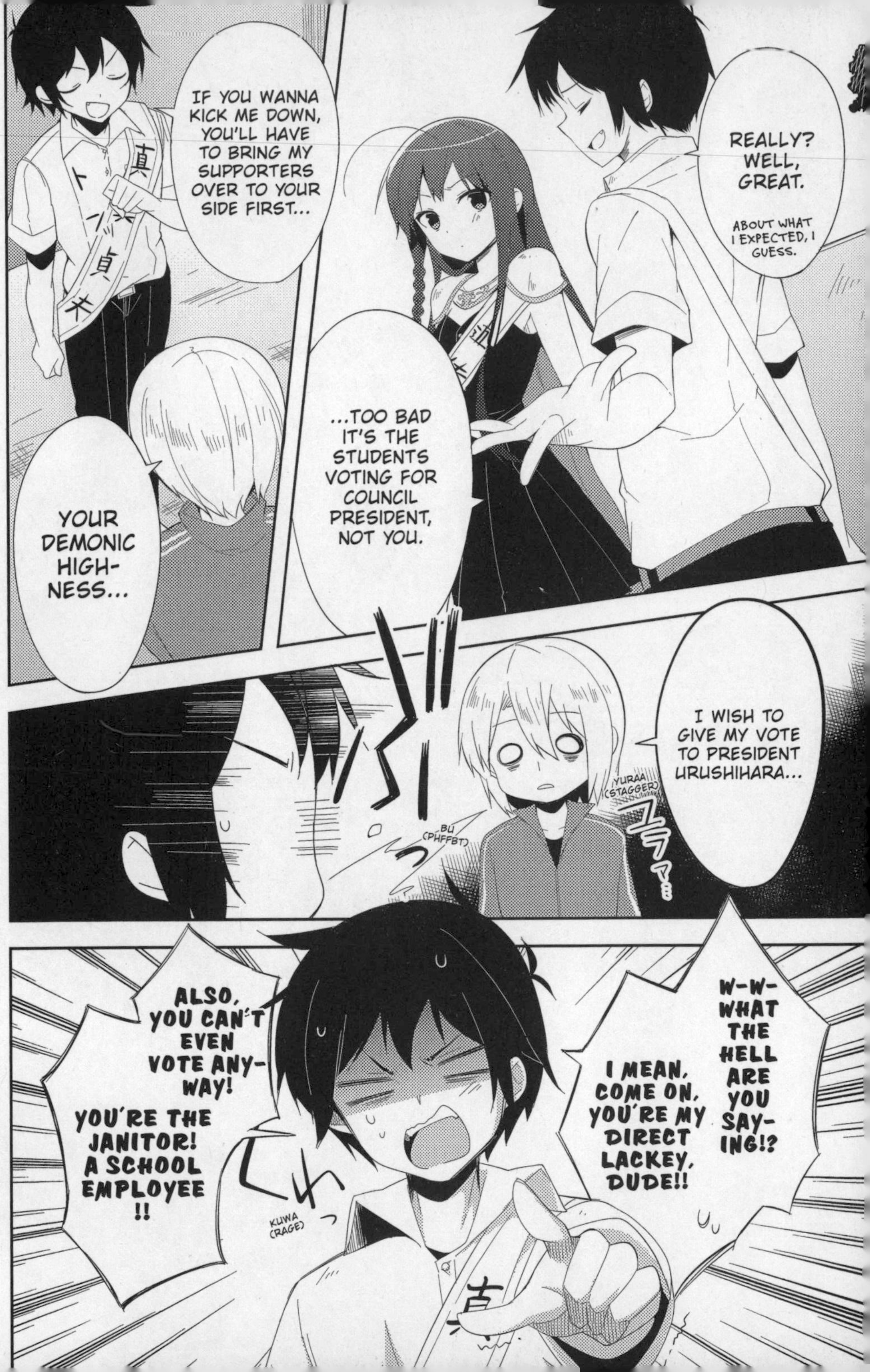
REALLY? WELL, GREAT.
ABOUT WHAT I EXPECTED, I GUESS.
...TOO BAD IT'S THE STUDENTS VOTING FOR COUNCIL PRESIDENT, NOT YOU.
IF YOU WANNA KICK ME DOWN, YOU'LL HAVE TO BRING MY SUPPORTERS OVER TO YOUR SIDE FIRST...
YOUR DEMONIC HIGH-NESS...
I WISH TO GIVE MY VOTE TO PRESIDENT URUSHIHARA...
YURAA (STAGGER)
BU (PHFFBT)
W-W-WHAT THE HELL ARE YOU SAY-ING!?
I MEAN, COME ON, YOU'RE MY DIRECT LACKEY, DUDE!!
ALSO, YOU CAN'T EVEN VOTE ANY-WAY!
YOU'RE THE JANITOR! A SCHOOL EMPLOYEE !!
KUWA (RAGE)

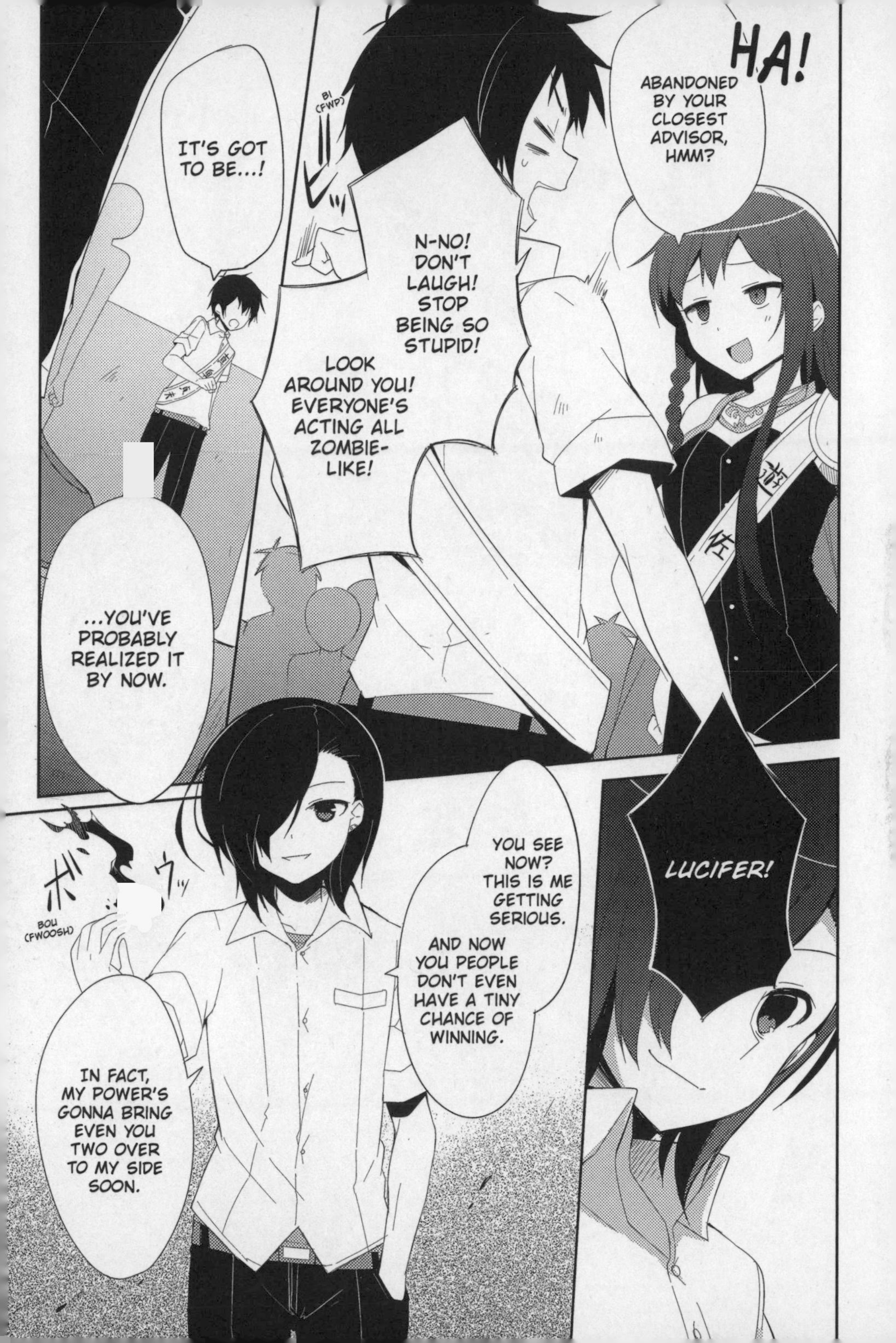
HA!
ABANDONED BY YOUR CLOSEST ADVISOR, HMM?
BI (FWP)
N-NO! DON'T LAUGH! STOP BEING SO STUPID!
LOOK AROUND YOU! EVERYONE'S ACTING ALL ZOMBIE-LIKE!
IT'S GOT TO BE...!
...YOU'VE PROBABLY REALIZED IT BY NOW.
LUCIFER!
YOU SEE NOW? THIS IS ME GETTING SERIOUS.
AND NOW YOU PEOPLE DON'T EVEN HAVE A TINY CHANCE OF WINNING.
BOU (FWOOSH)
IN FACT, MY POWER'S GONNA BRING EVEN YOU TWO OVER TO MY SIDE SOON.

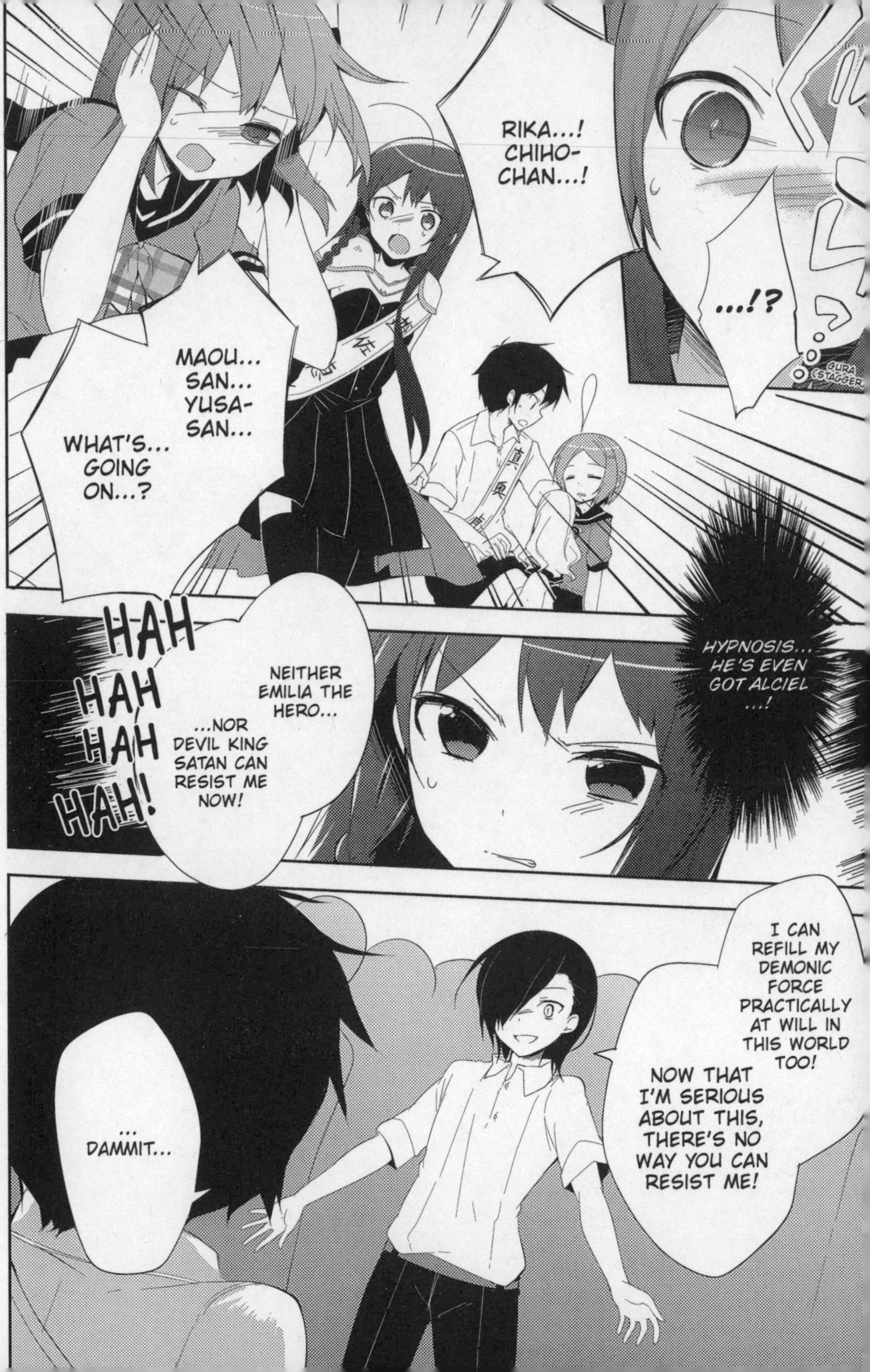
...!?
GURA (STAGGER)
RIKA...! CHIHO-CHAN...!
MAOU... SAN... YUSA-SAN...
WHAT'S... GOING ON...?
HYPNOSIS... HE'S EVEN GOT ALCIEL ...!
NEITHER EMILIA THE HERO...
...NOR DEVIL KING SATAN CAN RESIST ME NOW!
HAH HAH HAH HAH!
I CAN REFILL MY DEMONIC FORCE PRACTICALLY AT WILL IN THIS WORLD TOO!
NOW THAT I'M SERIOUS ABOUT THIS, THERE'S NO WAY YOU CAN RESIST ME!
... DAMMIT...

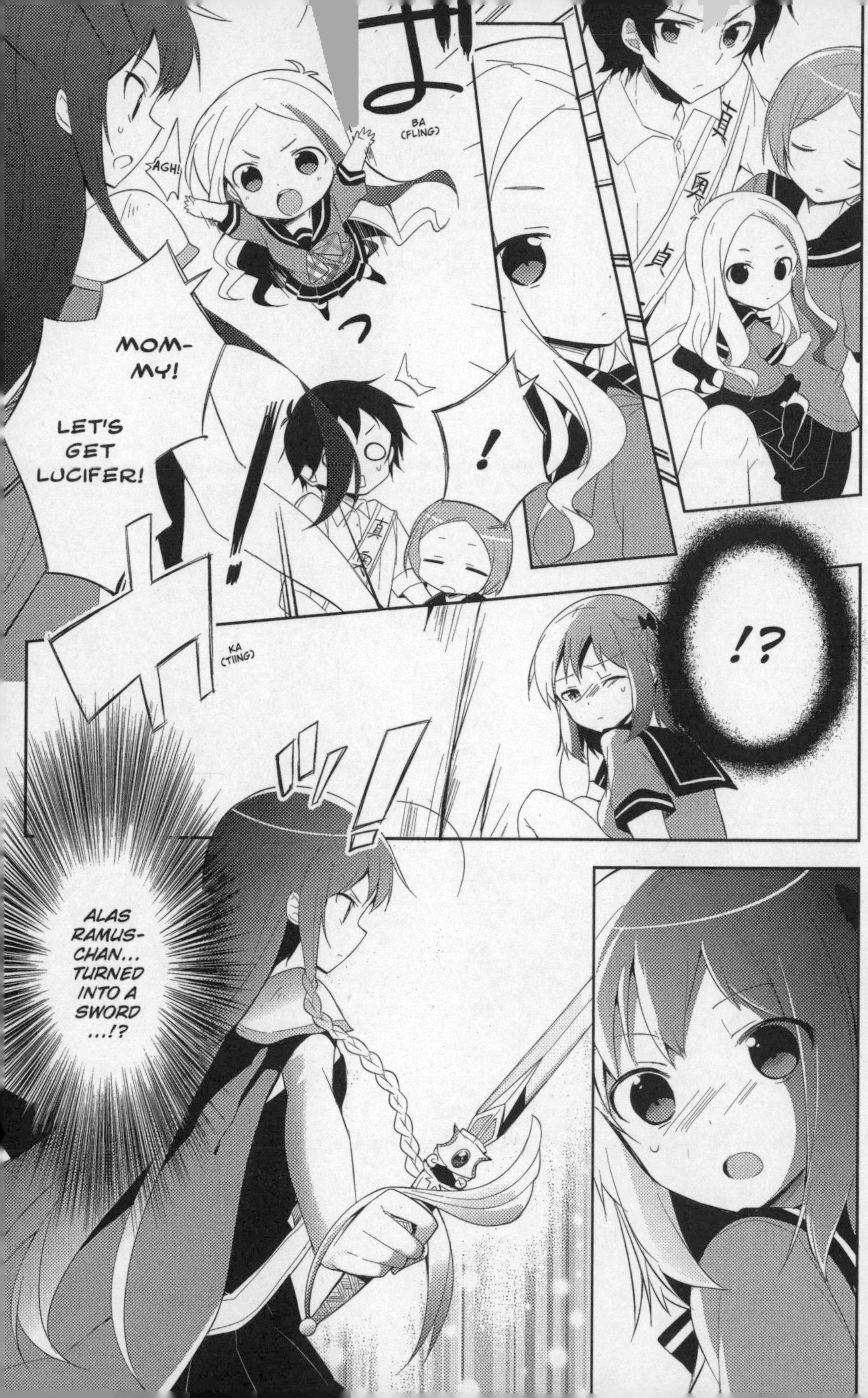
BA
(FLING)
AGH!
MOM-
MY!
LET'S
GET
LUCIFER!
!
KA
(TIING)
!?
ALAS
RAMUS-
CHAN...
TURNED
INTO A
SWORD
...!?

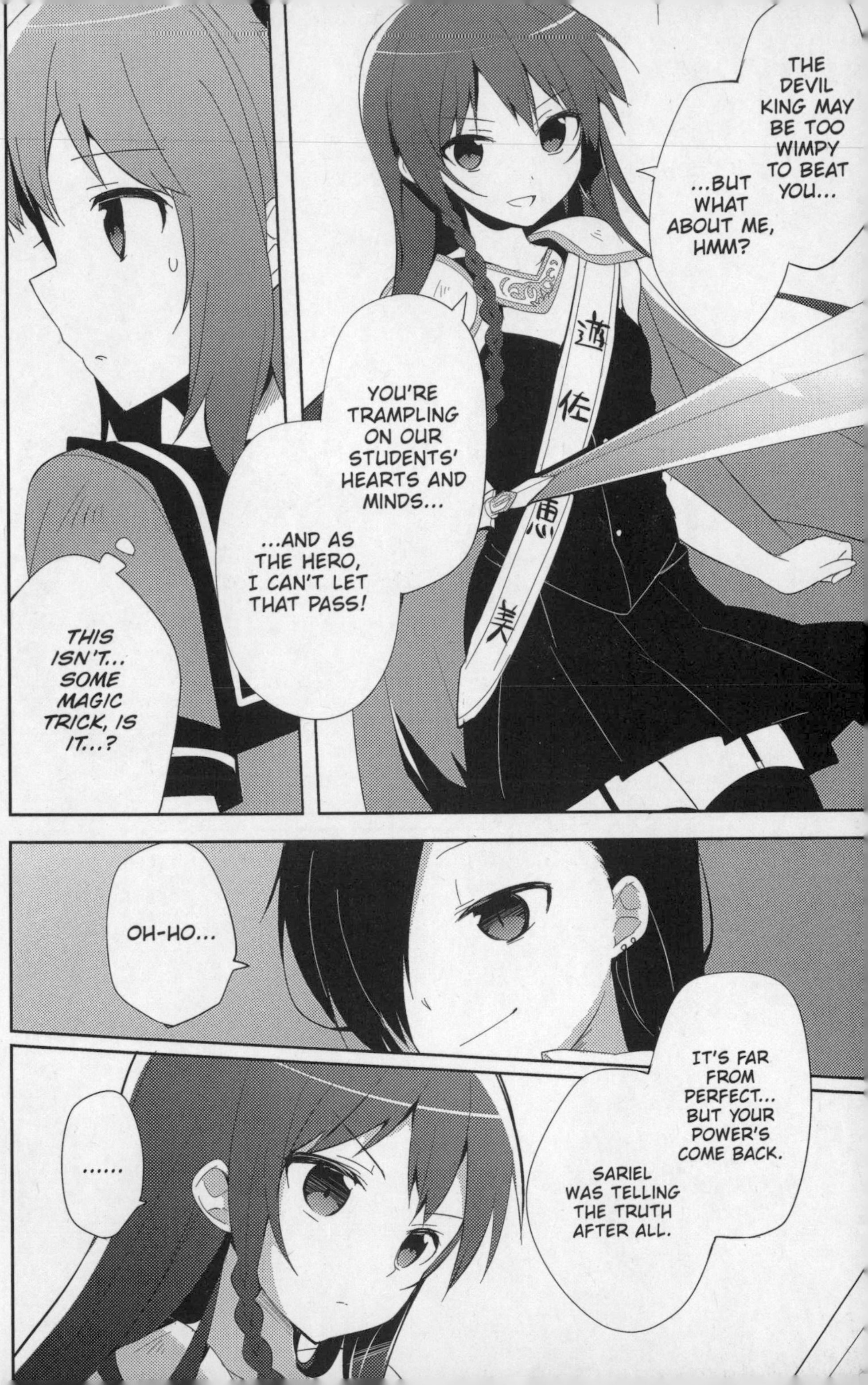
THE DEVIL KING MAY BE TOO WIMPY TO BEAT YOU...
...BUT WHAT ABOUT ME, HMM?
遊佐恵美
YOU'RE TRAMPLING ON OUR STUDENTS' HEARTS AND MINDS...
...AND AS THE HERO, I CAN'T LET THAT PASS!
THIS ISN'T... SOME MAGIC TRICK, IS IT...?
OH-HO...
IT'S FAR FROM PERFECT... BUT YOUR POWER'S COME BACK.
SARIEL WAS TELLING THE TRUTH AFTER ALL.
......

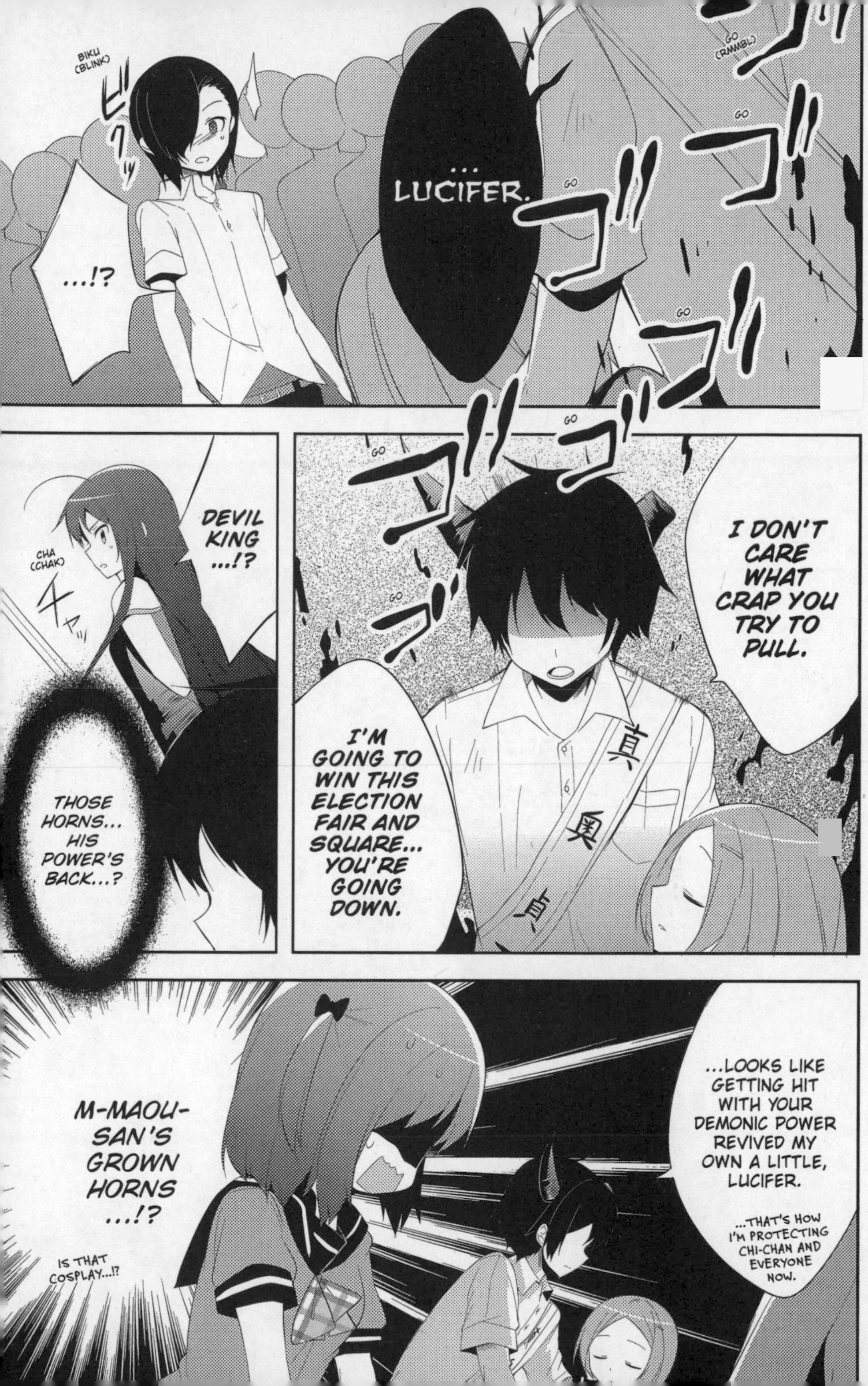
GO (RMMBL)
GO
GO
GO
... LUCIFER.
BIKU (BLINK)
...!?
GO
GO
GO
I DON'T CARE WHAT CRAP YOU TRY TO PULL.
I'M GOING TO WIN THIS ELECTION FAIR AND SQUARE... YOU'RE GOING DOWN.
DEVIL KING ...!?
CHA (CHAK)
THOSE HORNS... HIS POWER'S BACK...?
...LOOKS LIKE GETTING HIT WITH YOUR DEMONIC POWER REVIVED MY OWN A LITTLE, LUCIFER.
...THAT'S HOW I'M PROTECTING CHI-CHAN AND EVERYONE NOW.
M-MAOU-SAN'S GROWN HORNS ...!?
IS THAT COSPLAY...!?

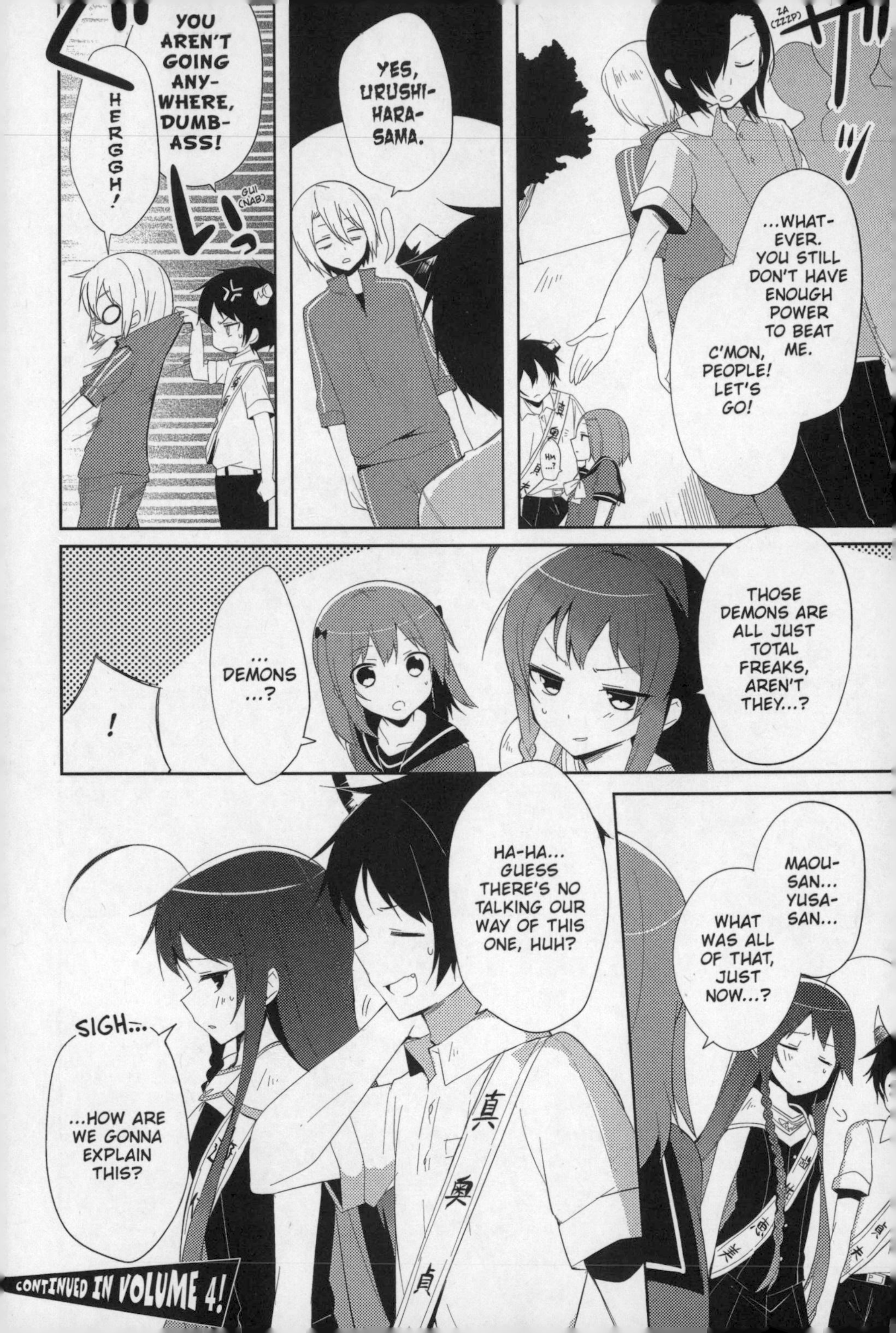
ZA (ZZZZP)
...WHATEVER. YOU STILL DON'T HAVE ENOUGH POWER TO BEAT ME.
C'MON, PEOPLE! LET'S GO!
HM ...?
YES, URUSHIHARA-SAMA.
YOU AREN'T GOING ANYWHERE, DUMBASS!
GUI (NAB)
HERGGH!
THOSE DEMONS ARE ALL JUST TOTAL FREAKS, AREN'T THEY...?
... DEMONS ...?
!
MAOU-SAN... YUSA-SAN...
WHAT WAS ALL OF THAT, JUST NOW...?
HA-HA... GUESS THERE'S NO TALKING OUR WAY OF THIS ONE, HUH?
SIGH...
...HOW ARE WE GONNA EXPLAIN THIS?
CONTINUED IN VOLUME 4!

THE DEVIL IS A PART-TIMER! HIGH SCHOOL!

AFTERWORD.

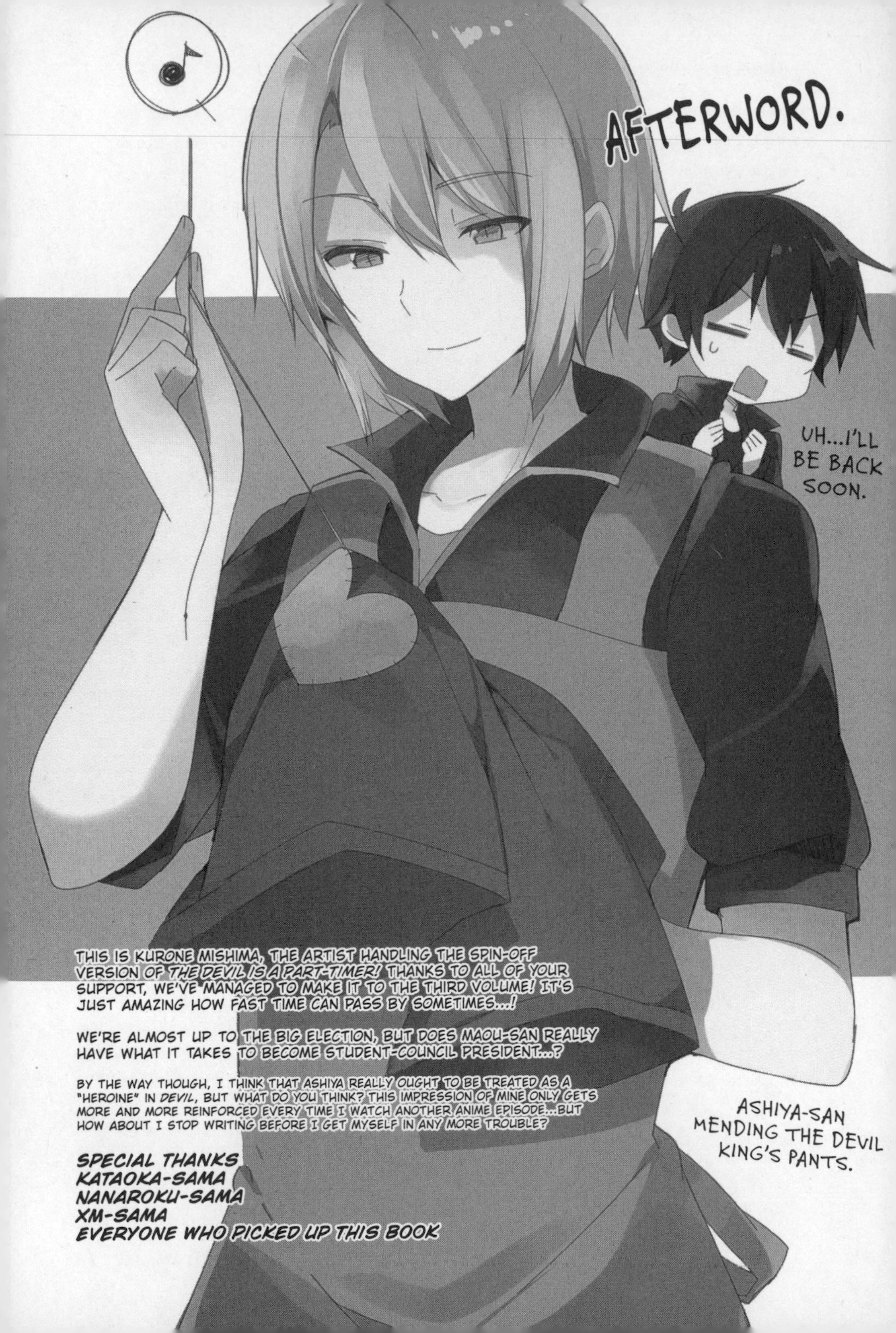
UH...I'LL BE BACK SOON.
ASHIYA-SAN MENDING THE DEVIL KING'S PANTS.

THIS IS KURONE MISHIMA, THE ARTIST HANDLING THE SPIN-OFF VERSION OF *THE DEVIL IS A PART-TIMER!* THANKS TO ALL OF YOUR SUPPORT, WE'VE MANAGED TO MAKE IT TO THE THIRD VOLUME! IT'S JUST AMAZING HOW FAST TIME CAN PASS BY SOMETIMES...!

WE'RE ALMOST UP TO THE BIG ELECTION, BUT DOES MAOU-SAN REALLY HAVE WHAT IT TAKES TO BECOME STUDENT-COUNCIL PRESIDENT...?

BY THE WAY THOUGH, I THINK THAT ASHIYA REALLY OUGHT TO BE TREATED AS A "HEROINE" IN *DEVIL*, BUT WHAT DO YOU THINK? THIS IMPRESSION OF MINE ONLY GETS MORE AND MORE REINFORCED EVERY TIME I WATCH ANOTHER ANIME EPISODE...BUT HOW ABOUT I STOP WRITING BEFORE I GET MYSELF IN ANY MORE TROUBLE?

SPECIAL THANKS
KATAOKA-SAMA
NANAROKU-SAMA
XM-SAMA
EVERYONE WHO PICKED UP THIS BOOK

FROM THE ORIGINAL CREATOR

WHEN YOU'RE TRYING TO INTERACT WITH OTHER PEOPLE, I THINK YOU NEED TO MAKE AN EFFORT TO KNOW THE OTHER PERSON TO SOME EXTENT, OR THERE'S ALWAYS GOING TO BE THIS SORT OF WALL BETWEEN THE TWO OF YOU. IN A PREVIOUS *HIGH SCHOOL!* VOLUME I WROTE ABOUT HOW THIS STORY WAS ONE POSSIBILITY FOR HOW *THE DEVIL IS A PART-TIMER!* COULD HAVE WOUND UP. NOW THOUGH, I'M SEEING POSSIBILITIES HERE THAT NEVER WOULD'VE OCCURRED TO ME WHILE WRITING THE NOVELS, THINGS THAT I NEVER IMAGINED WHEN THE MANGA BEGAN PUBLICATION.

WHAT I'M TALKING ABOUT IS THE MAIN CAST—MAOU, EMI, ASHIYA, CHIHO, URUSHIHARA, AND SUZUNO—TOSSED INTO THE SAME SPACE, NONE OF THEM KNOWING A GREAT DEAL ABOUT EACH OTHER. IT'S THE KIND OF PHENOMENON YOU SEE A LOT IN AN ENCLOSED ENVIRONMENT...SUCH AS YOUR TYPICAL NEIGHBORHOOD SCHOOL. I REALLY HAVE NO IDEA HOW THEIR RELATIONSHIPS ARE GOING TO GROW, AND THAT'S WHY I CAN'T TAKE MY EYES OFF OF THIS!

SATOSHI WAGAHARA

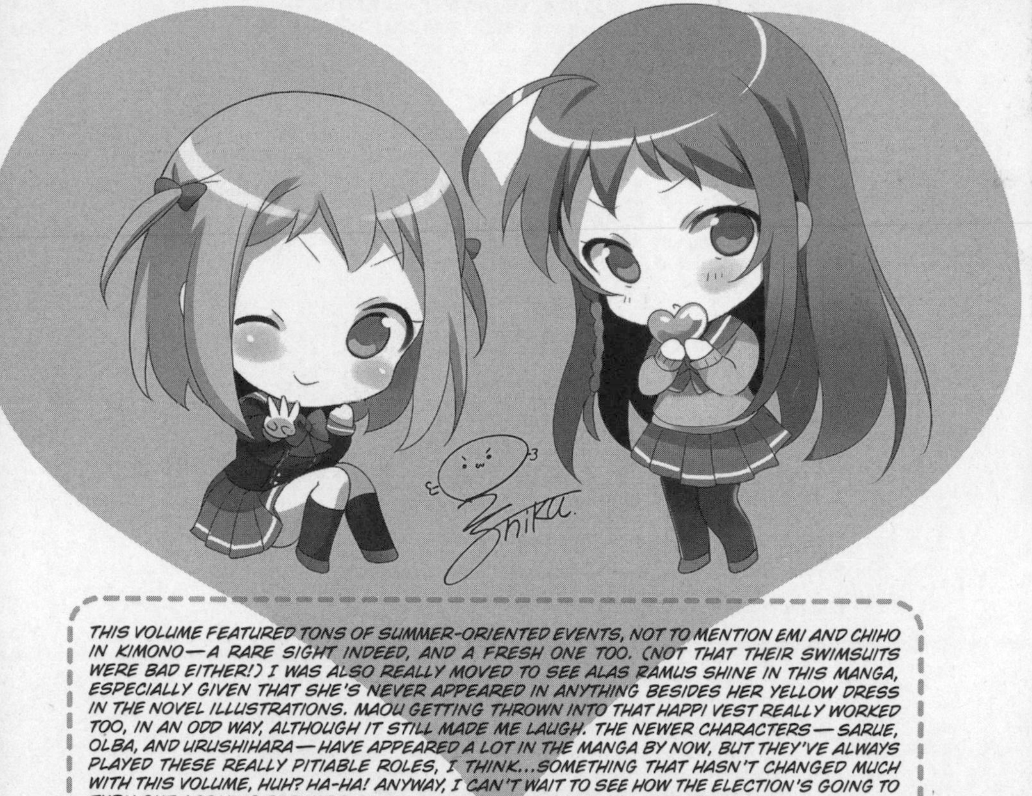

THIS VOLUME FEATURED TONS OF SUMMER-ORIENTED EVENTS, NOT TO MENTION EMI AND CHIHO IN KIMONO—A RARE SIGHT INDEED, AND A FRESH ONE TOO. (NOT THAT THEIR SWIMSUITS WERE BAD EITHER!) I WAS ALSO REALLY MOVED TO SEE ALAS RAMUS SHINE IN THIS MANGA, ESPECIALLY GIVEN THAT SHE'S NEVER APPEARED IN ANYTHING BESIDES HER YELLOW DRESS IN THE NOVEL ILLUSTRATIONS. MAOU GETTING THROWN INTO THAT HAPPI VEST REALLY WORKED TOO, IN AN ODD WAY, ALTHOUGH IT STILL MADE ME LAUGH. THE NEWER CHARACTERS—SARUE, OLBA, AND URUSHIHARA—HAVE APPEARED A LOT IN THE MANGA BY NOW, BUT THEY'VE ALWAYS PLAYED THESE REALLY PITIABLE ROLES, I THINK...SOMETHING THAT HASN'T CHANGED MUCH WITH THIS VOLUME, HUH? HA-HA! ANYWAY, I CAN'T WAIT TO SEE HOW THE ELECTION'S GOING TO TURN OUT. LOOKING FORWARD TO VOLUME 4 (MAYBE I'M BEING TOO IMPATIENT).

NOVEL ILLUSTRATOR ***029*** *(ONIKU)*

THE DEVIL IS A PART-TIMER! HIGH SCHOOL! ③

ART: KURONE MISHIMA
ORIGINAL STORY: SATOSHI WAGAHARA
CHARACTER DESIGN: 029 (ONIKU)

Translation: Kevin Gifford

Lettering: Brndn Blakeslee & Lys Blakeslee

This book is a work of fiction. Names, characters, places, and incidents are the product of the author's imagination or are used fictitiously. Any resemblance to actual events, locales, or persons, living or dead, is coincidental.

Edited by ASCII MEDIA WORKS
First published in Japan in 2013 by KADOKAWA CORPORATION, Tokyo.
English translation rights arranged with KADOKAWA CORPORATION, Tokyo, through Tuttle-Mori Agency, Inc., Tokyo.

Yen Press
Hachette Book Group
1290 Avenue of the Americas
New York, NY 10104

www.HachetteBookGroup.com
www.YenPress.com

Yen Press is an imprint of Hachette Book Group, Inc. The Yen Press name and logo are trademarks of Hachette Book Group, Inc.

The publisher is not responsible for websites (or their content) that are not owned by the publisher.

Library of Congress Control Number: 2015952615

First Yen Press Edition: February 2016

ISBN: 978-0-316-38514-5

10 9 8 7 6 5 4 3 2 1

BVG

Printed in the United States of America